WHAT LEADERS
90 DAYS TO LIFE

MW01283911

Ruble Chandy's book, 90 Days to Life, is a touching story about the importance of the connection of mind, body, and spirit to manifest abundance in all aspects of your life. More importantly, at this time in our world, it helps bring focus and attention to the importance of self-acceptance, self-love and what it takes to get there. It is a hero's journey and a healing journey. A great read for anyone searching to reach beyond the darkness or despair they may currently be experiencing.

~ Jim Blake, CEO, Unity World Headquarters

I love, love *90 Days to Life*! It is like a powerful awakened dream, filled with riveting, humorous, and life-changing paradigms, metaphors and business strategies. I was happy to realize the characters didn't go away after reading the last page. I can still hear Arjun's kind yet powerful voice in my ear, and I'm wildly grateful his teachings are still active within me long after reading the book. If you want to reignite your career and elevate your life to the next level, *90 Days to Life* is the book for you!

~Kelly Sullivan Walden, "Doctor DREAM"
Bestselling Author of 9 books, including *Chicken Soup for the Soul - Dreams and the Unimaginable*

"90 Days to Life is the iPhone of self-help books. Ruble Chandy has managed to innovate this genre by not only covering business success and productivity, but also personal and spiritual growth. Read it. You won't be disappointed!"

~ Christine Bell, New York Times and USA Today Bestselling Author

In his new book, 90 Days to Life, Ruble Chandy, takes you on a journey into your conscious and unconscious mind identifying strengths, weaknesses, habits, and fears. The heroine in this book goes on an amazing journey from tragedy to triumph.

~ Lynn V Andrews, NY Times Bestselling Author (The Medicine Woman series)

Ruble Chandy's 90 Days to Life, stands out as the book that integrates personal transformation and business success. Truly a must-have for any entrepreneur looking to maximize their business success and tune into their highest degree of true value.

~ Mark Mincolla PhD, Author of the best seller, Whole Health

90 DAYS TO LIFE

A Journey from Turmoil to Triumph

RUBLE CHANDY

Avante Publishing

Avante

First paperback edition May 2019

ISBN 978-1-094-71855-2 (pbk)
ISBN 978-0-578-48771-7 (ebook)

Cover Art : Devra Ann Jacobs
Formatting: Polgarus Studio

Trademarks and Copyrights:
Power Ceremony™
Power Questions™
ESCAPE™
The new ABC of Persuasion™
Pre-creation™
Flow Time™
Convert Stress and Suffering to Celebration™
C^3™

I dedicate this book to the three people who impacted me the most, Nisha my best friend and love, my Dad, my first superhero, and my Mom, who sowed in me the seeds of applied Faith; and the two people who inspire me the most, my children Rojelio and Fiona.

Contents

Introduction

I hate reading long introductions, so this is going to be short and sweet.

Through this book, we've created a new genre called Business-Fiction. It is one ordinary woman's epic journey from turmoil to triumph. By the time you finish reading, you will have grasped everything you need to know to start or succeed as an entrepreneur, small business owner, or professional. If you don't own a business, it will teach you how to treat your job like a business and accelerate your career and income as you do it. As a bonus, the stories within will align your psychology and mindset to victory and drive you to implement those nuggets you pick up on your way. The inspiring stories and new metaphors in 90 Days to Life will win your heart and linger long after you finish reading.

This book is not for everyone. If you are a business owner or aspire to be one, if you are a professional who wants to grow, if you work for someone today but want to claim your financial future, then this is for you. I intend to help you increase your bottom line by 25% or more in the next twelve months just by using the principles in this book.

If you are heartbroken, anxious, or overwhelmed, this book can help you achieve emotional mastery. If you've tried everything and you are still stuck and failing, 90 Days to Life can get you unstuck. If you are going through the motions but unable to find your true purpose, 90 Days to Life will provide the roadmap. If you are experiencing financial problems, 90 Days to Life will provide the solutions.

These are the gold nuggets from my experiences as a professional and entrepreneur, as well as everything I've learned from the best mentors for twenty-five years. Me and my research team absorbed information from countless books, high-end seminars, audio programs, and online courses to amass this knowledge and create the most entertaining, humorous, and empowering self-help book you will ever read. All you need to do is read it.

My note for you to get the best out of 90 Days to Life:

If you are reading the paper or Apple Books version of 90 Days to Life, download a QR code reader app on your phone, so you can access exclusive videos and training that complement the book. If you have the Kindle version, just click on the sentence right above the QR code or the code itself and it will directly take you to the bonus training.

PART I

MY INNER DEMON

"Just when the caterpillar thought the world was ending, she turned into a butterfly."
Barbara Haines Howett

CHAPTER ONE
Soulless and Penniless

The chill of the Pacific Ocean stings my toes as small waves crash and roll onto the shore. For a moment, the water pools around my feet, and I catch a glimpse of my own muddled, tear-stained reflection. I gasp and then cringe.

Who am I looking at?

What has happened to me?

My eyes are puffy and my cheeks are red and tear-streaked. *This is a face that could scare children.*

People have always told me that I'm attractive, and maybe I still could be if things were different. I hardly look or feel forty right now, though. More like sixty. The last few years have done a number on me, and now my face is gaunt, thin, bony even. My auburn hair hangs around my angular face in matted disarray. *God, I look homeless.* I can't even make out my turquoise eyes. They blend into the water, creating the illusion of a hollow, empty, soulless ghost staring back at me. Ha— *soulless and penniless!*

My heart pounds in my chest, and I wish the pressure would distract me from the crushing pain of this empty life, but it's useless—nothing can take my mind off this downward spiral. In a desperate attempt to break through this feeling of despair, I try to call forth an image of Jason Momoa, shirtless in Aquaman.

Nope.

Nothing. I just feel nothing.

I shudder, not sure if from the fear of what I'm considering or from the icy waters around my feet. *Come on, Lindsay, do it and get it over with. No one will even notice that you're gone.*

Sucking in a deep breath, I close my eyes. I can do this. I heard that drowning is an excruciating way to go, but that's what this piece of metal in my pocket is for. It will probably be the only backup plan that has ever worked for me. Yes, it'll hurt, but the pain will be far less than living my horrible existence for even one more day.

And whose fault is that, Lindsay?

Mine. I know it is. I'm here because I allowed myself to fall this far down.

Suddenly, memories ebb and flow like waves around my heart. A burning guilt stabs at my stomach and begins to creep upwards. *Your fault, Lindsay.* My eyes brim with unshed tears, and suddenly, they spill over and stream down my cheeks.

Drawing in a deep breath of sweet, ocean air, I savor it one last time before exhaling. Then, letting those memories drive me forward, I reach into my pocket and take one small, shaky step forward…

Three months earlier—

Before he even opens his mouth, I see it on his face—a new expression. And I know it's over.

Shifting uneasily in the chair of our stamp-sized galley kitchen, I wait while he begins pacing. In some ways, I always knew this was coming.

Why do I have to be right about the crappy stuff? Why can't I be right about knowing lottery numbers or where to invest my money on the stock market?

The room becomes stagnant with silence and impending doom. I've been holding my breath and quickly inhale, snatching in some air. My heart races as I tap my fingernails rhythmically against the slick dinette surface.

He stops pacing and looks at me with that blank look in his eyes. "Can you stop that?"

I stop. But I don't want to stop. Fury rages and fumes inside me and, like a five year old, I want to yell, "*You're not the boss of me! I hate you!*"

"Lindsay, there's no easy way to say this." He leans against the wall with a sigh, clearly hesitant to take a seat opposite me. "I know you've been trying to live your dream in spite of all your failures. But the truth is, you need to stop with this pie-in-the-sky nonsense. You need to come back to reality, get a job, and live a normal life. Unfortunately, that's something I can't do for you...or with you."

I stare at him. And, despite my precognition, his words sting more than if he'd slapped me across the face.

"Hello? Anything?" He raises his eyebrows.

"What are you saying?" I manage to whisper.

"What I'm *saying* is...I know you have some cool ideas, but let's be honest, you're not good at marketing or running a business. You can't play ball with the big boys. You tried and failed again and again. Now you're in debt up to your eyeballs, and your constant stress is dragging me down. Lindsay, I have to be honest with you—I *can't* love someone as selfish and unrealistic as you are."

His words are like little darts, stabbing me, one after the other. "So, you don't love me anymore." I barely get the words out.

Just last year, this man asked me to spend the rest of my life with him. Who knew the rest of my life, our life, could be outlasted by a sickly hamster or a semi-viral video.

He couldn't just stop loving me...could he?

We stare at each other for what seems like forever. This is the soul scorching, heart of darkness in hell, kind of forever. The answer to my question is scrawled all over his face. I try to speak, but a sob catches in my throat. He sighs heavily in a way that he always does whenever he has big news. I always thought it was cute, but right now, he's killing me.

"I need you to move out of my house," he says, his brown eyes focused on me. "And I know this may seem selfish, but...I need the ring back, too. It was my grandmother's."

I look down at the beautiful diamond and platinum creation circling my finger—the perfect ring. The ring that showed the world I was loved unconditionally, through good times and in bad. The ring that held so many promises for the future.

Humiliation makes my cheeks burn. *Not now! Hold back the tears, stay strong!*

I slowly slide the ring off of my finger and drift, zombie-like, toward the counter. My heartbeat thunders in my chest. Each beat reminds me of the things that had gone up in smoke this year—my business, my bank account, my attempts to get backing to start another company. Even my family thinks I'm a tragic failure.

And now Charlie does, too.

Gently, I set the ring on the counter, but somewhere inside of me, a fire ignites and courses through my veins. It takes every ounce of self-control for me not to pounce on him at this very moment. How dignified would that be? Instead, I keep it cool, turning on my heels and strolling out of the kitchen without a word.

Yes! I looked cool! Looked is the operative word, but that's good enough.

"Oh, and the car's in my name, so you're gonna need to leave that here, too," Charlie calls out soberly.

The dam holding back my roiling flood of anger cracks and then crumbles. Hot tears rise into my eyes, betraying me. How dare he treat me this way? I needed his support, not this BS. All at once, I turn back to him, disgust creeping into my voice. "Anything else, dear?"

"What do you mean—"

"You can keep your freakin' house. While you're at it, how about my pride, my dignity, my future, my hopes and my dreams. And don't forget, my Faith, my love. The ring! The car! How about the clothes on my back? Maybe you can sell them at a consignment shop! What else do you want from me, Charlie? How about my toothbrush? Would you like my floss? I know, you want my Zen coloring book collection! You can have it all!"

"You're being immature about this."

"I'm being immature?" I place a palm to my heaving chest. "I'm not the one bailing when things get too inconvenient. I was there for you when you weren't sure which direction to go in your life, but now that it's my turn...you can't handle it. You know what? Forget it." I turn, my nails digging into my palms.

"Now, wait a minute, Lindsay. That's not true…"

I whip around and rush up to his face, in spite of myself. "No, YOU wait a minute. Where the heck do you get off making me seem like some wimpy woman incapable of anything? Yes, I've been struggling to make ends meet, but it's not like I haven't been trying. Plus, I've worked my rear off around this house. While you go off to a secure job every day, coming home too tired to hold a conversation with me, I've been taking *risks*, trying to find new business opportunities while single-handedly holding this house together."

He scoffs and shakes his head.

"Oh, you don't believe me? Who do you think fixed the sink in the master bathroom? Or the garbage disposal when it stopped working? Definitely not you. You wouldn't know an Allen wrench from a monkey wrench. Did I call a plumber and spend hundreds of dollars? No. I watched YouTube videos and *poof*—fixed it *myself*."

"Wow, you're so awesome," Charlie says, folding his arms over his chest. "You fixed one sink while I pulled in a full-time household income. Good for you."

"You…" I seethe, "are *such* a douche. You want the car? The ring? Take them!" I pick up the ring and rush over to the kitchen sink.

He holds up his hands. "Lindsay? Don't…"

"Since you're so *awesome* at pulling in a household income and can afford to buy another one, I guess you don't need this." I let the ring drop into the garbage disposal and poise my hand on the switch to turn it on.

"STOP!" he shouts, running toward me, eyeballs the size of dinner plates.

His face contorts in fury as he realizes what I'm about to do. I grin coldly, spin around, and open the door, ready to walk out in a dramatic blaze of glory. Except as I exit, my toe catches on the uneven threshold that Charlie had promised to fix a dozen times and never had, and I go stumbling out with a muffled, "Oof!", like one of the Three Stooges.

Pefect, Lindsay. Just perfect.

Tears run down my face, unchecked now, as I scurry away. What a mess, and I'd only made it worse with my childish behavior. I could never grind his grandmother's ring in the disposal for real. She, unlike some people, was nice to me.

Down the hallway of the building, it's difficult to turn my brain off as it continues to berate me for all of my mistakes. *No one will ever take you seriously unless you can play with the big dogs like Charlie said. Forget it; no one will ever love you. Your ideas are stupid; you're stupid.*

"Shut up," I tell myself.

In my heart, I know I'm not worthless, yet my brain tells me otherwise. Always at war with myself. *You're a failure, Lindsay.* Just like the man at the venture capital firm told me when I pitched my idea for another startup company last month, just like my mother has told me over and over. The years I spent trying to prove everyone wrong is what I should have thrown down the stupid garbage disposal and shredded into a million worthless pieces, not the ring.

For all that time wasted, I could have flipped that switch a million times. Not that it would have mattered. Because, despite what I'd told Charlie, like everything in my life, the garbage disposal repair was a total failure, too.

The present day—

The water grows even colder than a moment ago. I take another step forward. Then another. Shivering, I feel around the inside of my shorts' pocket for the warm sliver of metal stashed inside. I'm careful while doing it. Funny how even as I prepare to obliterate my life, my mind still automatically protects me.

Suddenly, the air warms with nearby laughter. Turning to shore, I scan down the beach, which is covered in dancing dots of reds, blues, and oranges as the cheerful beach-goers play in their colorful swimsuits. A powerful swell cuts my legs out from under me. Disoriented and downed, I'm pulled into the depths of the ocean water.

Briny water fills my nose and mouth as I struggle to the surface, gasping.

Holy crap, I almost died! And that is my job ocean, not yours.

My terror-fueled outrage is kind of ludicrous, considering my purpose here today. I guess I forgot not to turn my back on the ocean because I was too busy turning my back on life. Another example of Lindsay's failures.

Check.

The buzz of the chatter back on shore is lost in the gentle breeze. A young man chases a woman down the sand as she shrieks with glee and lets out a chorus of laughter when he catches up to her. Another stab to the gut.

That was Charlie and me once.

I've never felt so broken, but I've never hit rock-bottom like this before, either. I try to come to grips with the reality of what is about to happen.

You're pathetic; you know that? You messed up your life beyond repair, so who's going to trust you now? No one. Ending it is for the best.

Pushing back tears, I pull the blade out of my pocket and stare at it.

Ever since I was a little girl, I imagined myself a successful businesswoman by now, making the big bucks with the best of them. Yet, here I am…lost it all…staring hopelessly at glinting silver in my hand—not the bling of my dreams, that's for sure.

The giggling woman's voice in the distance pulls me back to the present. Her laughter is beautiful but also a waterfall of salt in my bottomless wounds. I allow myself one last moment to look at her, to see what I could have been—should have been—had I done things right. I turn my face to take her in, but the happy couple has disappeared.

Better that way. No need to ever see what I will never have.

Turning back toward the ocean, a glimmer of light catches my attention. Standing about thirty feet away is a man in his early sixties. The sun reflects off his gold wristwatch. He has brown skin, a neat white beard, and well-groomed salt and pepper hair. He would make for a nice postcard standing on the shore, a picture of gentlemanly perfection in his white linen pants and loose Polo shirt, staring out at the peaceful water.

He senses me watching him and turns his gaze on me. His eyes are deep, kind and filled with compassion. A grin splits his face as he twiddles his fingers in my direction.

Not today, old man. I am not *in the mood to make friends.*

Still, he keeps his gaze locked on me. Moments silently pass, then minutes. I look away but glance back every so often.

He's still staring. Seriously? How can I kill myself with an audience, especially one so bright and cheerful?

I focus back on the task at hand and take another step into the ocean. The water level is now up to my thighs. The ocean water is so cold. I'm not sure which is worse, the freezing water or my cold, empty life—I can't stand either.

Still, I can feel his eyes burning holes into me. I turn to look. Sure enough, he's watching with a bemused look on his face.

What's his problem? Even though I shoot him a heavy frown, he responds with another broad smile, one that touches the corners of his crinkly eyes.

My mind spins with rage. Who does this man think he is? I shrug to let him know I am not at all happy about this staring contest.

Can't a girl properly end her life without a stranger mocking her for it?

Water splashes up as I stomp to the shore with a face full of gritty sand stuck to my cheeks and clinging to my hair.

The closer I get to him, the wider he smiles. When I finally emerge onto the sand, my shorts drenched, I stand in front of him, hands on my hips.

"So what! Today I don't look cover girl perfect? No sin in that. Why are you staring at me?"

He cocks his head to one side, looking confused.

"What? You can't mind your own business?" I cross my arms, waiting for his answer.

He blinks slowly and looks out at the horizon. "It's not your time yet."

It's not my time yet? What is he, some carnival fortune-teller or something?

"What do you mean?" I snap at him, sizing him up. He looks so calm and peaceful; I find it difficult not to hate him for it. "Who are you?"

"I'm Arjun," he says in a kindly voice. "And you?"

"Lindsay," I say, though I have no idea why I am even talking to this man.

"Lindsay," he says as if trying the name out on his tongue. "Very nice to meet you. I don't believe it is your time to leave this world yet. I sense there is more for you to do here."

My mouth swings open.

A pretty audacious claim, but is he right?

No. This whole thing is ridiculous. He doesn't know anything about me.

In fact, my life is none of his business.

I take a deep breath to collect myself. "What makes you think I was about to end it? I mean, who would try to off themselves at a public beach in broad daylight? As far as ideas go, it's a pretty dumb one."

The smile fades from Arjun's face. He contemplates his answer for a while. "I saw the way you looked at the ocean. The way you shook from the fear of uncertainty. I saw the way you looked at that couple on the beach and noticed the sadness you felt watching them."

My throat goes tight at his words, but I bluster through. "Really? Well, you're making a lot of assumptions for someone who doesn't know me."

"Was I wrong?" He raises an eyebrow.

I fold my arms tightly across my body and start moving away. "I don't see how it's any of your business."

"You're right, but you're the one who came to me. I didn't come to you."

"Well, to be honest, I was a little surprised to see someone *smiling* at me just as I was about to end my life. Anyway, being so smiley when someone else is so clearly miserable isn't exactly compassionate, is it, Mister?"

Arjun glances down and slides his hands into his pockets. "But it worked, didn't it? It stopped you."

He looks into my eyes, and I smirk.

Arjun lets go a small chuckle and shakes his head. "Well, Lindsay, I must say…at least you have a sense of humor going for you."

"Yeah, well, that's all I have. And right now, it's worth about a stinking penny." I let my arms fall to my side.

He looks straight through me. Something about his eyes calms me. Still, I can't help but ask this, "What exactly is it that you do, other than distract people during their private, really, really private, moments?"

He smiles, ignoring my question and shaking his head again. "Or you might choose to see that I was giving you a reason to walk back to shore. No one can make anyone do anything. **You are in charge of your destiny.**"

Okay, I don't know which mountaintop this Gandhi wannabe fell from, but I am not going to stand here and listen to this nonsense. I start walking away, wishing I'd never walked over in the first place.

"Great. Let me go take charge then."

"Lindsay," Arjun says, "weren't we having a conversation because you *do not* want to end your life?"

It's true that I want this pain to end, and while I was talking to him, I was at least distracted. "Sir, I can't seem to make it any better no matter what I do. You don't understand what it's like. I'm not even good at planning and executing my ending…no pun intended. I mean, coming to the beach during the day, and all the people? Just another bad idea."

"Then make me understand. I have the time." He plops his butt right down on the wet beach.

Ugh. I'm so horrible at everything; I can't even kill myself right!

I pace the stretch of beach in front of him, words bubbling up in uncontrollable waves. "I have nothing to live for. My friends and family have all written me off. Life has become one struggle for survival after another. I mean, look at me! I'm a forty-year-old woman! I look forty, right? You were going to say forty and not a day older?"

Arjun looks unfazed. "I think you look just fine. And it sounds like you have already decided nothing will work for you."

"What is that supposed to be, some reverse psychology crap?" I ask.

"No, I'm completely serious. You think life has not been fair to you. But you are so young. Who knows what else it holds?" His voice is challenging, yet, almost naïvely innocent.

"First of all, I think you missed the part where I said I was forty…"

He draws in the sand with his finger. "Practically a baby. My life didn't even begin until after forty. So tell me how you got to this point."

I sigh. "Okay, look…long story short, I was a top-performing software engineer for a successful company. But after some time, I started wondering why I couldn't just start my own company and make all this money myself. I had the industry knowledge and a good-sized nest egg I could dip into. So I started a social media company for conscious entrepreneurs. I didn't know much about hiring or managing people, but I hired a CEO and a few software engineer friends—the best I knew. When the great recession hit in 2008, companies couldn't even afford the small monthly subscription fee we charged. It all fell apart. I lost everything I had…" The tears well up again and begin streaming down my cheeks. I can't stop crying.

"Sorry," I mutter as I wipe my face with my dirty shirt. "I tried to make a comeback, but my confidence was completely shattered. Still, I pulled myself up and started a company to help small businesses with their technology needs. Bombed at that one, too, even though I tried everything. Now I have no money, nowhere to stay and the love of my life, my fiancé, Charlie, left me, and I'm forty years old with nowhere to go."

Arjun reaches out a hand and lays it right on my arm. I stare at it for a long moment. "I understand what you are going through, Lindsay, and I certainly appreciate the courage you have to start a company. I also appreciate what it is like to be successful at failing at such a young age." He chuckles lightly.

"Are you laughing at me?" I ask with a scowl. "Because it's not funny. I just opened up to you, you know."

"Of course not," he says. "I see so much of myself in you. I am not enjoying your failure, but did you know that most successful entrepreneurs in this world have failed when they were starting out? If you are going to fail, fail early in your life rather than later."

"Nope. I'm not cut out for this. I can't take it anymore. I can't even look at my family. They knew I was going to fail, told me I couldn't pull it off. They even tried to warn me before I started, but I managed to convince my parents and grandparents to lend me money to help keep me going. They were right. God, I'm so stupid! Why didn't I listen to them?"

Arjun flashes an all-knowing smile.

"Why do you keep doing that?"

"Can I ask you a question?" Despite my mild irritation at his constant smiling, Arjun's calm voice is like a sweet syrup of love and humanity.

It's strange, but I feel like I can trust him to some degree, even though I hardly know him. "Sure," I finally relent.

His eyes light up with joy. "Great. Who is the best-looking, most attractive guy on this beach?"

My mouth drops open. "Seriously? Do you need an ego boost today or a compliment or something?"

"Just humor me and answer the question seriously," Arjun insists with both a firmness and urgency that piques my curiosity.

"Fine." I gesture vaguely down the beach a ways. "I guess the guy in the black shorts…over there."

He nods and then points to the row of spectacular houses in the distance beyond the beach, perched in their glory overlooking the ocean. "And which of those homes do you think is the most beautiful?"

Tears spring to my eyes again as I recognize the futility of what we're doing. "This is silly."

"Please."

"Ugh." I shield my eyes from the sun and scan the row of houses. "That house, the one with the blue roof. There. Happy?"

"Yes, very." He smiles.

"Great. Now can I go kill myself in peace?"

"Lindsay, you didn't even have to look around to find the most handsome man or beautiful house. Love and wealth are two things you desire on a deep level, so you automatically noticed them when you arrived. Am I right? Your mind stored these images as important information that you could easily access."

I flip my palms up. "I guess so, but that doesn't seem so strange to me. Don't we all want love and money?"

He nods. "Certainly. So, if I were to show you how you can buy a beautiful house like that *and* have the most amazing love of your life, would you be willing to postpone killing yourself for just ninety more days?"

I let out a low, pained laugh. "Postpone killing myself so I can go chasing mystical unicorns and rainbows again? I think living in a fantasyland is what got me here in the first place."

Arjun studies me intently. "If unicorns and rainbows is what you want, Lindsay, we can make that happen, too," he says dead serious. "Would you choose to live for ninety more days?"

"You sound like a commercial," I said, suddenly feeling desperate to end this conversation. Regaining hope and having my dreams dashed again would surely kill me quicker than the ocean ever could. "Do you come with a money back guarantee, too? Or maybe a fancy set of knives that can slice through a can *and* a tomato?"

"No can. No tomato. But a solemn promise, with a get your life back guarantee. Maybe that's just a bit better than just the usual money back guarantee. Don't you think?"

I sigh. *Ninety more painful days on this planet...for what? More rejection, failure, and disappointment in the end?*

"Aren't you going to say, 'But wait! There's more!'" I ask. Maybe if I make it all into a joke I can stop that little kernel of hope from spreading.

"Nope. That's all I have to offer. What do you say?"

I stare at him for a long moment before whispering miserably, "I can't."

"You can't, or you won't?"

His words echo deep inside of me, despite my fear. And as I turn back to face the sea and begin to march toward it, I can't stop my cascading thoughts.

What had happened to my passion? My dreams? What happened to that determined young girl who was once on a mission to live an extraordinary life and change the world? What happened to me...who have I become?

From somewhere inside of me, a tiny voice calls out...*I'm still here. Just rub the genie bottle and I'll come out.*

I stop cold in the sand. Icy water pools all around my feet, dousing the fire and fight from my body and brain. I turn around and search Arjun's eyes.

"Okay. Okay, I'll do it."

He walks towards me and wraps me in his arms, hugging me close. I want to say that it feels awkward, that I hate being pressed up against a perfect stranger, but it doesn't. It feels nice. For once, someone cares about me.

And for now, it's enough.

CHAPTER TWO
The Ferrari

When he releases me, there are tears on his shirt and linen pants, but he doesn't seem to care. He gently pulls back and holds out his hand.

"What?" I scrunch my brow in confusion.

Arjun nods toward my pocket.

"Oh." I guess he was watching me from the beginning. I reach cautiously into my pocket and pull out the razor blade, carefully placing it in Arjun's palm.

"Thank you for believing in yourself." He smiles reassuringly, takes me by the shoulder, and leads me up the beach, away from the water.

Can he help me? I honestly have no clue, but I have nothing to lose by letting him try. We walk past beach-goers who frolic and play without a care in the world. "Let's get you a dry towel so that we can continue our talk."

"Yeah, I feel like a stinky wet dog who needs a good shake," I say, cringing.

As we reach the edge of the beach and step onto the hot pavement of the parking lot, I shake the sand from between my toes. Arjun leads me across the lot to a beautifully polished Ferrari LaFerrari.

Holy Shih Tzu! What does this guy do for a living? That's as expensive a Ferrari as there is!

As I stand there gawking, he pulls a set of keys from his pocket and disarms the alarm. Suddenly, I'm excited and nervous all at the same time. On one hand, I've always dreamed of having a fancy sports car like this, but on the other, what if I fail again?

"I don't want to mess up your beautiful car with my wet clothes. Maybe you should run me through the car wash first."

"Lindsay, it is only a car. Besides, believe it or not, wet and muddy, you are still much more valuable than this car! Jump in."

"Yes, sir."

How did this man make me feel hopeful again in such a short time?

Looking around at the shiny dash and fancy interior, I shake my head in disbelief. Never in a million years would I have guessed that my beach adventure would have ended this way.

Arjun climbs into the driver's seat beside me and flashes a confident smile.

I shrink in my seat, suddenly feeling less than confident once more. Here's this guy who looks like he has it all, but does he really understand the mess I'm in?

"You never answered my question," I blurt.

"Which one?" His calming voice rings gently as the car rumbles to life.

"What *do* you do? I mean, how did you…" I fumble for words.

He closes his eyes momentarily. "Ah, yes…well, are you asking *what* I do, or *how* I can do it?"

"Well, I guess both," I admit.

Arjun guides the car out of the parking lot, and I wince at the beat-up Honda Fit I'd bought with my last nine-hundred dollars after Charlie invited me to leave sitting in the first space. The old man notices me eyeing my junky car but says nothing. The Ferrari glides smoothly onto the Pacific Coast Highway. Picking up speed, the shoreline zips by in my peripheral vision. It's a beautiful day, and I'm sorry I almost missed this view.

"I own a few companies and also have consulted as a business growth accelerator for numerous others." His eyes flit to me every few seconds to make sure I'm listening. "My businesses have made me wealthy. After years of helping to grow Fortune 500 companies, as well as small businesses, I shifted my focus to teaching entrepreneurs and professionals how to gain freedom from the pitfalls that caused them to fail in the first place. I use what I learned over the years to help them succeed."

My mind swirls with a million questions to ask him but I remain silent.

"I sense that you are perplexed, Lindsay."

There he goes being Madame Cleo again, reading my mind. Arjun shoots a quick but pointed look in my direction.

I believe he's done well for himself. Heck, the car alone is proof of that. But, first of all, he's a man. And secondly, his life seems pretty easy breezy to me. Maybe his companies were well-funded. Maybe he has never had to deal with failure or struggle at all.

I don't want to alienate my new friend, but I want to be truthful…

I clear my throat and shrug. "Well, yes, to be honest, you come across like you have a perfect and easy life."

Arjun turns the car off the highway and takes a sharp left toward the city. He slows as we melt into the thick jungle of traffic that moves at a slow trickle throughout Los Angeles no matter the time, day or night. Upscale restaurants and polished marble buildings line the streets.

"Actually, I have been through quite a lot," he says. "And have gone through extreme financial failures in my life. So I do know what you are going through."

I look at him in disbelief. "Seriously?" His car was worth more than any house I've ever lived in.

"This happened when I lived in India. I was in my final year of engineering college. I was getting ready to go to class, but I didn't have any money—and I mean, not even enough to pay for my bus ticket that day. On the other hand, you arrived at the beach in a car, so right away, you have more than you think you do, Lindsay." He eyes me carefully.

I cross my arms. This time, I can't walk off on the beach when Arjun's words strike a nerve. I am cemented in his car, but if I'm being honest with myself, I wouldn't have left anyway. I'm intrigued, to say the least.

"I had no one to help me. I was alone in the world. I was so depressed because I thought I'd have to drop out. If I couldn't even pay for transportation to school, how would I ever pay for my education? I was ready to give up on school—I just couldn't afford it!"

I am shocked. All this time, I envisioned that Arjun had come from money. He seems so carefree.

He looks at me knowingly and continues. "Even back then, I used to talk to homeless people and would give them a little money when I had it. Well, on this particular day, I was visibly upset as I passed by one of the poor people I had talked to before. 'What happened to you today?' he asked me. 'Usually, you are very happy!' I shrugged him off, not wanting to admit my defeat to anyone, but he insisted I tell him why I looked so upset.

"I pulled myself together and tried to sound confident as I told him, 'I don't have money for my bus fare to college today. But it's okay. I will find a way,' and I started to walk away before he noticed the tears gushing in my eyes. He called after me and handed me an old piece of cloth. Inside were small coins and bills he'd collected. He said, 'Take this all!' and gave me everything he had. I just lost it right there. I started crying. I told him I only needed twenty rupees—about a quarter dollar—for my bus fare, and I gave him back the rest of his money."

I sit in rapt attention, barely noticing the traffic now.

"That man had nothing and yet was radically generous. It inspired me to pick myself up and find a way to make things work in my life even when things were not easy, specifically to find money no matter what the odds were so that I could finish my college studies, and to recognize that there are worse things that could happen to me. I had to go through many more challenging experiences, but that one was truly a significant, inspiring, turning point in my life."

"Wow," I say, dumbfounded. I had failed, too. How many times? I started to silently count my failures on my fingers. Forget it. I'll have to borrow Arjun's fingers and toes, too, for that math. But if Arjun was able to pull himself up from that kind of poverty, then why couldn't I?

"Yes, wow. Lindsay, back then, I tended to brand myself as a complete failure and get frustrated. It took me some time and deep thinking, but I decided on three things. One—I wanted to become extremely wealthy. Two—I wanted to help other poor kids, like myself, get an education. And three—I wanted to help those who suffer, and convert that into celebration."

I can't even imagine this confident, successful man in front of me as a depressed and penniless kid. Maybe Arjun really does understand. Maybe he *can* help. The tiny ember of hope inside my chest blossoms into a flame. "What happened after that?" I whisper, happy to be breathless with anticipation instead of from near drowning.

"I spent decades of my life trying to figure out financial success. I observed and interviewed and learned from the top one percent of successful people in the world. I dove deeper into neurology and psychology to understand the inner workings of these phenomenal entrepreneurs and world class proffesionals. Based on what I have learned and from my own experiences, I uncovered seven simple, but very powerful forces that shape most wildly successful people. I applied these to the businesses I now own, and then I became impassioned to help other entrepreneurs and professionals to do the same."

"Seven forces?"

He cracks a huge smile. "I call them, 'The Accelerators'. By now millions of businesses and professionals around the world have used my system to grow their business, life or career to the next level in a rapidly changing world," he says with such certainty, he almost convinces even me.

My curiosity pushes me to the edge of my seat. "So, you're telling me you have it all figured out."

"Not everything, but enough to guide you to be successful in *this* life." He smiles. "Listen, Lindsay, let's be real. In the past, women didn't have the opportunities they have today. Many women with whom I've worked tell me they were not taken seriously as female entrepreneurs. For the last four million years, men were the hunter-gatherers. Most women joined the workforce less than a hundred years ago. Due to this, the work environment is conditioned and built by men for other men. Quick and impulsive decision making, aggressive management styles, most places don't even have a facility for new moms to breastfeed their children. We need a major shift in mindset to adapt to women's aspirations and needs, as well as men's. I didn't want my daughters to grow up in a world where they were deprived of the opportunities that my son had. I wanted to change that and level the playing field for both female and male-run businesses through a new generation philosophy."

Sounds good to me.

"Most importantly, it is time for us to abandon the old philosophy that dictates the ABC of sales—'always be closing'. I propose the new ABC of Persuasion—always be caring. This philosophy has helped me grow a few billion-dollar brands."

He just said "billion".

With a "B".

I desperately want to believe in Arjun but all I can hear is Charlie's voice in my head, *"Enough with this pie-in-the-sky crap!"* I'd like to shove a pie in his stupid face.

But maybe watching him gobble up a huge helping of humble pie served up by your's truly would be even more satisfying...

"That sounds intriguing," I sigh, trying to take it all in. "But I'm sure luck has a lot to do with it, too."

"I can speak from my experience...today, I am what some consider a 'lucky person,' but my success has been anything *but* luck! I have created most of all that I dreamed of creating, and I have a fabulous life with my wonderful wife. Both son and daughters have very successful businesses and families of their own now. I am offering the same invitation to you."

I listen to the soft timbre of his voice and know that I want to be helped.

"Lindsay, a few minutes ago, you *chose* life. Let me ask you a question—what are the reasons why you feel you *must* succeed in life and business?" He stops and holds up a hand. "Let me rephrase that, why *do* you want to live, what drives you?"

I think about that for a long moment and stare at him solemnly. "I want your Ferrari, Arjun."

He chuckles. "You can have your own. You remember the story of the Tortoise and Hare?"

"Oh, come on. Are we going back to Kindergarten now?"

"Steve Jobs said 'Simplicity is the ultimate sophistication.' Have you ever thought about that story as an adult? You've heard of that tale as a child, but what does it mean? How does it apply to real life?"

"I have no clue, but something tells me you're going to explain it to me," I say with a half-smile.

He nods. "You would be right. Let me share my version of the story. There once was a hare named Bolton."

"Bolton? Come on, Arjun, couldn't you go with Bunny, or Harry, or even Peter? Peter is a much better name than Bolton."

"My story, my name," he says, turning the corner down a winding road. "So, Bolton was the swiftest in his country, revered by everybody who knew him. He was the fastest, the best, and he bragged about that fact to anybody who would listen or wasn't fast enough to cover their ears."

That rabbit sounded like a real jerk.

"Charlie," I said emphatically. "The bunny should be named Charlie. But if it was named Charlie, I'd have to hate the bunny and I'd want to throw a pie at it. No one likes to hate bunnies. Bunnies are cuddly and …"

"Lindsay, the bunny could be named Kanye if you like, but let's stick to the story, shall we?" Arjun said, patient as ever. "As it was with many heroes, when Bolton proved his strength, everybody listened. Most cheered him on, caught up in the glory that Bolton promoted in himself. Nobody challenged his authority, and Bolton used his name to intimidate everybody else. In his eyes, he was the fastest and thus—the best. But he also wasn't going to let anybody contest this fact.

"So this went on for a very long time, until one day, Sophie, the tortoise, was completely annoyed by his vanity and challenged him to race her. Everybody laughed, Bolton the loudest. After all, how could a mere tortoise beat a rabbit? On the day of the scheduled race, all the animals in the forest came to watch. The race began. Bolton was barely a visible blur; he ran so fast. In contrast, Sophie plodded along, her heavy shell slowing her progress."

I could almost picture myself trudging down the road like a sack of stones with feet while a bunch of slick rabbits in business suits went zipping by me.

"This is hitting too close to home, Arjun."

He nods knowingly but doesn't falter from his storytelling. "When the hare was well ahead of Sophie, he stopped to rest. He looked around—nobody was watching. He couldn't hear the cheering of the crowds any longer and knew he was far ahead. 'What is the big deal if I close my eyes for a minute? That silly tortoise could never beat me.' His heart slowing down,

Bolton allowed himself to relax and enjoy his well-earned lead, and he slipped into a pleasant nap with the finish line just around the next bend in the forest."

"I know where this is going…"

"Shh… Bolton slipped into a dream in which he was running toward the finish line. Suddenly, he heard loud cheering!"

"Was it the bankruptcy lawyers collecting his debts? Just drawing some parallels, you know."

Arjun shot me a warning look and went on. "In his excitement, he jumped up, out of his dream, to see Sophie approaching the finish line. He dashed to the finish line to great applause, only to see the crowd was wildly lifting a victorious Sophie onto their shoulders!"

"This story sucks for Bolton."

"But has a great ending for Sophie, doesn't it?"

"Yeah, sure, if you believe in fables and fairytales. I tried Prince Charming, and kissed the frogs, but nada for me. That story has been told a million times, yet I don't hear of anyone's life being changed by it. It certainly never changed mine."

"YET," Arjun adds. "But you know how Sophie, the tortoise, actually won the race, don't you?"

"Sophie got lucky that Bolton fell asleep."

"Hmm…let me explain, and you'll see how the story *is* part of real life. This story is far more than two animals in a race. It's about the lessons we can learn, and how we can apply them in your own life and business. Sophie was a forty-year-old woman and mother of two beautiful children. A wonderful wife. But she was shy and struggled her entire life to understand herself. Still, she always had great ambitions and the drive to move forward. Bolton was twenty-nine years old and a graduate from University of Oxford. He had all the attributes of a type A personality—intelligent, organized, driven, achievement and task-oriented. He talked fast and always thought about what to say next when someone else was talking. He bragged about his speed and, frankly, his presence was intimidating for Sophie and anyone else."

Yeah, you got that right, I think, giving his car's interior another glance.

"So tell me, Lindsay, what gave Sophie the courage to challenge Bolton?" Arjun pauses to let me process his question.

"I guess she was…unrealistic, like me." I flash him a grin. "She believed in fairy tales. And fables involving animals."

"Yes," he says to my surprise. "Not only was Sophie unrealistic, but also optimistic. You will soon learn about the power of optimism and how you can use that to become successful in your career and life. But for now, tell me, who would possibly make such an unrealistic, bold move like challenging that hare to a race?"

"I don't know…"

Arjun continues. "A person with clear goals and compelling reasons to achieve them, that's who. Now let me ask you this, Lindsay: why must you have strong emotional reasons to achieve your goals? Why do you think it is so important for you?"

I'm starting to feel overwhelmed by his questions, but I do my best to answer. "Compelling reasons motivate us to pursue what might seem like impossible goals. Or else we'd never even try."

"Exactly! Look at Mother Teresa, Mahatma Gandhi, Dr. Martin Luther King, Jr., and Nelson Mandela," he says. "All of them were ordinary people like you, with a few key differences. Why were they so willing to move mountains to make their dreams come true?" Arjun's eyes light up as he warms even more to the topic. "Their tasks were more challenging and way more *unrealistic* than Sophie's goal of running with the hare. Gandhi got his country of India to freedom from centuries'-long history of captivity from the British 'empire on which the sun never sets'. Dr. King had a dream that would require the Herculean task of leading the civil rights movement to overcome centuries of horrific injustice toward the black community in the U.S. If the tasks they had were this insurmountable, then how did each of them get the grit to make a difference and impact people's lives?"

"Yeah, but those people were special," I argue. "Born with that 'X' factor, the superhero chromosome. I don't know. But I don't think they were ordinary."

"Oh, Lindsay, I assure you, they were. But it's compelling reasons that enable ordinary people to do extraordinary things, and each of those people had reasons associated with their goals." He gestures to the glove compartment. "Get out a pen and paper and write this down."

I do as I'm told and sit with a pen perched over a scrap of paper as I look at him expectantly.

"The number one Accelerator that shapes all successes is this."

"Accelerator # 1 - Compelling reasons lead to creative answers."

A compelling reason, huh? I try the idea on for size as I scrawl the words on the page.

"Right now, my compelling reason is to fill my gas tank. That's what's motivating me, Arjun. Not exactly the stuff of greatness, is it?"

Arjun glances at me. I can tell he knows I'm not convinced. "I want to tell you a true story about Mother Teresa. This incident happened during the early stages of her work. As you know, she made it her life's mission to help the poor, the sick, and hungry. One day, she encountered a rich, unkind man. Think Ebenezer Scrooge of Dickens' fame. Mother Teresa asked the man for help, and even though he refused, she would not give up, holding her hands out, pleading.

"In his blind anger, the man spit on Mother Teresa's hand and yelled at her."

"What an ingrate."

"Yes, Lindsay. Can you imagine somebody rejecting you and being that hurtful toward you?"

I have no frame of reference for something so terrible, but I know how bad I'd felt when Charlie had rejected me in my time of need, and that had been bad enough. My eyes well with tears for poor Mother Teresa as Arjun presses on.

"Many people would have given up. But not this amazing woman called Mother Teresa. She quietly wiped the spit away, and said, 'I completely accept this gift for me. But what is your gift for my children?'

"Her peaceful response and persistent attitude shocked him. He hung his head in shame and apologized to her, even as she still held a heavenly smile. He immediately gave her the entire contents of his wallet and also became one of her devoted followers."

"But that's Mother Teresa. Not Lindsay Mitchell."

"There is no difference, Lindsay, if you have compelling reasons pushing you. Now tell me, why did our tortoise, Sophie, win the race?"

"Because she had a compelling reason," I say, hearing a little bit of confidence creeping into my voice.

"You are right. Sophie was vulnerable and emotional, thus strong. She could easily have felt rejected and quit when Bolton teased her. Sophie has a heavy shell that made it almost impossible for her to move quickly. She could have been paralyzed by her fear of being laughed at when she failed. But instead, she persevered because she had very compelling reasons behind her goals."

He skillfully maneuvers the car into a parking space on the street in front of a drugstore and cuts off the engine before facing me. "I am going to run inside and pick up a few things. I will only be a minute. Why don't you think about your compelling reasons in life while I am inside? I have complete confidence that you will be able to share them with me when I get back." He flashes me a reassuring smile.

Well, I'm glad *he* has total confidence in me because I sure don't.

I feel my forehead wrinkling with distress and rub it with my fingers, willing myself to relax while I sit back in my seat.

Compelling reasons… As I think on this, I watch the people on the street all shuffling along toward their destinations. Some are dressed in professional attire, but most are casual in their hip, trendy LA style.

After a few minutes, Arjun opens the driver's side door and slides into the car. The expensive leather seat squeaks as he reaches over and hands me a shopping bag. I peek inside.

Pens, a journal, and a touristy beach towel. I smile at Arjun in gratitude, pull out the towel, and wrap it around my damp legs. "We will get some clothes and something to eat soon, but I thought you might want these now," he says like he's my dad or something.

"Thank you." I smile. "What's the journal for?"

"You will see." The engine roars to life again, and I *so* want this car! Some people passing by turn to admire it.

Or maybe admire Arjun. With my homeless dog, damp, matted, dirty hair, and sand stuck in all the wrong places, I flush for a moment, thinking of what a wreck I must look like. Arjun guides the car smoothly back onto the street, then turns his attention back to me. "So, the answer?"

I sigh. This all feels a bit like lying on Dr. Freud's couch, but I suppose there's no harm in answering his question. "I want to show the world that I'm a powerful and wealthy businesswoman, a role model of possibility. I want to fall in love and stay in love for the rest of my life. I want to celebrate life with my friends. There. Tall order, huh?"

"Pretty awesome," he says, still driving purposefully. "I love your passionate reasons especially the one of falling in love, staying in love and celebrating life. It's beautiful and romantic."

I can't help but smile. Arjun's joy is a bit infectious.

"So, dry clothes or food first?"

"What?" I ask, thrown off for a moment. "Oh, uh...I don't have any money," I finally choke out, cheeks flaming with embarrassment. I've never felt more vulnerable than at this moment. Here's this strange man seeing me at my worst—sad, helpless and broke.

"Lindsay, money is only a tool. A tool to achieving what you desire, and one you can use to help others and make the world better," Arjun explains.

I eye him skeptically. For a moment, I don't know what to think. Am I his charity case? Does he want to sleep with me? Ugh, in my despair, the thought hadn't even crossed my mind until now.

Arjun glances at me. I must be wearing a wary expression on my face because he meets my discomfort with a gentle smile. "You seem uncomfortable, Lindsay. Is there something you want to ask me?"

I square my shoulders and look him directly in the eyes. "What do you want from me? I mean, what do you get out of all this? Do you expect..."

Arjun catches on to my thoughts and shakes his head with fervor. "I have no expectations of you. Eradication of stress and expanding joy in the world is my life's mission. It's my way of paying back the kindness others showed me, Lindsay. That is all. You can choose to accept this help, these lessons, and run your race and win, or...you can choose to walk away."

Truthfully, it's hard for me to imagine. Most people I have dealt with always wanted something from me.

"Think of me as a mentor or a coach," he adds.

A coach...*my* coach. I like that. I roll the phrase around in my head.

"Okay, my coach!" I smile at him, feeling even more hopeful.

"Good. Now that is settled, which is a higher priority for you right now, dry clothes or food?" Arjun asks patiently as we wait at a stoplight.

My shorts are wet but manageable. I'm still not entirely comfortable with the idea of this stranger buying me clothes, so food seems like an easier place to start. On cue, my stomach grumbles. "I'm starving. I haven't eaten anything since yesterday morning."

"Well, we must remedy that immediately!" he exclaims with whooping laughter.

Arjun pulls into the left lane and slows to a stop waiting for a break in traffic. As the cars whiz by on either side of us, I peek up at the cloudless California sky—a sheet of uninterrupted blue. The street is lined with tall, thin palms gently rustling in the breeze. I shiver, realizing that had Arjun not come along, I may not have ever seen another cloudless day.

Arjun presses down on the gas pedal, making the engine growl, as we shoot across the street and around the bend. He turns to me. "French, Italian, or sushi?"

"Italian," I answer quickly, thinking I could go for pasta.

He pulls in front of a cute little Italian café with a green, white and red striped canopy stretching over a small outdoor seating area roped off by potted jasmine vines in full bloom. It is a lovely sight. A valet quickly runs up and opens Arjun's door. Arjun climbs out and greets the valet, handing him the keys.

I reach for my door handle, but just as I do, the door swings open, and a younger valet pops his head into view and offers me his hand.

"Ma'am," the valet says.

Did he just take a second look at me? He must really be desperate.

I take his hand and step out of the car. The street is less busy than the one we were on a few minutes before. Everyone on the sidewalk seems so perfect.

I frown, looking down at my damp shorts and wrinkled T-shirt. Someday, someday, I will forget this embarrassing moment, if I'm lucky. I wonder if Arjun is a therapist, as well.

Arjun steps up next to me and leans close, whispering in my ear, "They are too caught up in their own lives to notice yours, Lindsay. Don't worry," he offers reassuringly.

I smile. A perky hostess interrupts the moment.

"Welcome to Angelini Osteria. Table for two?" she chirps.

"Yes, please," Arjun replies.

"Very good, right this way."

We follow her into the seating area to a small table in the corner where the intoxicating scent of jasmine fills my nostrils and brings back memories of a small village in the south of France I visited with Charlie. *When things were good*, I think.

My eyes swell up with unshed tears. Thankfully, a waiter steps up to the table and snaps a crisp menu, holding it in front of me, and the memories shatter into fragments and float away.

I order the Lasagna Verde, my stomach rumbling as I speak the words to the waiter. Eyeing the sugar packets on the table, I slap myself for even considering eating them right now in front of Arjun.

Arjun leans back in his chair, taking a deep, slow breath. Finally, he opens his eyes, fixing his gaze back on me.

The waiter brings us our drinks and asks if we would like anything else while we are waiting for our meals.

Crackers? Tortilla chips? Anything besides these sugar packets to gnaw on.

I know it's Italian, but my stomach is screaming at me.

Arjun focuses his intense, kind eyes on me. I can see the excitement building within him. "Are you ready to commit? Are you ready to find out what was stopping you from succeeding and kept you in the dark until today?" he asks, pausing dramatically.

I nod. I've come this far in just one morning. I can't stop now. I don't know where Arjun came from or why I've been listening to a perfect stranger all morning, but something about him—he's connected with me more in a few hours than anyone else has tried to do in the last three years. There's no question in my mind.

"I'm in."

CHAPTER THREE
Obstacles Are Opportunities?

After lunch, Arjun and I head to the beach where we park and get out to walk off our meals. Arjun tells me he has a conference call to make and that he will meet me at the Vista Del Mar Park a few blocks away in half an hour.

But he leaves me with one task...

"Imagine you are a seven-year-old at Christmas, dreaming without limits. What is something you want to achieve in the next ninety days?"

Seems so simple. But reducing all my hopes, dreams and wishes down to one single thing without instantly squashing the idea beneath my crushing self-doubt, before it even fully forms, is no easy feat.

As he drives away, I'm grateful for the time alone to let his question and all those lessons marinate some.

I'm going to need a lot of marinade, and a long time to steep in it.

Heat penetrates through to my bones as I walk, basking in the warmth of the mid-afternoon sun, which I almost didn't feel, had I taken my life. Conversational din and laughter from chattering tourists filters through the sunny air. Absorbing their sounds, I'm unable to place the accents of a few.

Cutting across the street between pedestrians and speeding bikes, I waltz into the small park—a stretch of grassy area lined with large palm trees and a low metal fence facing the ocean—the same ocean I almost ended my life in this morning.

Palms on smooth metal, *ouch, ouch,* I forgot how hot metal in the sun gets. I quickly hoist myself onto the picnic table. The ocean breeze kicks up my hair. I taste the saltiness in the wind. Looking at the ocean, I feel its vastness and calm.

Arjun's words filter into my mind: *Imagine you are a seven-year-old at Christmas, dreaming without limits. What is something you want to achieve in the next ninety days?*

What *do* I want?

To win the Powerball? Move to Mars and get away from it all? Travel to the past and invest in Apple Computer? Hey, Arjun *did* say to let my imagination soar as if I were a little girl.

Well, let's see... here's a biggie, I know I don't want to feel depressed and miserable anymore. I don't want to be broke and alone, either. I don't want to be a failure. As for what I *do* want...I know I want to be happy and successful. But how? I am *so* rock-bottom right now, reaching that goal feels insurmountable.

Speaking of bottom, my shorts are finally drying out from the heat on this picnic table as the sun warms my cheeks; I close my eyes.

I wish that somehow, all the answers would magically soak into my brain. I don't know how long I'm sitting there when I hear a familiar voice and open my eyes to find Arjun a few feet away with a wide smile.

I have to say; I'm a little jealous of his happiness. Then again, if I were super-rich like him, I'd have a smile on my face, too. Still, something tells me that Arjun's peace doesn't all come from his financial stability. I want to know how he does it.

Suddenly, I feel grateful and lucky and incredibly emotional all at the same time. A surge of tears rises into my eyes, and I blink them away.

"I don't know why you stopped me this morning. Why you're taking time from your busy schedule for me and my problems. But I'm glad you did. So, thank you."

Arjun looks at me straight in the eyes. "You are worth my time, Lindsay."

I choke the tears back down as Arjun pats my shoulder. We sit in silence for a while just staring out at the churning waves, listening to the soft whooshing wind through the palm fronds.

"Did you think about what you want to achieve in the next three months?" he asks.

I shrug, shaking my head. "I know I want to get out of debt, but that's like $500,000." Half a mil, ugh, talk about the impossible. I'm getting lightheaded just thinking about it. But saying the actual amount hurts more than I realize. I have a huge hole to crawl out of, but for once, I don't feel so hopeless about it. "I would love it if I could reduce my debt by $30,000 in the next three months."

Of course, there's probably no way—I haven't even been able to come up with enough money to rent a tiny apartment—but Arjun told me to dream big, so that's what I'm doing.

"Lindsay, that is an excellent thought. However, if you focus on avoiding debt as your *goal*, that is what you are going to grow. How can you rearrange your words so that you're stating something you want to **attract** instead of something you want to **avoid**? Also, since your goal is financial, make sure you add how you are going to serve others by earning that. **In a business or a career, money is the reward for adding extensive value.** The more value you add to the marketplace, the more money you will make."

"Okay..." I say, thinking it through. "I want to earn $30,000 in the next ninety days by adding value to small business owners who were part of my social media network. I want to do this using the software development skills I have. I'll help them automate and scale up their business and make more money."

"Terrific." Arjun nods. "You articulated it very well."

"Thanks. Now, all I have to do is find $30,000 and start my climb up the Himalayans." I grin sheepishly.

He chuckles. "We will talk about money soon and how to attract true abundance into your life. But for now, take the notepad we bought..." Arjun gives me a moment to retrieve my journal and pen from the shopping bag.

I examine my cuticles and pick at the tiny grains of sand still lodged there. I muster the courage to continue. "Arjun, I have to be honest. A big part of me still tells me I'm good for nothing. This voice has been the serial killer of my dreams for a while now. How do I fix that?"

"Lindsay, first of all...I commend you for the trust you are placing in me. The good news is that the moment you found your compelling reasons you have started the process of crushing your nagging inner voice."

"What you have is an inner conflict," he continues. "Part of you thinks you need to succeed financially, while another part thinks you are good for nothing. Let us say one person wants to become wealthy, and she works hard every day to reach that goal. At the same time, part of her brain says if she becomes wealthy, she might lose her moral values and become a corrupt person. Do you think a person with inner conflict such as this can become wealthy?"

"Probably not. You're looking at the poster child for inner conflicts."

"Why?"

"I wanted to be wealthy and successful. I tried hard, but deep down, I think I feel guilty about having excess money. Maybe that's because all the rich people I know are crooks. As a kid, I hated Ebenezer Scrooge and mean, stingy rich people. So, I always told myself, if I ever get to be like them, I don't want to be a bad person and lose my identity."

"Whoa, whoa…hold on. Is it true that *all* rich people are crooks?" He gives me a wide-eyed look.

My brain comes to a halt and does an about-face. "Well, not *you*, of course, Arjun."

"Oh, sure, insult me, then walk it back, why don't you?" Arjun says with a wink.

"I'm so sorry. I didn't mean that."

"It's okay. I'm not offended, but I can personally attest to knowing hundreds of people who are wealthy and are the most truthful, trustworthy and giving people on this planet, and nothing like Ebenezer Scrooge. Remember even old Scrooge had a change of heart."

"I know. I'm probably just jealous."

"There are good rich people and bad rich people, just like there are good and bad of any kind, Lindsay. My friend Warren Buffet put it quite well when he said, 'Of the billionaires I have known, money brings out the basic traits in them. If they were jerks before they had money, they are simply jerks with a billion dollars.' Morons become rich morons, and kind people become kind rich people."

"Yes, I get it. I'm sorry for generalizing. My bad."

"It's okay. But the real question concerns me is: *Is your belief about rich people stopping* you *from becoming wealthy yourself?*" Arjun pauses, a question in his smile.

Well, dang.

What other negative assumptions have I made, I wonder? I open my journal. "I feel like I'm in school again, and you're Mrs. Meyers, my World History teacher, about to start her lecture."

"Was Mrs. Meyers a good-looking older man with salt and pepper hair and an undeniable charisma?" Arjun wiggles his eyebrows and gives me his "good side."

"Actually, she was petite and blonde with big bosoms."

"Good for me!" Arjun claps once with a satisfied smile and then continues. "What are the five words that will describe you at your best? What words do you want others to use to describe you? It can be a word or a phrase. Think about that for a minute and let me know what you come up with," Arjun adds, hopping off the table and walking over to the seawall, leaning against it to gaze out at the sea.

What are five words that describe me at my best? Passionate, for sure. What else? Kind, maybe. And grateful?

I scribble down the first thoughts that come into my brain, writing and writing until my hand begins to ache. When I finish, I feel like my entire soul has purged itself on paper. Arjun knows I'm done, too. He strolls back and casually sits down on the picnic bench.

"I can tell you were passionate about what you were writing. What did you come up with?" he asks gently. I wish my father would have spoken to me the way Arjun does, instead of in his stoic, judgmental manner.

"I am passionate, kind, loving, caring and grateful."

"Those are powerful words." Arjun bows his head. "And, now, write down the five words you would never want to be associated with. These are words or phrases that you are disgusted by. You frantically hate the people with these characteristics…" I think about this for a while as Arjun sits silently beside me. Finally, I place pen to paper and begin writing, slowly at first; then the ideas pour out.

"I am not lazy. I am not weak, I am not untrustworthy or a loser, or insincere, or selfish. I'm not like Scrooge, either," I read aloud. "That is seven already, you want more?" I close my journal and drop my head into my hands, suddenly overwhelmed again.

"Let's work with those. Those are your negative identities or shadows. You believe that you are *not* weak, *not* untrustworthy, *not* insincere, and *not* selfish. But if you look closely, you will see that the focus of these words is on what you do **not** want. These are the areas you are resisting the most. What you resist the most persists as your shadows. For example, not selfish—you are giving energy to being something you don't desire to be...investing energy into protecting yourself from being selfish. Similarly, you are protecting yourself from being untrustworthy. Shadows are the biggest waste of your mental energy. This resistance is the number one cause of failure in life, career, and business."

Hmm. *So how else am I supposed to think of five words that don't describe me?* "But isn't that a good thing that I'm protecting myself from being selfish? I'm confused on this one."

"I understand. But here, let me ask you another question. Why are you trying to be *not* selfish?"

"So I can be selfless," I say. "Isn't that the point? To be the opposite?"

"But then, why don't you say *selfless* as one of your identity traits, rather than *not-selfish?*"

"Because you told me to think quickly off the top of my head."

"Fine, but if you were to say *selfless* as your identity word instead of selfish as your shadow, how would you feel differently?"

"I might feel more excited about my identity as a giving person." I don't know if I'm on the right track, but again, I think my mind is opening up to new ideas. "Is that what you mean?"

"Exactly. What do you think would happen if the entire world chose '*being selfless*' as who they are?"

"We'd have a perfect world," I reply with a laugh.

"That is not true, Lindsay. You will have a lazy and boring world. We can debate that later. But your selfishness is here to serve you, to inspire you to action. If a person doesn't have aspirations to motivate them, how will they progress? Unless and until you stop resisting your selfishness and start embracing it, you will not find your true freedom. Love yourself in spite of your vices. Now, let us look at your shadow identities, find the one with the highest emotional intensity. Which would you avoid or resist the most?"

"I would say being untrustworthy." I look out across the ocean, feeling a wave of melancholy sweep over me, in contrast to watching the rolling, sparkling blue waves glinting with joyful light. "That's one of my biggest pet peeves, when I can't depend on someone. I went through a lot when I was younger, seeing my mom unable to depend on my dad, and I guess that affected me a lot."

"I'm sorry to hear that. Well, that would be what I call your prime shadow, the one that is limiting you the most. Once we integrate this shadow into your identity, you will immediately see the most amazing changes take place in your life. *Your strength lies in your gift—your true identity. Your massive opportunities lie in your weaknesses—your shadows.* Are you ready to tap into those massive opportunities now?"

I tear my gaze away from the ocean and focus on Arjun's patient smile. "I am."

"That's good to hear, Lindsay. If you listed *untrustworthiness* as a shadow, it means trust was an important part of your original tribe—your family. Perhaps you haven't received enough validation from those who are most important to you. This might be why you feel so strongly about untrustworthiness because they might have told you you were untrustworthy. Some people might have gone through trauma, hurt or abuse that redefined them, but as you didn't mention it, I'm guessing that wasn't the case for you?"

"Unless you consider having my hair cut too short in sixth grade and everyone calling me Larry because I looked like a boy trauma, then no."

"That's debatable," Arjun says with a smile in his voice.

But as I examine my childhood now as an adult, I realize that there were some tough times that really did define me as a person up until now. Seeing my mother do the work of two people deeply affected me. She was my mother *and* my father, took on both roles since my father couldn't share in the hard responsibilities of raising a child. He was there for the fun, but never the true parenting. In many ways, it was this that had made me a strong woman…back when I was one, at least.

Arjun stares at me. "Where did you go, Lindsay?"

"Just thinking about why I have a strong association with that word." I don't feel comfortable telling him the rest. Arjun may be a great coach and a wonderful man, but he isn't my shrink. "So, you're saying I feel inadequate as a trustworthy person, and that's why I assumed this as a shadow rather than my identity?"

"Precisely. Your mind believes you haven't done things to show trustworthiness. Your mind attaches trustworthiness onto you as a shadow because it is too important for you. You may have done a thousand things to show that you are trustworthy, but your mind chooses to disregard them. So what can you do to fix that?"

"Go shadow boxing and use some big gloves to eliminate that shadow," I laugh, "or just take the darn thing and shove it down the InSinkErator."

He chuckles but shakes his head. "You know, I don't believe in eliminating anything. I want to integrate that shadow to be a coherent part of you."

"I had a feeling you wouldn't make it easy."

"Exactly!" Arjun stands and leans back against the railing, crossing his legs in front of him. "According to Dr. Daniel Siegel, integration is a central organizing principle for how the human mind develops across your lifespan. Integration creates a rhythm in which energy and information are free to flow across your entire self, helping you to be childlike again. I believe integration is the pinnacle of emotional and social intelligence."

"How do you remember all this stuff?"

"Lindsay, you seem distracted…"

"Yeah, well, I have good reason to be a little distracted today, but I'm trying. Come on, hit me with intelligence stuff again." I cup my ears with my hands, "I promise to listen better."

He sighs and glances at his watch. I have to remember that I'm not paying him for any of these lessons, and he's a busy man, though I fully intend to pay him back one day.

Arjun continues, "Tell me three instances where you displayed incredible trust to someone or something."

Okay, it's time to pull up my big girl panties, even if they are still full of sand. I can do this. I take a deep breath and let it out slowly. "With Charlie, my ex-fiancé. I never gave him reason to doubt me. I never cheated or betrayed him. He was the center of my world, and I gave him the benefit of the doubt all the time."

Arjun seems to contemplate me a minute before continuing. "Excellent. Share another experience where you were completely trustworthy, possibly from your childhood."

"My parents could trust me from the time I was young. I didn't lie to them, even if the truth might get me in trouble."

"That was good of you, Lindsay. Now, please share one final one from your business life."

"Alright. Here's the thing. I was always a hundred percent trustworthy to my business partners, even when I was bleeding money. I have never taken a single penny that didn't belong to me. I may not have been the best businesswoman, but I was extremely trustworthy to my clients."

Arjun nods approvingly. "Do you see how, even after all these examples of your trustworthiness, you wrote it as a negative. 'I am not untrustworthy' vs 'I am trustworthy.'"

"Yeah, why is that? I guess we always see ourselves in a more critical light, huh?"

"Yes, but it is also because you haven't allowed this characteristic to be part of you. All these years, you have been trying to avoid being untrustworthy, but not necessarily *be* trustworthy. Does that make sense?"

"Sort of. Why am I doing that?"

"Because your entire relationship network is built on the foundation of the relationship you had with your primary influencers, whether it be your father, mother, or another role model. In your mind, your inner child does not want to be rejected by these figures, even though you are forty years old. So you either imitate your parents or you become the opposite. But you are not a child anymore. You can own yourself and integrate the trustworthy part of yourself."

"I'm all for it, Arjun. Let's integrate away! Where do we start?"

"Very well. Take the first example of your trustworthiness and in your imagination bring it closer, bigger and more colorful."

"What does that mean?"

"It means magnify the experience by really listening to what you heard, really visualizing what you saw, and feeling what you felt. Bring the experience closer and closer to you. Bring it one inch away from your nose. Then, step into this experience."

Red linoleum tiles shine as a woman leans down on her mop. Her daily apron is tied around her back, and her brown hair is pulled up in a knot. My mom. The worry lines in her face smooth away and she smiles as I set the car keys on the table, five minutes before curfew. It had taken a lot for her to let me go to the school dance alone that night. Especially since I'd just gotten my license, but her trust in me had proven to be merited. She could count on me to honor my commitments.

After the first experience, Arjun asks me to do the same for the other two, and I do, really visualizing and stepping into those memories. The one with Charlie is particularly difficult because he dumped me even after I was completely devoted to him and bailed him out many times over. Still, I do it, and I feel stronger because of it.

"What do you feel now, Lindsay?" I hear Arjun's voice cutting through the ocean breezes.

"It was easier than I thought. I am starting to feel that I am trustworthy. I usually overlook this about myself, but I have to say...I've been a model daughter, boss, and girlfriend in this respect, I really have. I never associated these experiences as part of me being trustworthy. When I deeply connected with those just now, I saw myself in the mirror of trustworthiness."

"Excellent. Your identity is just a collection of your most cherished memories. When you deeply recollected the memories that demonstrated your trustworthiness, you felt it as your new identity. It will wear off sooner than you think. That is why you need to install this new identity into your psyche permanently."

"How?" I mean, forty years of thinking a certain way is not easy to change, but I suppose that's why I'm here with Arjun, to try and rewire my brain.

"By religiously practicing the same remembering exercise for three minutes for the next ninety days. Showing your brain that you are a heck of a trustworthy person until it becomes ingrained in you. Do it as soon as you wake up and right before going to sleep."

"So, let's see. All I need to do is remember the three instances I was trustworthy and experience it as if it is happening then and there. That is a lot of imagining to do." I laugh, a low, sardonic chuckle.

"You can do it, Lindsay. It's all about conditioning your mind. You can do the same for all of your shadows, and you will be a better version of yourself starting today. Once you build your empowering identity, you will automatically align yourself to true north. Your identity defines your destiny. Even criminals and sociopaths act in a way that is consistent with who they believe they are. One of the strongest forces in human psychology is to be consistent with their definition about themselves—their identity."

"That makes complete sense."

"Time to build a solid identity. When I was young, I did not have a great role model for business in my community. I admired Peter Drucker a lot as a great business strategist. So early on in my business career, I built this identity for myself: I am the Peter Drucker of Business Strategies."

"Hey! I like that."

"And then I went back and asked myself, 'What are five words that define Peter Drucker? What is the prime question that 'Peter Drucker' would ask on a consistent basis? What values does Peter Drucker have? What beliefs would Peter Drucker have about business? What state of mind would he live in most of the time?'"

"That's some serious idolizing, Arjun."

"It was, and in less than an hour, I had built a new identity."

"Dang."

"Dang is right."

"So, what have I learned here? Like, if you could roll it all into a little ball and present it to me."

"You've learned that the goal is not for you to become Peter Drucker, but to become the best version of yourself. You can start building upon yourself, spending years and years working on the next version of yourself. Or, you can re-engineer what successful people in your industry have done and build that in less than one hour by modeling them. Which one do you prefer?"

"I'm all for less work, Arjun. Remember the 20-80 rule. 20% of the effort creates 80% of the results?"

He laughs. "Precisely. That is your opportunity today. But remember that for your new identity to stick, you need to spend time daily declaring your new identity. Tell me, who could be a great role model for you in business?"

"Billionaire entrepreneur and founder of body shapewear company, Spanx, Sara Blakely. I am the Sara Blakely of Technology," I exclaim.

Not only is she an amazing businesswoman, but on a personal level, her product has saved me from a tragic case of muffin-top more than once.

"Yes, okay, good. And what are the five words that describe the one and only 'Sara Blakely of Technology?'"

"Passionate, adventurous, creative, successful, and trustworthy." I don't hesitate a bit. I admire this woman like no other, except my mother.

"Perfect. These are the words that now describe who *you* are—your new version of yourself. Notice you said trustworthy?" He winks at me. "Now, let me ask you the magic question that will help you discover your rule for stepping into this new identity. What should happen for the Sara Blakely of Technology to feel successful?"

"If she gives her best to her customers, then she knows she is successful. If she gives more value than she receives, she'll be able to acquire massive wealth. And I'm pretty sure she wears clothes that don't have seaweed and barnacles stick to them," I add with a smile.

"Okay, Lindsay, let's take this all the way home. Later tonight, sit down and ask yourself the same question for all the words that describe the Sara Blakely of Technology's identity. What should happen for the Sara Blakely of Technology to feel *blank*? Okay?"

"Roger that, Captain."

He playfully swats my arm. "Lindsay, you have much humor, passion, and intelligence to offer the world."

I can feel my eyes getting watery again and I clear my throat. "I'm glad you found me, too. Thanks for believing in me."

"Now, time for shopping!" he announces, glancing back in the direction of the shops.

"You've been too kind already! It's no problem. Really, I've gotten used to smelling like a mermaid."

"And it's no problem for me to help you. Besides, my sister tells me there's nothing like some new clothes to make you feel a fresh start!" He laughs heartily, that laugh I envy.

"Smart sister."

After another winding ride through the posh LA streets, Arjun finally brings the Ferrari to a halt in front of a beautiful, modern building.

"Uh, J.C. Penney?" I ask, knowing it's anything but.

"Barneys of New York." He smiles back, putting the car in park and pulling up the emergency brake. He may as well have said, *You-Can't-Afford-It Land,* for that matter. I've heard of the famed Barneys, but my wallet had never granted me access before.

Arjun reaches into his pocket and retrieves his wallet, pulling out a handful of one hundred dollar bills. "Buy what you need."

I flush with embarrassment at the wad of cash in my hands. On one hand, I'm too full of pride to take it, on the other…well…he's handing me a bunch of Benjamin Franklins. He always was my favorite almost-president.

I've never felt so pathetic, but special at the same time. This man has managed to care enough for a lifetime in just a single day.

"Go buy yourself the basics, and I will come back and meet you here, out front in two hours, okay?"

"Arjun, if you want me to buy basics, Target or Old Navy will suffice. I just don't feel right taking—"

"Lindsay, stop." He takes my hands and shakes them lightly. "This is all part of your education. The first step to wealth is to get out of a scarcity mindset. You understand?"

I nod reluctantly and slink out of the car. He flashes me one last smile before I shut the car door. The little Ferrari drives off down the street, and

I'm left standing in front of the store with my new friend Benjamin Franklin. "Here goes nothing…"

Pushing through the large glass doors with beautifully polished brass handles, my breath catches in my throat.

So *this* is how the other half lives. Everything sparkles and smells of big money, but I tell myself to hold my chin up. A few older sales ladies smile at me with slightly raised eyebrows, à la *Pretty Woman,* but they say nothing.

They're no different from you, Lindsay. That's for sure.

But it's a hard sell, even to myself, as I feel the grit of sand between my toes.

Walking through the store, I catch my reflection in about ten different mirrors. Besides looking like a sea hag and my hair needing color and a trim, the most noticeable thing about me is my posture. My shoulders sag like a deflated Macy's Day Parade balloon. That's been the hardest part of all this— dealing with being let down. But did life let me down, or did I do that all on my own?

If the latter, I need to forgive myself. Today is a new chance to change all that. I mean, it's not every day someone hands you Ben Franklins to go shopping with. *So suck it up, Lindsay. Straighten those shoulders and find something in this store that makes you smile.*

Retail therapy at its best.

A four-pack of Benjamins and ninety minutes later, I stroll through the glass doors into the bright sunshine—maybe not a new woman, but at least a better smelling one. I spot Arjun sitting in his car by the curb, eyes closed, smiling at the sun.

God, I envy his ability to disconnect and enjoy simple pleasures like that. The shopping bags rustle against my legs, as I jog over to his car. A few sharply dressed pedestrians glance at me as they walk by, as though I don't fit in, but I don't give a rat's ass anymore.

He looks at me inquisitively. "Looks like you found what you needed."

"Hell, yeah! I've been wanting five-carat diamond earrings my whole life! Thanks, Arjun!"

He raises an eyebrow at me but doesn't blink.

"Fine, I wish I'd gotten five-carat diamond earrings," I say, climbing into the car. "Instead, I just got some shirts and pants and undergarments. I was beyond reasonable and trustworthy. Thank you," I said sincerely as I hand him back the remaining cash.

Arjun takes it with a smile. "It's nice to see you smiling, Lindsay."

Yes. Sure, it's just clothes, but for the first time in a long time, I feel more hopeful. Until I remember the diamond ring I had to give back to Charlie. If I had a voodoo doll of him, it would go right into the InSinkErator, and the disposal would actually work this time.

He glances down at the shopping bags by my feet, and a concerned look comes over him. "Do you have a place to stay?"

"Well, since I decided against permanent residency in that under-the-ocean condo earlier today…" I shake my head, refusing to make eye contact with him. Crashing on my friend Erin's sofa had been home as of late, but… "I *was* staying with a friend."

"And how are those living arrangements going?"

I force a smile. "Not well. I don't think I can go back. It was causing tension between her and her husband."

"Has she told you that?" he asks, dark eyes full of concern.

"No, but I overheard them arguing about me last night. He made it pretty clear I'm not welcome."

"I'm sure that is one reason why you ended up on the beach today," Arjun said gently.

He's probably right, though it's a combination of everything—their argument last night, my feelings of inadequacy, frustration, anger, but mostly…hopelessness. "Though I feel much better right now."

"That's great to hear. Is it because you are focused on the ideas that you are learning?"

"No offense, but it's mostly because the new jeans I got look amazing on me" I say with a laugh.

"Good what a few new things can do. But tell me…do you have anywhere else to go?"

I shake my head. I hadn't thought that far ahead. After all, I'd figured I would be dead by now and real estate wouldn't be exactly a priority.

"Honestly? I'll probably have to move back in with my parents in Kentucky. They have to take me in, right? God, I feel like such a loser." I begin feeling the weight of failure all over again.

Arjun gives me a side-glance. "You can stop beating yourself up, Lindsay. *You may have failed at a few things, but you are not a failure!*"

I rub my forehead, aching from the mental whirlwinds of the afternoon. I wish I could tilt my head to one side and drain all negative thoughts out of my ear, just like I did with the ocean water. Wouldn't that be nice? "I'm trying. Really. It's just so hard…"

"Yes, it is. Change is never easy. But it's going to get better." He pauses to consider something, then continues. "I actually have a proposition for you. My company has several apartments in the city we use for traveling consultants."

How can this man be so generous and invested in my well-being? I look Arjun dead in the eyes and shake my head vehemently. "I can't accept any more from you. You've already given me too much."

"Lindsay," he says, his voice full of fatherly concern. Maybe that's it. Maybe he sees me as a daughter he wants to help. "It's not a gift. You said you're a software engineer. I can certainly use your technology skills on some things over the next few months. And the apartment is temporary. We will need it back for an upcoming project next quarter. You can stay there for the ninety days and work on yourself while also doing some consulting for me in the interim. By the time you leave, you will have rediscovered yourself and will be ready to find your place. If not, then you can go home to your parents. Sound fair to you?"

"I don't know…I just…" I'm completely flummoxed is what I am. It was too much to accept.

"The kitchen is stocked. The apartment is furnished, and there is Wi-Fi and a laptop, so you can keep moving forward with your business. My only other caveat is that, if you ever feel despair like this again and are thinking of taking your life, you will call this number." He handed over a piece of paper with the following phone number written on it 'National Suicide Prevention Lifeline: 1-800-273-8255'.

My throat aches with unshed tears. This is real. Someone is helping me.

Real help. Not just pretty words that sound great in theory. I don't even know what to say.

"This is not a hand-out," Arjun says, as though he can feel my uncertainty. "This is a help up. Remember, a few decades ago, I accepted money from a homeless person. I was in a similar place as you are now. What I am doing for you is paying his kindness forward while also getting something in return through your expertise."

Arjun pulls the car over to the curb and puts it in park. Resting his arm across the steering wheel, he leans toward me.

"Lindsay, you've had a long day, and we have talked about many things. I have work to finish today. The apartment is over there." He points over my shoulder. "And the beach is that way," he says, pointing to his left. "It's your choice. Where shall I take you?"

He's not being difficult, nor pressuring me, just asking what I want, life or no life!

It's going to be a struggle. I still feel pain every time I think of Charlie and all my failures. At least now I have a friend, and that's something.

But is it enough?

I swallow the dumpling of emotion clogging my throat and meet his unwavering gaze. Mustering up all my courage and strength, I nod. "To the beach, please."

Arjun's smile wanes, and he looks stricken. "You sure about that?"

"Well, yes. It's no Ferarri, but I can't just leave my custom ride on the beach, can I?"

He shows me the below QR code on his iPad to his complementary training. It will help me reinforce what I am learning with him. I use my phone's free QR reader app to scan it. *I am ready.*

CHAPTER FOUR
My World is Upside Down

On time for our planned 7 a.m. meeting a few days later, I ring Arjun's doorbell and wait. His house is gorgeous, one of the most spectacular on the beach, but as welcoming and warm as Arjun himself.

I'd found the lovely apartment he'd brought me to a few nights before to be the same. Like a warm, safe hug.

Once he'd gotten me all settled in and I'd fawned over the awesome accommodations, he'd left me to my devices. Naturally, the first thing I did was fire up that laptop and Google him. It hadn't taken long to find his name on the list of Forbes' wealthiest people, which listed his net worth, and the number had been jaw-dropping.

Arjun is a multi-billionaire.

And his humble, giving air only makes me realize how wrong I was that wealth and bad character go hand in hand.

On the other side of the door, feet scuffle along tiles, and Arjun opens it. He stands there, smiling mischievously. "Good morning. Come on in, Lindsay. How do you feel today...Oh, I see you are free of seaweed and sand, so things are already looking up!"

Smiling, I volley back, "Yes, and I'm still alive, which is the icing on the cake! Even better, I have this amazing coach. He's really a life and game changer. So yeah, things are looking up."

He turns, leaving the door open so I can enter his home. "All settled into the apartment?"

I nod, closing the door behind me. "Yes, thank you."

"You are welcome. What was the most exciting thing you've done this week, so far?"

"Well, let's see...I got that high fashion modeling job I wanted, I made the cover of *Forbes Magazine,* and oh, hey—I won the lottery!" I smile, dropping my purse into the chair by the door.

"Oh, good, then I can send you an invoice for my services." He smiles, showing his perfect white teeth. "That will be two million dollars, please."

I laugh and then shrug. "Nothing too exciting happening yet. Except that I started seeing the world differently. I feel like I have a second chance, although I wish things would move a little bit faster."

I follow him into the courtyard where he keeps a variety of potted plants in colorful, mosaic planters.

"Soon, it will. And you've already done some great things on the project I sent you. My project manager is very impressed with your skill so far!" His words fill me with pride as he takes a seat in a chair next to a bamboo plant. "Have a seat, Lindsay. Can I get you some water or tea?"

"Oh, no thank you. I'm all set." I sit across from him, enjoying the warmth of the afternoon sun on my face.

"Then, tell me, what do you remember from our conversation last week?" Arjun folds his hands in his lap.

I let out a slow, deep breath. "Hmm. Mainly, that I need to find compelling reasons to achieve my goals."

"Very good. What else?"

"The concept of role modeling," I go on, "as simple as it sounds, gave me an 'ah-ha' moment. I am the Sara Blakely of Technology."

"Good, good. Did you do your assignments?" He raises one eyebrow.

"Yes, I did," I say, my smile wavering a little.

"You're wondering why I am so adamant about you doing the assignments." He tilts his head and watches me carefully. "Is that right, Lindsay?"

"Yes," I admit. "I'm a responsible person. I'm not going to mess this up."

"Of course you're not, but I wanted to check your level of commitment."

"I'm ready, Arjun." I'm surprised by his more serious tone today. Then again, I know he's pushing my buttons and pushing them hard, to test me.

He smiles, satisfied. "I can see that. Now, what did you learn from doing your intelligent actions?"

"More than anything else, I learned the power of momentum, of taking action immediately and generating energy. Finding solid, compelling reasons to achieve my goals helped me redefine what I believe to be possible. Honestly? Last night, I was starting to feel confident again, you know? Like I used to feel back before...we'll just call it my sand and seaweed free days."

"Before...what?" His eyes narrow.

"Nothing." I look up. I don't feel like talking about that. "Before I forgot how strong I was."

Arjun's face lights up like the right words have settled on his heart. It makes me feel more relaxed and receptive. "Incredible job, Lindsay. Now let me ask you this—are you feeling happy today?"

"Okay, let's not get carried away there," I say with a chuckle.

"So, no to happiness."

"My Ferrari is in the shop today." My grin fades, and I shake my head. "No, Arjun. I mean, I've made some progress, but how could I be happy when my life is still so messed up?"

"Lindsay, happiness is not an outcome. It is a state of mind. No matter what happens in your life, you can give yourself permission to be happy. Look at babies. They are happy all the time, except when they are hungry, in physical pain, or when they need their diaper changed. But adults often unlearn how to be happy, because we focus too much on material pleasure. We ignore happiness. Let me prove it—you said you had some good things happen this week. What did you feel then?"

"Well, I felt happy for, like, two seconds, but I thought you meant *in general*."

"But those two seconds were gifts to you, correct?"

I sigh. "You know, Arjun, you're starting to make sense right now, and I'm really not cool with that." I laugh, shaking my head.

I did have some pretty awesome moments this week, so why wasn't I thinking about them?

"And that..." He reaches for his tea kettle and pours himself a cup. "Is how we selectively ignore happiness. See, the key has nothing to do with the Ferrari."

His words simmer in my brain. They simmer so long; my brain turns to soup.

"What you're saying makes perfect sense, in theory, Arjun. My problem is how can I be happy when there are so many problems."

He nods fervently. "But happiness does not come from external sources. You should enjoy the world's beauty as much as you can, enjoy all it has to offer, including material things, but true happiness comes from within."

I try wrapping my head around his idea, but I still have trouble with it. We need a certain amount of money to be comfortable, because let's face it— I don't live in a hut at the top of a mountain. I live in LA. I'm going to need a few things.

He sees that I'm having trouble swallowing this concept. He tries again. "Lindsay, if somebody owned a Ferrari, and they think the Ferrari is making them happy, they are totally wrong. It is the feeling of significance, of excitement making them happy. You don't need to *own* anything for this internal feeling. The moment you focus on the Ferrari as a source of your happiness, your happiness becomes pleasure. **Pleasure has an expiration date—Happiness is eternal."**

"That's sounds beautiful. It does. But what if you're homeless? What if your air conditioner is broken, and you live in a small apartment? How do you tell someone, 'just be happy!' Isn't that a bit irresponsible and a lot unrealistic?"

Arjun closes his eyes, a peaceful smile materializing on his face, as though he's been waiting for that question. "If you tell yourself that your happiness will come only when you get x, y, or z, then no, you'll never be happy. But look at babies...they come into this world with nothing at all, and as long as they are taken care of, they are happy. That is everyone's natural state."

Him and these baby comparisons.

"But the baby still has conditions," I challenge him. "He wants to be fed; he wants to be comforted, he wants sleep. Only then, is he happy. Have you seen a crying baby, Arjun? It's very unsettling. An adult is no different, except he wants other things besides his bottle and a clean diaper. The Ferrari replaces his bottle, and the mansion replaces the clean diaper."

Arjun smiles. "And let's continue with that example. For babies or adults, wanting food and comfort are biological. Yes, you must meet those fundamental needs to be comfortable. What I'm saying is, out of peer pressure, the adult *chooses* the Ferrari to replace the milk bottle, *chooses* the mansion to replace the clean diaper and opt out of true happiness. You can have them all. But you can be perfectly happy without them. We are not born wishing we had material things. As we grow up, we learn to be fearful by modeling our parents and our culture. I call it psychological fear. Since we don't know how to process this fear, we associate it with everything we don't have; the cars, the relationship etc. We manufacture and distribute psychological fears that enslave us into sorrow and keep us from happiness."

Arjun wins again, the little bugger.

He's right. If I tell myself I'll only be happy when I own the Millennium Falcon, then I'll forever be scouring the galaxy in search of happiness. Better to search a little closer to home. "Darn you, Arjun," I mutter.

He laughs so hard; he almost falls out of his chair. "Lindsay, a few minutes ago, you asked me how could you be happy when your life is messed up. My question to you is: **how could you *not* be happy when your life is messed up?**"

I narrow my eyes at him. "Is this a trick question?"

"No, it makes perfect sense. You believe that happiness will come after you succeed, whatever you define as success, right? Nope. It is the other way around. **Happiness directs you to success**. A great state of mind will lead you there. So, if it's true that your life is totally messed up, you should focus on creating happiness and celebration more than somebody who is already successful."

"Wow. I never thought about it that way." What if he's right? That would mean I've been approaching my search for success all wrong this whole time.

"Good," he says. "Think about a time you made a huge mistake in your business or life."

Right away, my thoughts go to Charlie. Never saw that one coming.

"What state of mind were you in just before making that decision?" he asks, crossing his legs and getting more comfortable.

I had just come out of a bad place in my life and thought Charlie would be the one who could fix it for me. "I was stressed and in a stupid state of mind."

Sitting there, staring at Arjun's potted plants, I'm transported to one afternoon with Charlie. Setting my keys and work briefcase on the kitchen table, I was completely frustrated and exhausted.

"Ugh, you wouldn't believe the day I had! There is this client that I've been meeting with for the past three months, and today she decided…Charlie? Did you hear what I said?" Charlie was glued to the t.v. "ESPN?! Can you just give the basketball game a break for a few minutes?" I begged.

Scowling, Charlie retorted, "Hon, this is a playoff game. 'nuff said. Right? We can talk later."

Dropping into a chair, I went numb. Then, I yelled. I accused him of not caring, anything to get his attention. He got so mad, he left the living room, yelling, "I come home for peace and to forget work. I try and help you do the same, but every time you complain and I try to fix things, you shoot me down. What am I supposed to do about your problems if you don't want solutions?"

"Lindsay, come back to earth." Arjun brings me to the present. His kind eyes smile softly.

"I'm sorry. I was thinking about the huge mistake I made. I'd completely lost control of my life and was so stressed, I said some terrible things," I say, fighting the swelling sadness behind my eyelids.

"It's okay. Do you think your stressful state of mind influenced your behavior?"

"Maybe." I think about it a minute, as my mind plays over the situation again. Hesitantly, I nod. "I guess so."

"Is it safe to then say that your state of mind affects your decision-making? If you're in a good state of mind, you're more likely to make a better decision than when you're in a bad state of mind?"

"That seems fair," I say.

"So, why do you think losing control was a mistake?" he asks, pouring himself another cup of tea. Maybe Arjun's happiness is in that tea he's drinking. Maybe I should buy myself a whole case of it.

"Because…" I sigh, standing up to pace the courtyard. His questions make me a little antsy, and I have to walk around or go crazy. "When I cooled down from that bad experience, I went back to him—my ex, now—and we talked about it. I told him how I felt. He explained that he *did* care, but he thought the only way he could show it was by either offering solutions to my problems or giving me space. He didn't realize I was looking for understanding, not a solution."

"I see. That must have been frustrating. Now, tell me, would you have made a different decision had you been in a different state of mind?"

"Probably." I reach out to rub a leaf from one of his hanging ferns.

"*Probably,* or *yes?*" he asks.

"Yes."

He stands to stroll around, picking up a watering can to begin watering his plants. A person like him could hire landscapers and housekeepers to do that for him, yet he waters his plants. Wonder if it has to do with his theory that material things don't bring happiness. Maybe watering his plants makes him happy.

"And have you ever thought of the possibility that if you had altered your state of mind, your result might have changed, too?"

Well, dang.

"I think I'm gonna need a drink, Arjun."

"Tea?"

"Vodka."

He chuckles. "Not good for your clarity, Lindsay, and that is what we are striving for."

"I was just kidding," I say. *Mostly.*

"I know. Now, think of a time when you took a risky decision that turned out pretty well."

"Let's see…about a week ago, I decided to get in the Ferrari, which is pretty much the adult equivalent of a child getting into a white van to take candy from a perfect stranger. Some might say *that* was a risk, but I met you, and my life suddenly changed for the better." I smile across the courtyard at him.

He pauses watering his plants to point at me with the watering can. "I like the way you think. Thank you, Lindsay. Any others? Before you and I met?"

"Uh, let's see..." I think back to my few, elusive positive experiences. "Despite all the stuff that's happened to me, I still think deciding to be an entrepreneur at the age of twenty-five was one of the greatest decisions I ever made. I was so sure of myself back then, so convinced I was going to be a force for good in this world. I felt significant, powerful...I was a business woman! I started building great connections and networking with ambitious women like me who wanted to change the way women thought about business." Eyes glowing with nostalgia, I relax significantly.

Chin up, I can feel the difference in my posture.

Arjun grins, watching me. "Sounds like you were in a great state of mind then."

"An amazing state of mind."

"Do you see a pattern here?" he says, setting down the watering can and sliding his hands into his pockets. "**Your destiny is shaped by the decisions you make. Your decisions are determined by the state of mind you make those decisions with. Your state of mind is decided by the meaning you associate with your daily experiences.**"

"So you're saying it's all one, happy cause-and-effect relationship? Like eating ice cream. Eating it in a good state of mind, it's delicious and satisfying, no guilt. But in a bad state of mind, you end up eating ten gallons of it, and having guilt worthy of a therapist."

"Precisely. And if you are integrated most of the time, you will make great decisions most of the time. In Eastern tradition, this state of mind has a name. It's called **Ananda**. Living in Ananda is the second force that shapes all successful professionals and entrepreneurs."

Accelerator # 2 - Live in Ananda.

"Ananda." I repeat it just the way he says it, with the accent on the first syllable—*Ah-Nuhn-dah*. "Awesome. What does it mean, exactly?"

"It is a Sanskrit term meaning 'extreme happiness.' Living in Ananda means that you are essentially in one of the highest states of being that you can achieve."

"Ah. I understand," I say, snapping my fingers. "It's like when I've just finished eating an entire bag of Lindt chocolate truffles."

He raises an eyebrow. "Sea salt caramel?"

"Is there any other kind?" I raise my hand for a high-five, and Arjun, older man billionaire, LA Gandhi, reaches up and smacks it like a boss. "I knew I liked you for a reason," I tell him.

He sits down in a lounge chair and puts his feet up as he crosses his arms over his stomach. "Anyway, there is a part of your brain called the limbic system, which controls your emotions. Within the limbic system is an almond-sized area called the amygdala that is associated with fear and stress. Let us call it an almond, for now. One of the purposes of this almond is to help protect you from future problems through anticipation. Isn't that what we are doing when we are stressed? Are we not predicting what is going to happen next, through our emotions and physiology?"

I take a seat across from him to listen. It's a perfect day, and there could be worse ways to spend it than listening to Arjun talk about parts of the brain. "I guess so. Go on, please."

He nods. "Now...imagine you spotted a stick in front of you, and you thought it was a snake. Your almond alerts your body in a fraction of a second and predicts what needs to be done next. There are three commonly accepted responses—you could 'freeze' and be bitten by the snake, you could 'fight' the snake and defeat it, or you could 'flee' the scene. But it is only a stick, so your brain immediately lets every system know there is no harm. This process happens so fast it might not even make logical sense to us until later."

"Wow, go amygdala," I cheer.

"Yes, go. Imagine a long time ago, two brothers, Joe and Jeff, without an amygdala. They both see a snake while hunting in the woods. The snake approaches Joe, and Joe walks toward it. The snake bites Joe, and he dies. What do you think Jeff will do the next time he sees a snake?"

"Set it on fire? He was the caveman with fire, right? Unless it was his brother who knew how to make the fire, in which case...'

"Lindsay..." There's a twinkle of laughter in his eye.

"Ugh. Come on! Jeff will run away. Obviously."

"And why would he do that?"

"Because he can predict what will happen?" I ask, unsure of my answer.

"Remember that Jeff doesn't have an almond to predict danger, though, so he'll walk toward the snake, get bitten, and possibly die."

"What a great story, Arjun. A real pick-me-upper." I roll my eyes playfully.

"I know, right?" he says without missing a beat. "So what did you understand from Joe and Jeff's story?"

"Besides avoiding snakes, that the almond in my brain will help me predict what will happen. But what does this have to do with Ananda?" I ask, shielding my eyes from the sun coming up over the edge of his roof into the courtyard.

"Because whatever emotions you feel alter your current state of mind. What happens to you when you think you see a snake?"

"I am going to feel fearful, and not run towards it, most likely."

"And what is fear?" he presses.

"An emotion."

"Perfect. So your emotional state changes when you think you see a real snake in front of you—true or false?"

"True?"

"Are you asking, or telling me?"

I smile. "Telling you."

"Good. So, why are emotions evoked when you see a snake?" His hands waver around and around when he talks, and I'm starting to love the sound of his voice, like hearing an old friend.

"To alert me of impending danger."

"Exactly." He nods. "Alert is the key word here. Your brain is a prediction machine, too. Your amygdala works together with other parts of your brain to evoke emotions to *alert* you to take action of imminent danger. In business or life, the danger isn't a snake. It can be an angry customer, a disgruntled employee, or even an insensitive spouse."

"That's all good," I say, scratching my head. "But I still don't get how everything you're saying is related to Ananda."

"Lindsay," he says, sitting up suddenly and leaning forward. "Imagine a pond that is perfectly still — something you might see on computer desktop wallpaper. Now imagine someone drops a rock into that pond. What happens?"

"You see a big splash."

"Let's suppose there's a devastating winter one year, and the pond freezes to protect itself. The winter ends, and the spring comes, but the pond still is afraid of the winter of life. It still has a layer of ice on top. In order to protect you from the winter of life, your mind does the same thing. It freezes so emotions cannot come out. If you drop a rock onto the frozen pond, will there be ripples?"

"No, the rock is going to bounce right off the ice."

"But the pond is not getting enough of the sun's energy for the plants to thrive. So, the sun pokes a hole in the ice to reach beneath the frozen surface. It allows the sunlight to help nourish the plants. Just like that, your mind cannot exist frozen forever after the winter of life is gone, or it becomes eternally depressed. So it pokes a hole so emotions can come out. But all the emotions that were suppressed by the frozen icecap want to rush out of it. Guess what kind of emotions come out first – negative emotions like anger, guilt or sadness."

"Aren't the plants supposed to be happy that it is not dark and that there is a hole with sunlight after all?" I ask.

"Great question." He shifts in his seat, seemingly impressed with my question. "That would be completely true if there was no fear. But remember the pond is still afraid of the catastrophic winter. So it reacts with negative emotions. If a stone falls in that place, the ripples created are bigger because the ice around doesn't allow the rest of the pond to absorb the ripples."

"That makes sense," I murmur, enthralled with his tale.

"The problem occurs when the pond reacts more than it should to the dropped stone in that melted area, and the ripples are too large. The result is *chaotic* ripples in an ice-filled pond. The same way you might be reacting to the spring of life with unproportioned guilt, anger or sadness or some other negative emotions. That is how our minds ruin the springs of life, the opportunities of life.

"The pond by itself is almost never too chaotic, but it thinks it is chaotic because the waves are out of control in one spot. Your emotions work exactly in this same way, Lindsay.

"When we are out in the field trying to grow our businesses, people might reject you, or worse, be indifferent to you. You might feel lonely that you are in a boys club and might not feel the confidence to overcome the roadblocks that you face on a daily basis. You might fail miserably."

"I know that all too well."

"In our minds," Arjun goes on explaining, "we might create that layer of ice, too. The ice of *rigidity or certainty*. Like the pond, we freeze our minds, so we do not feel the impact of any rejection or failure. It's a defense mechanism, but remember, if we do not allow ourselves to be open to the rocks of rejection or failure, you won't feel the magic of the flowers, the success, or the fulfillment that might fall into your mind's pond, either. You can't get to Ananda being in this state."

"So again, it's up to me to change my state of mind. I understand it, but it's so hard to do that sometimes." I pick up a piece of dry plant leaf from the glossy tile floor and start ripping it apart.

"I understand, Lindsay, but yes, it's up to you. Just like the pond, most of us have the same frozen surface with one small, unfrozen area, which will help us vent our true feelings. The ripples of *chaos or uncertainty* that we feel through this unfrozen area is the major negative emotion that we experience. I call it **prime negative emotion**. It is through the eyes of this emotion that we see the world. Some people say, 'I feel guilty all the time.' Other people say, 'I'm sad all the time.' Others think, 'I'm angry or depressed.' We associate our identity to our primary emotion. I used to say, 'I am angry,' as much as I said, 'I am Arjun.' As I've mentioned before, if your primary emotion is negative, like sadness or guilt, that is what your pond will feel. Soon, the pond starts to believe that this is who you are."

I take it all in. It's a lot to absorb. I'm not sure I understand everything he's saying, but if only a small fraction finds its way into my brain, then I'm already ahead of the game.

"Are you following me, Lindsay?"

"I'm trying."

"Okay, for us to live in Ananda, we must do what I call Power Ceremony. Power ceremony is the process that manages your prime negative emotion and returns your mind to celebration. A non-reactive state, reducing those ripples of negative emotions until they are transformed to achieve Ananda."

"Like what?" I ask, challenging him.

"Power ceremony is the process of opening the edges of the holes or vents in your pond's ice. You experiment with different emotions than you're conditioned to feel. Good, bad, positive, negative, as long as it does not hurt others. Just let those vents start to break through the ice. And what happens when the pond is one large hole?"

"It's time to fish?" I say, trying to relieve a little of the stress I'm feeling now by not understanding him. "The bigger the hole, the less ice there will be on the pond."

"You got it!" he cries.

Wow, and here I was thinking that all of this was flying over my head.

"What if another winter of business failure or relationship rejection comes? Your mind will think, 'It is too cold. I'm concerned that my master is getting too exhausted. Let me help you to protect yourself by building more ice.'"

It all makes sense to me.

"What emotion do you feel most of the time in your life?" he asks, tilting his head.

"Not sure."

"Think about it. For a lot of people, it is guilt. For others, it is sadness or anger. Some people feel overwhelmed all the time. And for some, happiness or joy is their primary positive emotion."

"Let me see…I ate ten gallons of ice cream with a Kahlua drizzle, I didn't pull through for my family, my business went belly up, and I have a nagging sense that I did something wrong. I would say I feel guilty all the time."

"It doesn't have to be that way," Arjun says, leaning forward again. His eyes gaze at mine, as his hands fold across his knees. You don't need to feel guilty for anything."

"But I do."

"Then, guilt is your prime negative emotion. And unfortunately, this is one of the primary emotions many women see their world through. I used to get really angry when I was younger. Like a lot of men, it was my primary negative emotion. We project our primary emotions onto others. For a good part of my life, I even thought that anger was the prime negative emotion for everybody. Since your primary emotion is guilt, your neural pathway is paved like a highway to help you feel guilty. Your mind is conditioned to ask questions that produce guilt. **It has a simple enough recipe for you to feel guilty.**"

I nod in agreement. Mine sure does.

"Power ceremony is the process of regulating emotions so that you can choose to feel Ananda most of the time. You brush your teeth every day. You put makeup on every day. Power ceremony is the brushing of the mind and putting on makeup for your soul.

"During power ceremony, your whole brain, including your emotional brain, your amygdala, and the front area of your brain work together to achieve great outcomes. *In the initial stages of power ceremony, you are simply managing your primary negative emotion.* For me, it took years to practice to move out of my primary emotion at the time—anger. You can do it in weeks. Power ceremony simultaneously helps you neutralize your prime negative emotion and amplify a positive one."

"What does that mean?" I ask, thinking how I want to go back to the apartment and process all he has said so far, assess what I need to do to reach Ananda then make a game plan for doing it.

"It means you will be not only able to manage your guilt more effectively, but also become more aligned to Ananda by simply following the steps we are going to explore. But let me ask you a question, first: if zero represents absolute depression and ten represents being in total ecstasy, or Ananda, what number would describe the state you are in right now?"

"I would say a four, and that's a huge improvement from the sand and seaweed stage earlier this week."

"Will you be able to live at your full potential in this number four state of mind?"

"No way, dude."

He nods emphatically. "Yes, how can you manage something if you cannot measure it? How can you improve your state of mind until you measure and assess your current state of mind?"

"So measuring is the first step?" I mutter.

"Once you know where you are emotionally, change your physiology. By **changing your physiology, you feel any emotion on demand.** Your body is made up of chemicals, you see. Mostly carbon, hydrogen, and oxygen. It releases a wide variety of hormones based on what you feel."

"Like what?" I wish I had paid more attention in high school biology.

"If you feel fearful, cortisol and adrenaline are released. If you are happy, you release dopamine, oxytocin, serotonin, etc. You release estrogen or testosterone when you feel aroused. As a woman, the more oxytocin you naturally have, the more stress-free and relaxed you will be. Power ceremony will do exactly that. Part of it had been recently proven by a Harvard study to simultaneously reduce your stress level by twenty-five percent and increase your charisma by twenty percent. Power ceremony is the act of celebrating you, your life and goals in advance until you reach your true destination. Are you ready for celebrating your life?"

"Of course, I am, especially with a scoop of ice cream, and only chocolate on top, no more vodka."

Arjun's bemused smile appears. "I will show you. But first, you must stand up!"

"Ooh! This power ceremony thing sounds powerful, indeed," I say, bubbles of

effervescence popping off inside me like a bottle of freshly opened champagne.

What is he going to teach me?

I'm not sure, but for the first time in forever, I can't deny it. I am EXCITED.

CHAPTER FIVE
The Power Ceremony

I had no idea Arjun wore so many hats. Now, he's a Yogacharya as he stands tall and straight, holding his arms out wide like the Jesus statue in Rio de Janeiro.

"If you stand straight," he says, "bend slightly backward, lift your head, and expand and widen your body by extending your arms for two minutes, you instantly reduce stress hormones by up to twenty-five percent."

"Really?" I say, wondering where Arjun gets his facts.

"Yes. The same action helps to increase your charisma levels by twenty percent or more," he adds. "Your body is like a mystical treasure box. It can make you feel magical if you choose to."

My eyes widen. "Magic, huh? Can it produce the five hundred thousand I owe? Now *that* would be magical!"

"Lindsay…" Arjun opens one eye and gives me that playful chastising look to which I've become accustomed. "Your skepticism is part of the problem, which we will address another time."

I wrinkle my nose at him but nod. "Okay, continue."

"Do it exactly like this—stand the way you would if you were absolutely unstoppable. Stand the way you would be standing if you truly were Sara Blakely of Technology."

I close my eyes.

Dressed in a dark navy tailored suit, I stride onto an expansive stage. There, a female colleague holds a crystal engraved award plaque. The award, for my business savvy, is placed in my palms as the audience claps and cheers. My family cheers. Even Charlie—the bastard— is there. So sad, too bad, Charlie, I show him the amazing businesswoman he missed out on.

"You're doing great. Now, lift your head," Arjun says, reaching out to lift my chin with two fingers. "Stand straight, open your eyes, and look up towards the left. Feel the center of your body, about two inches below your navel. Imagine that your core has grown roots to the ground like a tree. And now, take one step forward, feeling absolutely successful. Take one more step forward, as if you're unstoppable."

I do as he says, taking one step, then another, feeling like I have made a billion dollars selling Spanx.

Arjun's gentle voice guides me through the power ceremony, which should, for all intents and purposes, be easy, but for me is difficult.

"Now, stretch your hands sideways, heart level, as if you're flying, and think of an experience when you felt loved by someone."

Okay, now he's pushing it. I haven't felt that in years, but I will do my best.

"Physically grab that experience with both your hands and gradually reel it into you, dropping it into your gut, like you're hugging your own experience."

As silly as I feel, I do it anyway. Warm, soft arms enfold me. Clear green eyes gleam with love towards me.

My grandmother releases me from the soft, welcoming warmth of her bosom, handing me an ice cream cone.

"How was school today, Lindsay?"

I'm almost in tears, but I grab the vision with my grandmother in it and reel it in towards me.

"Now," Arjun adds, "bring your hands back to your sides again and think about a time you felt grateful. Experience the feeling of your Gratitude throughout every cell of your body. Physically grab that experience with your hands and embrace it, and again, drop it into the center of your body. Now, stretch your hands to your sides and keep them at your waist, as if welcoming a two-year-old who is running toward you. Think about a time you felt proud and confident and feel that in your entire body."

Pomp and Circumstance, the graduation march, plays in a gym crammed with families and friends. Butterflies of excitement flit around my belly as I walk the red carpeted stage to receive my diploma. Not only did I represent the first woman in my family to go to college, I graduated from UCLA with honors in engineering. I remember feeling so proud of myself and everything I had accomplished.

"Again, grab that experience and pull it to your center, open your fists, and drop it right below your belly button."

I follow Arjun's instructions, waiting to see what comes next.

"Now, think about a sensual experience in your past. Do the same with that—open your arms to it, take it, and pull it back in. Drop it into your gut. Allow yourself to feel it with total intensity, and lastly, think of a spiritual experience you've had and stretch your hands at the level of your head, as if you've crossed the finish line of a 100-meter Olympic race and earned a gold medal. Open your arms out wide in total joy. Grab this spiritual experience into your fists and gradually bring it closer and closer to your body, then drop it into your gut. Feel the unstoppable certainty from within."

"I'm feeling a little light-headed and hungry."

"Lindsay..." His lilting voice lowers as he gives me a mischievous smile.

"Alright, alright...I feel the unstoppable certainty. That's me—Lindsay Mitchell, full of unrelenting awesomeness! Whee!"

It's not that I don't respect his exercise—I totally do. It's just that it's not easy making myself feel this way from one day to the next, but I'm doing my best. I take a deep breath and try to imagine myself like I used to feel in those early days of my startup companies.

"Lindsay, how do you feel now?" Arjun asks me.

"A little better than last week—about a seven out of ten. That's all I can ask for right now."

"And if you do it every day, you will only improve. Now, with your hands at your sides at waist level, think of a successful moment you've had in your life. Envision it larger than life. Hear what you heard at the time, louder than when you heard it. Feel the touch you felt at that time. Amplify these feelings, see them larger than life, stack them, so you feel completely unstoppable."

I do as he says, imagining my graduation day like it was yesterday. I amplify all the feelings, like he says.

"On a scale of one to ten," Arjun says, "what is your number now?"

"I would say a nine, way better than the zero I was last week." I smile.

Honestly, I'm more excited than I've been in a long time, but I have to be careful. It could be fleeting. In the past, whenever I was this stoked about something, I've gotten hurt—whether I failed in business or a relationship, the end outcome was always either depression or guilt. Depression or guilt? Really, that's all I've got?

"Excellent," Arjun said. "Continue power ceremony, and you'll go up more and more each time. When you reach seven and above, you might feel fear, Lindsay, and that is normal. Fear that you failed in the past— fear that you do not deserve to succeed. Psychological fear is your mind's way of protecting you so that no one can break your heart. Your brain does not want you to open up the unfrozen areas of your pond and be vulnerable to rejection and failure. But that is when you need to trust yourself the most and focus on your outcome and ignore everything else, including fear. Once you do, you'll reach the next levels of success and fulfillment you always dreamed of. Will you trust yourself enough to allow yourself to be passionate and unfreeze your pond?"

I nod, feeling almost completely certain that I'll allow it. "I'll try my best."

"Do better than try. Just do it, Lindsay. Okay? You have nothing to lose."

Arjun's gentle smile tells me that he's right. I don't have anything to lose, really, no home, no honey, no money, and not even my favorite Zen coloring books. I've already hit rock bottom. I may as well believe in myself without fear.

"Have you ever watched people when they listen to something super inspiring? They lift their chin like they feel proud. That is precisely what I want you to do every time you feel low. Lift your chin, open your arms wide, bend backward slightly, and flood your mind with the deepest thoughts of love, success, pride, spirituality, and sensuality as you possibly can. Gradually, you will begin to open your eyes to a new world, a new beginning where you set out for this adventurous, rewarding journey of successful entrepreneurship. Plus, you might even grow a little taller and pass for thirty-something." Arjun winks.

As my arms lift, my posture opens, this time with true excitement. Call me crazy, but I think I'm starting to feel what Arjun says I should feel – true passion, plus, I definitely would like to lose all those stress wrinkles that age my face.

"How are you feeling?" he asks.

"Incredible. I really am. Thank you, Arjun."

"I am so happy to hear that. I truly am, Lindsay." He pats me on the shoulder. "Now, for this next step of power ceremony, imagine there is a fly in your nose, and you are trying to push this fly out by blowing your nose."

I cock my head suspiciously, but his face is as serious as a heart attack. Arjun is crazier than a bat, but I'll humor him.

"Yes. Just imagine you are pushing air out from your gut. You do not need to breathe in. Your brain will automatically do it. Let's spend three minutes blowing the fly away from your nose. Remember, you will do it in a guttural way."

As silly as I feel, I continue standing and breathing, thinking of the imaginary fly as the poisons in my relationship, and I'm pushing them out of my body. The stains of my failures go away with every push out of my nostrils, face, and body. How will I look ten years from now when I'm successful? Younger? Thirty might be pushing it, but what the heck. Who will I be in a relationship with? Someone that makes me laugh for sure. How will I dress?

"Okay, it's been two minutes already…one more to go," Arjun says quietly. "The first time you did this, I wanted you to allow yourself to daydream, but for the next minute, focus on your forehead right above the center of your eyebrows."

How does he know that I'm daydreaming? I wonder. Regardless, I move my thoughts away and focus on my body's core.

After a minute, he announces, "Okay, time's up. Now close your eyes and slowly breathe into your heart and breathe out from your heart. Imagine for a few seconds that you do not have a head and breathe in and out of your heart. Your body stops at your shoulder. Imagine you are breathing directly from nature into your heart. Breathe directly out to the nature. Keep doing it for one minute and open your eyes when you feel like it."

I open my eyes some time later to a smiling Arjun. He folds his hands in his lap. "What if you could feel this way the rest of your life?"

"Arjun, if I could live this way even half the time, I'd already be rich and famous."

"Great! Well, what you just did is a brief introduction to what I call Accelerator Breathing, which is a great tool inside your daily power ceremony. It is a simple technique I developed using five thousand year old Vedic traditions from India. Vedic knowledge has been passed from one generation to another to help them to keep their energy high while fasting for weeks, if not months. It's a tool you can use to alter your state of mind anytime, anywhere, in any circumstance in your life. It will help you give energy for working hard to attain the things you want, such as financial growth or a positive love relationship, if that is what you seek."

I shake my head. "Maybe I should get a dog instead. At least a dog is loyal."

Arjun laughs, shaking his head. "Lindsay, I love how you think. So you know, Accelerator breathing will also activate the front area of your brain called the mid-prefrontal cortex. Let us call it the imagination brain. With a strong imagination brain, you will feel more and more empowered and able to handle stressful situations with a smile on your face. According to Dr. Daniel Siegel, your imagination brain, just behind the center of your forehead, is primarily responsible for a laundry list of things, including *connecting with other human beings, regulating fear created by your amygdala, imagination, choice of response, empathy, morality, intuition*, and last but not least, physical regulation of the body helping you to be more healthy."

"Wow. That's a lot," I say. Who knew such a tiny part of the brain could do so much? "Amazing things really do come in small packages, don't they?"

"Indeed they do," he agrees. "If you lived in this physical state every day, you could do the unimaginable. Do you think you could start every day feeling this way? Because if you start each day with the power ceremony for the next thirty days, your life could be completely different."

"You're right. I've always been jealous of people who can manifest wealth and the things they most want in life. I'm going to give it a try, though. I think I can do it."

"Good," Arjun says, nodding encouragingly. "It is worth it. You'll need to practice, just like you learned to drive a car, ride a bike, or anything else in your life that required practice."

"I get it," I say, thinking back to my teenage driver years when I started out driving stick shift on my beat-up, old Mustang.

He demonstrates how to do accelerator breathing.

Arjun continues. "Just like you mastered driving, you will master Ananda. Practice makes perfect! When you practice breathing and activate more of your front area of your brain, you will feel empowered to confront your problems with confidence. You will step up to the plate and say, 'Let me handle that,' when everyone else is afraid, which is another feature of your imagination brain. That is when a true leader is born within you." He pauses and pours himself a glass of water.

I take a seat opposite him and smile at the new feelings of empowerment creeping back into me slowly.

Arjun goes on, "Throughout history, we've seen these kinds of people. Remember when we talked about Dr. Martin Luther King, Jr., Gandhi, and Mother Teresa? They weren't that different from you. They all stepped up because they all had great missions in life. I strongly believe they each had very active front brains, which is something we all need to use! It's the most *human* part of us. Many people believe **the brain is designed to survive. I believe the brain is designed to thrive, but we are conditioned to survive.** We need to stop focusing on limits and start using this front area of the brain-operating system, which was perfected to do its job around 75,000 years ago."

"Wow!" I exclaim.

"The final step of power ceremony is to focus all your energy using Power Questions."

"Sounds intriguing."

"It is," he replies without missing a beat. "What is the mind, first of all? It's a process that regulates the flow of information and energy into and from your body. It decides whether the water should splash a little bit, a lot or not at all when a rock is dropped on the pond. Lindsay, do you know how the pond decides how to respond to a rock?"

"Sure. How dare you jump onto me without permission?" I smile.

"That is it! That is how ponds do it. It is not that simple for human ponds. We use our mind to respond to rocks using thoughts. You have around sixty thousand thoughts a day, of which around fifty-eight thousand came directly from yesterday. You and I are creating the same reality for yourself every day of your life by having the same recycled thoughts. What exactly are thoughts?"

"Okay, you're going a little meta on me. It's like asking me to describe a color to someone who can only see in black and white," I admit.

"**Thoughts are questions and answers.** Every moment of your life, you are asking and answering questions. If so, is it possible that your sixty thousand thoughts a day are thirty thousand questions and thirty thousand answers?"

"Sounds mind-boggling, but logical."

"Okay, so is it safe to assume that, *if* you change those questions, then you could change your thoughts, too? If so, how do you change your thoughts, Lindsay?"

"By asking *new* questions. Holy Smack. I get it now." All this time, I've been asking the wrong questions!

He smiles and wiggles his eyebrows. "See? There is a method to my madness. And this is why we conclude our daily power ceremony with power questions. Think about Google. You use Google to search for things. When you search for something in Google, what does it do? First of all, even if you try, 'How do I train my dog?' or 'How do I buy a cat?'— These are the questions. So if you type into Google's search box, you're typing a query. And what does Google do, Lindsay?"

"Uh…Google provides me with more search results than any one human would ever know what to do with?"

"Well, that's true, too," he laughs. "But what is its basic function?"

I sigh, letting out a deep breath. "It searches data servers in different parts of the world and accumulates information related to your topic, then returns the answer to you," I say with pride.

"So the first thing Google does is focus on one outcome, right? When you ask Google the question, 'How can I manage stress?' does it give you the answer for how to peel a banana?"

"Only if Google is on crack, Arjun. Or tired at the end of a long day and wishing to mess with me."

He laughs again. "If Google did that, then they would be out of the search engine business in a week. **Questions help you focus on a specific outcome.**"

He makes so much sense, it hurts. Like he's doling out little nuggets of goodness, much like a perfect chocolate truffle that I've been starved for.

Arjun leans closer to me, and by now, I've learned that he does this when he really wants me to understand something.

"This is exactly what your mind does, too. When you ask, *Why am I so unlucky? Why is God doing this to me? Why does my life suck?'* you are focusing on that outcome. If you ask, 'Why does my life suck?' What answer are you going to get? Something like, 'Because you are a complete screw-up, and your childhood was bad.' Is that the answer you need, Lindsay?"

"I would say no. I would say that's my mind being a little witch to me."

"But that is what your mind does. It will be a little stinker to you if you ask the wrong questions. So focus on questions with answers you actually need."

I stare at Arjun. I have a deep love/hate relationship with him right now. He's so right! I can hardly take it, and I have to change my questions. "You're going to tell me changing questions is as easy as changing socks, right?"

"The second thing the question does," he goes on, right through my humor armor, "**questions eliminate alternative possibilities.** So, let's go back to our Google metaphor because I know how much you loved it." He shoots me a grin.

"Loved it so much, I could explode from happiness."

"Don't explode yet, Lindsay. Wait until you have reached your goals to be blown away, okay?" He chuckles and puts both hands up in a gesture to stop me. "If someone asks, 'Why don't aliens come to Earth?' that question assumes that there *are* aliens, but it also assumes that aliens *are not* coming to Earth. So while it opens up one possibility, it eliminates another one. So, when you ask a question, be careful not to eliminate certain possibilities. For example, if you say, 'Why am I sad?' naturally, it eliminates the possibility of being happy. If you ask yourself why you are sad, do you think you're going to get an answer that will make you happy?"

"No," I say, staring straight ahead. Because that is the question I've been asking all this time.

"And the third thing that a question does—let's keep with our Google example—if you keep asking how to be happy, or how to be sad, Google will suggest what you are interested in. For example, if you search, 'how to make a girl laugh,' then Google learns that you are interested in making girls laugh. Next time you start typing, 'how to,' Google will autofill the rest of the information to: 'How to make a girl laugh.' What is the next thing Google does?" he asks.

"It sends you advertisements for things that make girls laugh, like watching a man try to squeeze into Spanx undergarments."

"Yes!" he cries, clapping. "And your mind does the exact same thing! Your mind will habituate your repeated questions and auto-fill your questions just like Google for your own simplicity. **Questions habituate and autofill your thoughts!**"

I let out a low chuckle.

He pours me a glass of water and offers me a cookie off a plate. God knows, with no perfect chocolate truffle in sight, I need a cookie right now after a revelation such as that one.

He takes a bite of cookie and talks with crumbs on his lips. "By **habituating our questions and answers, we are solidifying our thoughts.** Through these solidified thoughts, much like the ice in the pond example, we habituate our emotions. Through these predictable thoughts and emotions, we stagnate our mind. Through all these, *most of us become slaves of our own minds; our past.*"

I stare at him so hard; I think my eyeballs are going to fall out. "I think I need a drink after this discussion."

"The fourth thing a question does—"

My eyebrows fly up. "There's a fourth thing? Man, these questions seem more integral to living than food."

"You need good questions to keep you healthy more than you need food, Lindsay. Here is a classic example. If I ask, 'Why is my life a failure?' or 'What are three reasons I failed in business?' What does this question assume? It assumes that you are a failure. Assumptive questions are the most dangerous—or the most rewarding ones. So again, asking the right questions is imperative."

"I can see what you're saying. It's like I've suddenly begun wearing new glasses. This time, with clean lenses instead of ones covered in grime."

"Great! So, tell me...why are assumptive questions important for you, Lindsay? If you were to ask the question, 'What are the reasons for my success?' Your brain assumes that you *are* successful. Naturally, your brain selectively seeks those reasons that made you successful. It is not only eliminating the possibility of failure but also assuming that you are already successful. Asking a question like that one might feel weird initially, but you keep asking it, and after some time, it's going to eliminate the negative possibility."

"So, I'm practically rewiring my brain," I say. "Wow, this is all so amazing. Seriously, Arjun. I might have to go boil my head after this; it's so overwhelming."

"No, no...please don't boil your head. It would completely ruin your hair." Arjun smiles. "By the way, I believe that your mind is capable of answering any questions. It's far more powerful than Google. The fact that Google has become a verb, or Amazon has revolutionized shopping, or Apple has become almost a trillion dollar company today is because a few people were willing to ask quality questions. Sergei Brin and Larry Page of Google asked how they could become the epicenter of this new thing called the internet? Jeff Bezos of Amazon asked how he could create the most customer-focused company in the world that delivers goods and services to peoples' homes in a more convenient, inexpensive way? And most importantly, Steve Jobs asked how he could innovate technology in such a way that it will make people stand in line to get it? Sony was in the music business for decades, and all of a sudden, this computer company called Apple showed up with something called an iPod. Apple kept asking the question, 'How can we make it even more convenient for our raving fans? How can we improve our products dramatically and create a cell phone with no keypads? How can we use everything we know to create a new type of device called the tablet?' No matter what the outcome was, all solutions came from asking and answering a series of high-quality questions."

The realization that I've been doing it all wrong for years sets me back on my proverbial heels.

What questions can I ask instead? Not, *Will my day suck again today?* Or, *How will I ever make my minimum payment on my credit card?* Or, *How many scoops of ice cream with* Kahlua *does it take to drown my sorrows?* Those questions assume a negative connotation, and ice cream should always have a positive connotation.

"People ask me all the time: 'What is the big deal about this question thing? Why is it important? How is this going to change my life?' What they don't realize is that they are asking me a question!" Arjun laughs at the thought. He gets up and stretches in the way he taught me earlier. It's nice to see someone practice what they preach.

"Follow me inside, Lindsay. It's getting hot out here."

He heads into the house, and I follow. Arjun's home inside is full of beautiful, homey things. Not at all like a billionaire's home, but more like someone who enjoys art, pottery, and simple furniture. He stops in the kitchen and begins pulling out foods from the fridge, laying them on the counter.

"Salad?"

"Oh, uh…sure, thank you," I say. I'm stunned to realize it's already lunchtime.

As Arjun prepares a salad, he says, "Think about the five things questions do:

- They help you focus on the outcome.
- They eliminate other possibilities.
- They help you habitually internalize questions themselves.
- Pre-assumed questions help you pursue your success and dreams.
- They help you innovate through imagination.

"By consistently asking questions, you will tap into those inner resources which will help you to be happy." He washes his hands in his beautiful, polished steel sink and begins breaking a head of lettuce apart.

Taking a seat at the counter, I sigh and rest my chin on one fist. "Well, you've told me all about questions, and I understand it will help me grow to the next level. But what questions do you think I should ask?"

He takes out a knife from a drawer and starts chopping up cucumber and peppers. "The questions you ask need to make you feel profound, so ask questions that trigger empowering, positive emotions. Let's start by asking some that make you feel grateful.

- What are you grateful for right now?
- Whom are you grateful to?

"Ask those questions, and you intellectually begin to understand what you are grateful for. But you need to understand it emotionally, too. How do we emotionally understand something? You ask the *why* question, like 'Why are you grateful to that person or for that experience?' Let's try it now:

- What are you grateful for?
- Why are you grateful for that experience?
- Whom are you grateful to?
- Why are you grateful to that person?"

"Okay, I think I can do that. It's funny. It all feels like common sense, but I've been forgetting to do it—I've been forgetting to ask myself who I might be grateful to and for what reason."

"And I am here to remind you," Arjun says, munching on a slice of red pepper. "Now that you intellectually understand it and emotionally feel it, it's time for you to internalize. How, you ask? By asking the question, 'How does that make you feel?' Let's experiment with a different set of questions. Stand straight and ask yourself these questions:

- Who do I love?
- Who loves me?
- Why do they love me?
- How does that make me feel to be in love?"

I think about all these questions, but it's hard, knowing that Charlie is no longer in my life. My five year old, stubborn brain tells me "good riddance," but my heart has had trouble internalizing this.

"I know you're probably gritting your teeth thinking of those questions, Lindsay, so now ask a few that will help you feel your best, such as…

- What are the three most exciting experiences in my life?
- Why are those the most fulfilling experiences?
- How does that make me feel to have these amazing experiences?

"Integrate these questions into your power ceremony and feelings deep into your body. Then rank the answers. If '0' means you are feeling the worst, and ten means you are feeling the best, what number are you in right now?"

"Right now? I am totally at ten after this enlightening lesson, Arjun. Seriously. Thank you for this fabulous experience." I reach out for a napkin and dab the corners of my eyes. I am so emotional today, but it's liberating knowing there's hope for changing the way I think.

"You are welcome," he says, searching the refrigerator before holding up a Dijon mustard and then continuing when I nod my approval. "There are the questions that I ask myself every day. You don't need to use my questions. You can create your own. Do you know who else is creating questions for you?"

"Hmm, the U.S. Government. I know about the deep state," I say with a sage nod.

Arjun looks around playfully, as if he's being watched. "No, Linsday, the people in the tribe that you belong to."

My ten plummets straight down by a good five points.

Is this a requirement? I want to demand. Because what Arjun doesn't seem to realize is that I lost that support system a long time ago.

I'm tribeless, and suddenly, I've never felt so alone.

CHAPTER SIX
What Tribes Do You Belong To?

"I can almost read your thoughts right now, but we're all part of some tribe, Lindsay. A group of people who believe the same way and act similarly. If you and I believe that rich people are crooks, then we are part of a group with similar beliefs—a tribe. If you are an entrepreneur or you want to be one, then you are part of that tribe. If you have a team of people who you work with, that is a tribe, too."

"Then I'm part of the Lindsay Has Messed Up, But She's About to Fix Her Life Tribe. Is that a real tribe?" I ask, feeling slightly better.

"Yes," he laughs. "I believe you just made it one and became the president, the secretary, and the janitor. You might be wondering why it is important to learn about tribes. Here is the simple answer; your tribe makes or breaks your dream. Is that compelling enough? You see, Lindsay, an amazing or awful thing happens as part of that tribe. A few decades ago, there was a small group called the Seekers living in a suburb of Chicago. One of their group members claimed to be receiving messages from outer space about the end of the world. She believed there would be an apocalyptic flood before the dawn of December 21, 1954. She received the messages that a UFO would land on that day, and it would rescue true believers. Within their group, they started talking about it and believed it with every cell of their being. Suddenly, people around the neighborhood started observing this group and became curious about what was going on. More and more people joined the group. A few researchers from Minnesota, interested in studying the phenomenon of cult behavior, joined the group to observe and find out what would happen at the end when there was no flood.

"Although it may seem far-fetched to many, the group convinced themselves that the information channeling through was accurate. The more they believed, the more they convinced others. The more convinced others were, the more their own beliefs went over the top.

"The leaders of the group then instructed their followers to cut all communication from anyone outside of the group. With the external influence removed, which could have convinced the followers of the impossibility of their claims, the only proof the group had was social proof. At this point, people started showing greater commitment to that truth by selling their own homes and giving the money away to charity. Others quit their jobs."

"God, this sounds awful. There's no Kool-aid involved, right?" I said, as Arjun placed a bowl in front of me full of yummy salad. I couldn't wait to dig in, but first, I waited to hear how this story ended.

"Although some members were college students, most followers were made up of people who would normally be considered rational and scientific, including one doctor. These so-called rational people made others commit even more drastically. Some of the group members left their non-believer spouses and all their earthly possessions. They were preparing for their departure to the imaginary planet, Clarion.

"Finally, the day arrived. The group expected a visitor from outer space to escort them to the spacecraft. As instructed by the message, they got rid of all zippers, bra straps, and other metal objects when midnight approached. The clock struck midnight. The spaceship did not arrive to save them from the anticipated cataclysm. Ten minutes, twenty minutes, thirty minutes went by. The group was stunned — not even a drizzle. A few hours later, the leader received another message that the God of Earth decided to spare the planet from destruction. The cataclysm was called off. The little group, sitting all night long, had spread so much light that God had saved the world from destruction."

"Wow, talk about spin-doctoring. The Enquirer couldn't have done it better," I murmur.

"What do you think happened, Lindsay?"

"I think it was a form of mass hysteria, social proof playing at its best," I respond with enthusiasm.

"Excellent," Arjun says, pouring us two glasses of water and pushing one toward me. "Social proof played the greatest role here, but what is the essence of social proof? How does it work?"

"I'm not sure," I reply. It's hard to think with this delicious salad staring me in the face.

"Go ahead and eat, Lindsay," Arjun says, watching me take my first bite as I nod happily. "Cult groups or tribes get their negative traction through what I call **Tribal Push**. Tribal push works, first by **creating limiting questions inside of the person directing her towards fear.** We can only hypothesize about the questions that might have been asked, but I would think they might be somewhere along the lines of, 'How can I be special and be saved *when* (not *if*) the world ends? **When** (again, not **if**) a catastrophic flood destroys the world, where will I go? How did I become so lucky to be a chosen one? Who will be lucky enough to come with me? How much will I miss out on if I am not part of this group?' On the opposite end, when group members started to ask their questions, for instance, 'What if the flood doesn't come?' They were squelched. Another component of this was that, even within the group, the followers were instructed to support the leaders if there was a difference of opinion. So if one person would raise the slightest hint of doubt through a question, the others would align against him or her. **The tribe pushed the group's questions to each indvidual,** so they were conditioned to ask **only** those."

Swallowing a bite of salad, I mumble, "But this doesn't apply to me. I'm not part of any cult, though; I might consider joining an Arjunian cult."

"Well, that's good news. And no, there's no Arjunian cult," he says, smiling, pulling up a stool and sitting to eat next to me. "You are not part of any cult, but we all are part of some groups, tribes who believe in something with absolute certainty. **They are either empowering or disempowering you, or doing both at the same time.** It could be your religion, denomination, ethnicity, nationality, work, your family or even simply a group of friends. Believe me, each of these groups are unknowingly pushing their questions to you. Questions of scarcity and sadness, or abundance and freedom!"

"Almost everyone has an agenda," I clarify. "Whether they are consciously aware of it or not."

"Precisely. **The second way tribal push works is by adaptation of vocabulary.** We are trapped into our current reality through our limiting vocabulary we use to experience life. The vocabulary you use is how you associate meaning in your body. Traditionally, if you think about it, most people use about two thousand words in English. Even most writers use less than five thousand words, generally speaking, in their books. Shakespeare used around fifteen to sixteen thousand words in his works of literature."

"He did it well," I add.

"He did," he says with a nod. "But what is so important to realize is that, most of the time, your experience in life is limited to the quality of the vocabulary you have. If you say 'good' about how you feel, and you mean it, you are going to feel good. And if you sincerely say you are excellent or outstanding, then that's what you're going to feel. Have you ever seen people or children who are impatient? They don't know what to do, so they go to a psychotherapist. Suddenly, they have this new term for what they might be feeling: ADD - Attention Deficit Disorder. We don't even take the time to say the whole name! They have a shortcut for the disorder! 'Yes, I'm ADD. I don't have enough attention or time to say Attention Deficit Disorder!'" Arjun laughs, and something inside of me splits and lets out a rolling chuckle, as well. "Yet they feel good that they have ADD. Why? Now they have a name for what they are going through. 'There's nothing wrong with me; I just have ADD.'

"What this means is, through vocabulary, people generalize how they feel. For example, for an extended period in my life, I believed I was feeling anger. Anger was the only emotion I felt. Whenever I felt something, I thought it was anger because it was the only label I had for every negative emotion I felt. Whenever I felt something different, I would still generalize: 'I'm angry.' I could have been feeling overwhelmed, frustrated, or even annoyed, but I would not have known this, because the vocabulary bucket word I kept using was *anger*.

"If you're a child, and your father says, 'Rich people are crooks,' and your mother says, 'rich people are alcoholics,' you will most likely have a negative association to money. You start to think, 'Being rich is bad,' because you have negativity associated with it. Even if you have the opportunity to become wealthy, will you do the right things that will get you there?"

"Sounds like my life," I say. "You're hitting a nerve with a freight train, Arjun."

"Tell me, how so?"

I put down my fork and stare into my salad, a mishmash of different foods, much like the mishmash of emotions I feel whenever someone talks to me about wealthy people. "Well, on one hand, I want to be independently wealthy. I don't want to worry about paying my bills all the time. I wish any children I have in the future would not have to worry about college, but on the other hand, all the wealthy people I know gloat. They gloat about their vacations on Facebook; they gloat about the wonderful private schools their kids go to and, internally, I know that I don't like those qualities in a person. So maybe I don't want to become one of them, and I'm subconsciously keeping myself from achieving that."

Arjun nods. "So you avoid wealth without realizing it. Let's look at a similar example: You enter a store as a child and ask your dad if he can buy you a book or toy. Your dad says, 'That's **expensive**. We cannot **afford** it.' So, 'afford' becomes part of your vocabulary. When 'affording' becomes part of your vocabulary, do you know what you're going to say even when you are a full-grown adult? 'I don't think I can afford this car. I don't think I can afford to lose my job, or this person.' This is because the word 'afford' was added to your working vocabulary through tribal push without you even noticing."

"Okay, I get it, but what am I supposed to do, completely change what everything means to me? I can't just change my past and my associations, Arjun."

"You can. You rewire yourself, and transform your old vocabulary with a new one. Catch yourself doing this. When you say, 'I cannot afford this", ask the question: is it really true that I cannot afford it today? For example, 'I cannot afford a vacation.' You cannot afford NOT to take a vacation! In reality, if you're not going on vacation, you're limiting your income by lowering your performance and creativity. If you have a vocabulary that allows you to say you cannot afford a vacation, you need to start questioning it. Ask questions like, 'How can I afford a vacation?' 'What will I do to afford this vacation?' Or change the vocabulary altogether! 'How can I *enjoy* a vacation instead of *affording* it? How can I pay for a vacation and enjoy it at the same time?' Remember, quality of your experience in this planet can be raised through the quality of your power questions."

Arjun dances a little on his stool at the counter and begins eating his salad. I laugh out loud at his antics.

"So you raise your standard by raising your vocabulary," he adds for emphasis. "By raising your vocabulary, you're essentially telling your brain that you have higher standards. Don't settle for 'good' or 'very good.' Demand 'remarkable.'"

"I get it," I say, polishing off my salad. "When you start changing your vocabulary, the emotions associated will also change."

Arjun smiles and returns to his lunch. Even as he eats, he continues to talk. "People who upgrade their vocabulary with higher quality words create higher quality emotions that can transform their lives. In the Seekers cult, I would suggest the vocabulary they used could be something like *believers, destruction, apocalyptic, channeling, preparing, commitment, giving up, contributing, emulating*, and so on. By itself, consistent use of this vocabulary would force people to act on their false conviction."

"To the point that they would sell their house or to give up their spouses?"

"And their children," Arjun adds.

"What?" I can't help the bark of astonishment that erupts from my lips.

"The doctor and his wife left their two kids with their aunt, supposedly to make the arrangements. The aunt was worried that the children were neglected and took the children in. Can you imagine the sense of abandonment?"

"No. I'm still amazed at how people get swept up in this," I say.

"The third way tribal push works is through Social Attunement," Arjun adds. "Ours is a social brain. You get socially and neurologically attuned to the emotions and beliefs of the tribe. Do you know that a person in a mob operates from 50% of their intelligence? For us humans, there are three types of neurons - cells in our brain, that are specifically built to help us be social. We use them to connect with each other deeply. Your brain has cells called spindle cells that will help you identify the emotion of what another person is feeling. And yet another type of cell, called mirror neurons, get you to mirror what others are feeling. Then, there's another type of cells called oscillators that allows you to affect them. It's like Hitler giving his hate speech to Nazi Germany. He would have used his spindle cells to get a feel of his audience, mirror neurons to experience what they feel and oscillators to influence them. It can be good, bad or ugly depending on the leadership of the group. I call it synchronization. Through social attunement, a cult or a group will attune its members to whatever the group feels through synchronization."

"The power of suggestion," I say. "Always influencing behavior."

"Exactly. Members have no idea why they are feeling what they are feeling. Have you ever had an experience where you were happy all day, but then, you talked to a friend who was depressed, and then you felt bad for the rest of the week?"

"Not that I recall, but I'm fairly sure my friends felt that way after talking to me." I frown. "After talking to me, they probably felt compelled to go home, listen to some Nirvana, wear dark clothing, eat five large pizzas by themselves, and become incoherently depressed. I'm sure I had influenced people with my state of mind at some point. Why do you bring it up?" I ask.

"Because if you associate with a group of people who believe that life sucks, a group of people who believe the economy is going to go bad or believe the world is going to be in a worse place in the future, then you are part of that tribe and, naturally, this is going to be part of your reality. Your reality is your perception of the world, and your tribe greatly affects what you see in the world. With tinted glasses, you only see what is wrong in the world. They will guarantee you will experience only bad things. You are the average of the five people you emotionally associate with. *You are the average of your inner tribe.* In other words, your income is the average of the five people you emotionally associate with, so is your relationship or health. I have seen this time and again in the millions of people I worked with."

"Wow, this is sobering. But many of the people I associated with were successful," I say.

"Even Charlie?"

"Oh, heavens no! Charlie was the biggest loser of all, yet I spent three years with him. So I suppose…listening to him that whole time greatly affected me." Suddenly, I can't believe I let myself listen to negative words for so long.

"Lindsay," Arjun says softly, "would you rather be part of an empowering **Super Tribe** or one that is enslaving you?"

"Super Tribe, for sure," I say. Mama didn't raise no dummy.

"Exactly."

"So how can you shift out of your tribe?" I ask.

"You need to begin the process of detaching from your enslaving tribes. You need to find new tribes that have better beliefs than what you have today."

"Right now, I really have no tribe, Arjun."

"Good. That is better than having an enslaving tribe, Lindsay. Join a **Super Tribe or start your own. Connect two of the most amazing people whom you know, and the three of you start a Super Tribe.** Then, find other like-minded people to join you, one at a time. There are exciting people on this planet, plenty of them. For you to attract them, you need to become one first. If you do, they will come find you."

"How do I select my Super Tribe members?" I ask. "I'm sure there is a fine line, but where is that line between being a healthy individual to part of a limiting tribe?"

"Great question. There's a huge difference between a positive tribe and a negative, dangerous one. If you are looking for growing your wealth, find people who are wealthier than you. If you want better health, find those who already have that. Ultimately, listen to your gut brain."

"Gut brain?"

"Yes. According to the latest research from Stanford, you have three brains. Your head brain, a heart brain, and a gut brain. When you did breathing through your heart, you activated your heart brain. Your gut brain is even more powerful. It produces 90% of the serotonin and 60% of the dopamine in your body."

"Holy moly!"

"Your gut will give you a more accurate reading on people and situations than your head brain. Listen to your gut. It's been scientifically proven to work to our advantange, and should be used when selecting people for your Super Tribe in personal or business life." He is clearly pretty thrilled about these discoveries he is sharing.

"That is truly astonishing," I say.

"Look at your current tribe from a bird's eye view. Is this a positive tribe? Is it a group of friends meeting for some lunch and laughs? Is it driving you to perform better? If so, that is an empowering tribe. Associate more with these people. Then, ask yourself: Is a group constantly negative, or trying to isolate you from your friends and family? Then you should question their motives, and run away from this tribe. **Abandon the tribes you no longer belong to.**"

I feel good about this. I should have run away from Charlie long ago, because I knew his views were not aligned to mine. He was bringing me down, pure and simple. It all makes sense to me now.

"Once you create a Super Tribe," Arjun goes on, "the best way to get the optimal outcome from the new tribe is by consciously start asking power questions of the tribe. Not only in your personal life, but also in business. In fact, your business becomes exponentially more successful when you create it as a Super Tribe. Do you want to know the key ingredients to a highly successful business Super Tribe?"

"I do."

"Then listen close, my young protegé, and prepare to have your eyes opened!"

CHAPTER SEVEN
The Three Flairs in Business

"There are three flairs in businesses," Arjun begins. "One is the technician—the doer, who performs the hands-on part of a job in any business. I call them **Artists**. There are also the **Managers**, who inspire and empower these artists and build the teams. The managers talk about efficiency and performance improvement. The managers are the result focused, getting-things-done folks! And third, there are **Leaders**, visionaries with a million ideas, the innovator, the creator. She shows her vision to the team and heads the whole operation. She doesn't carry out the Artists tasks. You need all of them in proportion to create your business as a Super Tribe. But they also need to learn to coexist without killing each other. We'll get into that more another day but let me give you an example why that is important, and then we'll be finished for today."

"Okay! I'm all in to flair, as long as it doesn't turn into 60's hippie jeans with the little embroidered mushrooms down the leg," I say, cheerfully spinning in my chair to face him directly. I've listened a long time today and want to absorb every bit of knowledge as I can before we're through.

"Imagine a plantation filled with crops perfect for harvesting. The leader, who owns the business, her manager, and her artists decide to meet on the edge of the plantation before they begin harvesting. They agree to meet at 9 a.m., although the manager and artist secretly didn't believe the leader would arrive on time. After all, she is always late. She is always thinking about new ideas and envisioning new products and services. Besides, she is in constant contact with the customers who will purchase the crops. They couldn't possibly understand how many things she needs to do to move the business forward…and thus, keep all of them employed.

"As expected, the manager and the artist arrive on time. And, as expected, the leader sends them a text that she's running behind, but will be there shortly. After some time, the manager makes a decision. 'You know what? It's about efficiency. We're wasting our time, and lost time means lost revenue. I know what our leader needs. What she wants is results.' So, he instructs them to start harvesting. The artists are so skilled; they harvest almost half the plantation in a short time.

"The manager assesses their progress and considers some process improvements. 'You know,' he says, 'there is one way you could increase your harvesting efficiency.' He articulated and implemented his super-efficient harvesting plan and then had them stop, taking a break every half hour.

"Their efficiency increased dramatically," Arjun explains. "Soon, the last crop was harvested, well ahead of the deadline. The manager felt so proud. Just as they were shutting the machines down, the business owner, the leader, arrived. The manager practically ran to her in his excitement to have finished without her guidance. Before he could even open his mouth, she was staring in slackjawed shock. 'Oh my gosh! You harvested the wrong plantation!' she exclaimed."

"Management is doing things right. Leadership is doing the right things. Peter Drucker," I say, familiar with his ideas.

"Correct, Lindsay. The leader is the only person who knows where they should be harvesting. Leaders ask questions like: 'Are these the right plantations to harvest? In other words, is this the right market to explore? Who is our niche? How can we innovate and add more value to our clients than anyone else in the market?' The manager is always thinking about efficiency. All he knows is that there are crops that need to be harvested. 'Why do I wait? Let's be efficient. Let's harvest it.' The artist is simply following the instructions of the manager, cutting wood in the best possible way. Now the question for you, Lindsay, is which of these three roles describe you in your business?"

This is a toughie. Considering I'm the one who does—or did—everything in my business, I would have to say the artist, though I also managed myself, and I was also the leader. But for the sake of simplicity...

"I'm the artist," I say finally, since I was the engineer coming up with the business solutions.

He smiles widely and taps his fingers on the counter. "Precisely. And you know what? Most small businesses in the U.S. are run by artists. Because at some point, we worked for a company as a technician for a long time and realized that we could do better. So we started a business and ran it like an artist. Who do we think like? Who do we hire? Whose mindset do we have? Artists'. We hire more artists like us. Our company becomes a sorority for artists!"

"That sounds like my company," I say hesitantly. "I would never have thought about it that way. I thought I was the manager and the leader. I hired other software engineers like me to run my software company."

"Ah, Lindsay, that is the artist's mindset. If you are a true artist, then you need to eventually hire a leader for your company or you must become that leader. When you are just beginning, it might be very difficult financially. So what do you do?"

"Easy. I clone myself. With three Lindsays, one can be Wonder Woman, one Athena, and one an Antigone, then I can do everything!"

He laughs, shaking his head. "Where will you get the money to hire a leader if your business is not doing well, much less purchase a cloning machine?"

"That's true. Cloning machines are quite pricey these days, and I think they only spit out sheep. We may have to settle for the store brand knock-off Lindsay."

"Yes, and they always break down right in the middle of cloning. Last thing we need is a half a Lindsay, with the leg of Athena, a bracelet wearing arm from Wonder Woman, and the rebellious spirit of Antigone." He smiles. "Okay, here is your answer: You have a manager and a leader inside of you, even though you were an artist for a long time. That's why you started your business. You believed that you could come up with new ideas and manage it at the same time. But what happened was you ignored the uncertainty and focused on what was known to you – being an artist. So what is unknown here?"

"How to innovate and manage effectively?" I take a guess, totally feeling his vibe. I get it.

"Excellent! You consciously set aside time to **master your business** as a leader and a manager. **Remember, your strength lies in your gift; your true identity. Your massive opportunities lie in your weaknesses; your shadows.** So today, you work as an artist. Tomorrow, you work two hours with a manager's mindset. Every day, you think like a leader for at least one hour. That is called mastering your business. Most entrepreneurs don't master their business. They work **in** their business, being artists all the time and not devoting enough time to managing or innovating."

It makes total sense.

"If you are in the business of creating mobile apps, *working in your business* is making more and more apps and not paying attention to anything else of importance. Now you became the operator of the business, not the owner. It almost feels like it's yet another full-time job. The only difference is, you're working eighty hours for less money. Sound familiar?"

Guiltily looking away in mock shame, I gulp heavily. "That's what I was doing. So, how do I master my business?"

"Mastering **your business** is finding and claiming new markets for selling more apps (marketing), finding better ways to make more of them (innovating) and delivering to your clients, and managing the inventory of the apps (optimizing). But most importantly, it's about building a great apps team. At this point, you own the business."

And yet again, my mind is blown. All this time, I've been working, working, working—like a hamster on a wheel, wondering why I wasn't getting anywhere. It was because I was neglecting the other two people in my business—the manager part of me and the leader within me. Darn it…*where was Arjun before I dug myself a half a million dollar hole?*

Oh, wait, that question implies that Arjun was not around. It also implies that I needed help, but didn't receive any. I need to rephrase my question to something more positive. Here I go…

"Arjun," I say, putting my plate in the sink and smiling at him. "How will I do things differently now that I have Arjun as my business acceleration coach?"

He smiles, closes his eyes, and nods. "And that, dear Lindsay, is an empowering question, as well as a compliment. Thank you. Are you ready to learn how?"

"I'm ready." I smile.

"See you next week, same day, same time."

CHAPTER EIGHT
Conquer Your Past

The following week, Arjun requests that I meet him at the Sequoia and King's Canyon National Parks Visitor Center. Although I've lived in LA most of my adult life, I've never been to Sequoia National Park, even though it's only three hours away. I have no idea what this man has in store for me, but knowing Arjun, some life-altering, mind-bending lesson is involved.

As I drive to our new meeting place, I mentally prepare for our meeting, even smiling to myself quite often to trick my brain into thinking that I've achieved a complete state of happiness.

Believe it or not, I think it sort of works. But then I start thinking of Charlie, of what he would think of me, getting all this psychological-slash-business training, and a dour mood comes over me.

Just as I reach the exit for the park, I plaster the smile back on, the biggest smile yet, like one that Lincoln wears on Mount Rushmore, and tell Charlie's ghost to suck it.

After wandering the park's visitor center for a bit, Arjun walks in with a big, Arjun-like smile on his face. "Hello, Lindsay!"

"Hi, Arjun." I smile. "What's with the natural setting today? Are you going to have me harvest a field or something?"

"It's a beautiful day, and we all need exercise, don't we?" Arjun chuckles.

"I guess." Truth is, I feel like exercising right now about as much as I feel like a wheatgrass enema, but I shrug, follow him toward Boyden Cave.

He laughs. "You don't sound too enthusiastic. You know, exercise has

94

been proven to release endorphins, which in turn, makes you feel happier, Lindsay."

"Alright, alright…" I don't want to admit I let myself go over the last few months…okay…maybe a year, but I'm sure he can tell. Not to give excuses, but I *did* get swept up in work, then the deep descent of my misery.

Once we're on the hiking path, though, I can't deny it. I can barely keep up with Arjun's spry pace. Who's the older one here? *Sheesh.*

"Lindsay, you need to exercise more," Arjun teases as we walk beneath the giant towering trees.

"Yes, I know. Thanks for rubbing it in, *Mom.*" I puff my breath heaving in my chest. "This trail has gone on forever. Is the worst of it behind us?"

Arjun laughs. Always so jolly, he is. "That reminds me of a story."

"Oh, boy, here we go…"

He side-glances at me. "What? You don't like my stories?"

"I love your stories! I kid." I smile, realizing that he and I have developed a rapport with each other, and I can say anything that pops into my mind. It's…nice.

"Okay, good, because I packed them for you today," he says, quickening his pace, and I have to boost my energy to keep up with him. "A woman is in labor. It's been a long day, but the pain only gets worse. She tells the nurse, 'It has been going on for a long time. You are an expert on this. Tell me…is the worst part over yet?'" Arjun breaks off and looks me in the eye. "Don't we ask that, too, in our lives? When the economy was really bad in 2008, you probably asked that question—are we at the end of the tunnel?"

I nod fervently. "Yes, not just in 2008."

Arjun continues. "So, then the nurse says, 'Oh, no, no, no. This is the *easy* part. The hard part is the next eighteen years!'" He breaks into a hearty laugh and comes to an empty bench surrounded by lush, giant trees.

I chuckle, thankful I don't have kids to complicate my issues yet. "Are we going to rest here?" I tease. "Or are we waiting until I collapse?"

He gestures for me to sit and then follows suit.

"Lindsay, one who does not enjoy the journey may not enjoy the destination," Arjun responds, holding up a finger. "And one who focuses only on the journey may not even reach the destination. Either case, it is a failure. So, let's talk about failure."

"Yay, failure! *Aced that one!* A topic I finally know something about!" I roll my eyes. "Shoot. Ask me anything."

Without giving in to my negative reaction, he goes on without missing a beat. "Okay. When you lost your first business, what did you feel?" he asks.

Ugh, I had no idea this would be our subject matter today. Regardless, I answer, knowing that Arjun is on the road to some method with his madness.

"Let's see…where do I even begin?" I sigh. "I felt like I had let people down. I felt like people stopped believing in me, supporting me. And could I blame them? They trusted me, and I couldn't be entrusted with money anymore. When everything failed, they probably thought I was a big loser."

"So you felt horrible," Arjun summarizes.

"Of course. I still do. I feel like if people trust me again, I will let them down again."

"What else do you feel if you fail again?" Arjun asks.

"I'll lose what's left of my credibility. I'll lose business partners and even more of my friends. I'll feel completely rejected, and to me, rejection is like being hit and run over by a truck, a big, double-rigged logging truck. I want to avoid it at all costs."

"I understand, Lindsay. But when you started your business, were you thinking of letting people down?"

"Of course not. I felt fearless, like I could win and accomplish anything. I was certain I would succeed. I don't know what happened." I stop and drop my face into my hands.

Hold it together.

I feel a gentle hand on my back. "Lindsay, when you start a new business venture, you don't think about failure. No one does. But when you began losing money, what immediately came to your mind?"

"Everything I just mentioned. Like, what if I fail and let my family down?" I do my best not to let the tears out. If I'd have known I'd have to drive three hours to cry amongst the trees, I would have stayed in LA and cried in private, where I would have had lots of tissues. Not to mention, I'm not exactly a pretty crier. If I really broke down, there would be red, snotty nose and swollen eyes in my near future.

Even more of a reason to pull it together, woman!

"Okay, now listen…**when people focus on failure, they are blindsided by their fear and the failure snowballs.**"

"So, it's like I took a tiny little snowball and rolled down the side of a mountain, turning it into a village-crushing size avalanche that I skied headfirst into? So again, am I perpetuating my fears?" I ask.

"Something like that. But we're working on skiing lessons," Arjun replies, smiling and crossing his legs out in front of him as if getting ready for a detailed explanation. "You said you wanted to avoid rejection at any cost. Let's talk about how rejection can destroy your business. Here is one example: suppose there are race cars that race in a desert. Every mile, there is a pole marking the distance. When these expert drivers race, they still somehow manage to hit this pole. But why? It's a lone pole in a wide open space. How could they possibly accomplish it?"

"Maybe someone's hitting the sauce too much?" I say in confusion. "I mean, they could go in any direction they want."

Arjun nods his head. "You would think. However, they focus on avoiding the pole, and while trying to avoid it, they drive straight toward it."

"So, in trying to be overcautious, they could end up being killed." I'm not sure I buy that. "Imagine how much worse it would be if you don't take precautions, Arjun."

"I understand," he says, nodding. "I am all for being intelligent in business. I teach my clients intelligent optimism. We can discuss more about it another time. But precaution is one thing and focus on not failing is another thing. Here you shift your focus from what you want (success) to what *you don't want (failure)*. You get more of what you focus on or what you want to avoid. Thus, when you want to avoid rejection or fear at all costs, you are driving a hundred miles an hour straight toward it. **Your success lies at the intersection of your highest aspirations and biggest fears.**"

"I'm not sure I understand what you're saying."

"Okay…" Arjun says, using his hands a lot to make his point. "Being an entrepreneur, you know if you don't get at least five no's, you haven't even started selling your idea. If you feel rejected on the first no, how can you market who you are and what your business stands for? You might think you don't need to do this. You can build a marketing and sales team. How can you possibly show someone a path if you are blind yourself or suffering from a snowball concussion? Even better, what if you cannot budget for a sales team yet?"

It's not hard for me to agree with that concept. "You're right," I say. "I cannot afford a sales team. Marketing and sales were always two of the biggest challenges in my business. I felt guilty for not getting involved in sales activities, but I always told myself this was not my area. I used to get mad when my salespeople didn't bring me the results I wanted, but I knew secretly that my results would have sucked even more. Ugh, I hated marketing and sales."

"Now back to fear, let me ask you, if you get over your fear of rejection, will you be able to succeed in business?"

"IF is the important part. IF I can get over the fear, yes, I can."

"No, you can't," he counters.

"What?" I laugh. "You are so frickin' crazy, Arjun!"

"The first time someone fails in business, you can blame their fear of rejection as one of the reasons for failing in marketing and sales. After the first time, though, it's highly likely they will have fear of failure when they start their second business."

"Which is the vicious cycle I get caught up in," I explain without a shred of confidence. "It sucks to fail all the time."

He smiles gently. "I will help you overcome your fear of rejection, Lindsay, but just curious…how do you think you will change this pattern?"

"I have no clue, Arjun. At all. If I knew, I wouldn't need you. For me, rejection is like being hit by a truck and then run over by it." I nervously laugh, shaking my head.

"Then, let me tell you another story," Arjun begins, facing me and crossing his legs. "In a village in India, there lived a rich man named Kubaer. One day, he met Puchel, a poor farmer who once was his classmate. Kubaer invited

Puchel to his house. Puchel's clothes were filthy and tattered—"

"This sounds very familiar, Arjun. *Very* familiar."

"It's not the story of Arjun and Lindsay," he laughs, then continues. "So, as per their Indian tradition of treating guests like gods, Kubaer gifted his only best outfit to his poor friend. Puchel refused his gift, but Kubaer insisted until finally, Puchel wore the beautiful threads. The poor Puchel looked like a king, while rich Kubaer appeared to be his servant. Even though he was rich, Kubaer already felt inferior. **He was a poor man with a lot of money.**"

"In his mind," I add.

"Yes, in his mind, where it matters." Arjun winks at me. "The two friends went for a walk. They met up with some of Kubaer's rich friends. 'This is Puchel, my old classmate,' Kubaer said, '**but his clothes are mine.**'"

"Wow, what a jerk," I say, aghast.

"Yes," Arjun continues with his story, "Puchel felt horrified. 'Why did you tell him these clothes weren't mine? There was no need for that. I didn't even ask for your clothes!' Kubaer felt horrible. 'I am so sorry. I don't know why I said that. I guess I was embarrassed and felt like explaining. I am so sorry, I won't say that again.'

"They kept walking and met another friend of Kubaer's. He introduced Puchel and said, 'This is my friend, Puchel, from the village, **but his clothes are not mine.**' Again, Puchel was totally embarrassed this time. 'Why do you keep mentioning the clothes? There is no need! Nobody asked you whose clothes you are wearing. You gave them to me to wear, and now you are embarrassing me. I was fine the way I was! I work hard. I'm proud of my sweaty clothes. Yet, your clothes shame me.'

"'I am so, so sorry,' Kubaer said. 'I didn't mean to make you uncomfortable. Please forgive me. I will not talk about the clothes anymore, I promise.' They continued walking and met another person. Kubaer introduced Puchel again. 'This is my friend from the village. Please don't ask me anything about what he is wearing, because I promised **I would not talk about his clothes.**'

"The poor man threw his hands up, frustrated. 'You know what? I am going back to the village. I want to live my life without being embarrassed.

Goodbye, Kubaer.' On a broader scale," Arjun sighs, "this is the ultimate story of human conditioning and how we are trapped by our minds and our pasts. You either embrace it, fight it, or pretend to be cool, but we are almost never free from it. I will teach you a powerful technique that will help you break free from the mental jails we build for ourselves.

"For now," he begins, "let's focus on today's outcome—overcoming fear of rejection. Kubaer felt rejected first, right? He tried to avoid it by denying it. Once that was challenged, he became indifferent. But all along, he was controlled by his insecurity and fear. When people try to change their patterns, most of the time, this is what happens—they move from smoking to drinking, or drinking to overeating. Emotionally, they move from negative emotion to negative emotion like guilt to anger. What we really want is lasting change even *after* we overcome our challenges. Successful entrepreneurs and professionals conquer their past."

Accelerator # 3 - Conquer your past.

I nod, totally empathizing. Up and down like an out-of-control yo-yo on the end of a tight string is just like how I managed dieting. Sometimes that yo-yo caught sight of a dessert bar, or justified a couple pints of ice cream to de-stress. I mean, how many times in the past had I started a diet, done very well the first few weeks, then fallen back to the same old patterns? But we're talking about business, so I stop Arjun a moment.

"Okay, so let's suppose I have a new business. As the owner of the company, what can I do to address my fear of rejection?" I ask, curious to hear his thoughts.

"Excellent question. Let me answer your question with another question..."

"Ack! You and your questions!" I laugh.

"Yes, yes, you're going to hate me by the time this is all over." He smiles.

"Trust me; I won't. Continue, sir," I say gallantly.

"Okay, tell me, Lindsay, why must you overcome your fear of rejection today?"

"Because I need to succeed," I reply.

He winces a little. "From a deeper sense, though...why else must you change?"

I try to dig a little deeper past the yo-yo within. I should have known he wouldn't accept the first answer my brain spat out. "Because I don't deserve to feel like this, let alone live this way."

"Why don't you deserve to live this way?" he asks. I know he's playing devil's advocate.

"Because I'm a good person, and I try my best, and I have a great product," I say, willing my unconfident brain to believe it.

He nods slowly. "So…if zero is you are not at all interested in overcoming fear of rejection today, and ten means you absolutely want to make this change right away, what number are you?"

"I think a seven or eight," I say.

"Great. Let me follow that up with another question. What is most important for you?"

"Most important…in what?" I ask.

"Doesn't matter. Just tell me what is most important to you. In life, business or in general," he clarifies, but not by much. He's leaving it open-ended to hear my thoughts.

I have to think about this for a minute. At one point in my life, I thought it was my relationship. I thought having someone to share life with was my highest desire. Recently, I want to succeed in business. I feel like if I cannot stand on my own, I'm not fit to be in a relationship. After some deliberation, I reply, "I want to be extremely successful."

"Do you mean extremely successful or wealthy?"

"Both." I smile.

He nods as if saying, *fair enough*. "Okay, what do you feel this extreme success gives you?"

"More money. More recognition."

Arjun is unrelenting. "Whose recognition are you losing out on because you have this fear of rejection?"

"My family's, my colleagues', my business partners'…all of them." Familiar feelings of sadness and despair threaten to take over me. I don't know why it's so important I have everyone's validation, but it is.

"How do you feel about losing all that recognition?"

"Insecure."

"Insecure about what?"

I sigh loudly. "About myself, business...everything!" I can feel myself stressing out just talking about this. Though it's not Arjun who made me feel this way, I can't help but feel a bit annoyed by all the tough questions.

"If you continue to allow yourself to feel rejected, will you ever be able to feel secure?"

"No."

Arjun arches one eyebrow. "Now, on a scale from one to ten, what is your number for overcoming fear of rejection?"

"A nine."

He grins. "Had you overcome this fear ten years ago, how could your life be different today?"

"Don't remind me. I could have succeeded. I could have lived my own life. I could have applied my creativity to innovate in my business. Like you said last week, **I could have mastered my business, not been enslaved by it.** I could have been a successful businesswoman. Plus, I would have been able to stop eating ice cream after just one bite. Ugh, this is so disappointing."

"Lindsay, I do not ask these questions to make you feel disappointed but to teach you what you could do differently, so it doesn't happen again," he says, laying his hand on my back again. It truly feels comforting. "If you had overcome this fear ten years ago, what types of people could you be connected to right now?"

Thinking about this is difficult. "The most successful entrepreneurs in LA. I might be married to a successful, understanding and supportive man. My family and friends would have looked up to me."

"And how would you have grown your business differently had you been fearless a decade ago?"

I feel the tears rising in my eyes from the pressure of these answers, but I give in anyway. "I would have built a business empire. I would have had hundreds of employees working for me who felt secure and respected. I would have fed thousands of starving children around the world real food, plus a bit of ice cream for fun." I wipe quiet tears from my lids while trying to stay light.

"Lindsay, what is your number for overcoming fear of rejection now?"

"Through the roof, Arjun. Twenty."

Arjun nods happily. "That's right. I see that you are truly ready to overcome the fear of rejection that is stopping you from succeeding in business and life."

"Heck yeah, I am."

"Heck yeah, this is the first step of changing anything. You must give yourself emotional consent to change. You have great leverage on your mind and your past right now. According to neuroscientists, when you are emotionally activated, you can easily change your brain's wiring for good," he agrees, and something about Arjun saying *heck yeah* makes me smile. "Have you heard of Swami Vivekananda?" he asks.

"Doesn't sound familiar."

"He was an Indian Hindu monk who traveled around the world teaching Indian philosophies to the western world. Long ago, he was challenged to prove himself in a king's court in India. 'If you are truly a holy man, can you take this stick and make it smaller?' the king challenged, placing a large stick before the swami.

"Vivekananda thought for a minute and said, 'Yes I can.' Everybody gathered to see if he would be able to change the size of the stick. After some consideration, Vivekananda asked two men to retrieve a large log from the castle grounds. Finally, the men returned, hefting the log and stood before Vivekananda and the king. 'Now, place it next to the stick,' Vivekananda said. Now, the old stick looked tiny next to the large log. 'Is the stick smaller now?' he asked the king. The king was humbled by the new perspective." Arjun cocks his head to one side. "What did you learn from this story?"

"That it's all about perspective," I reply quickly. "Maybe I've been looking at fear of rejection as bigger than it is. I need to work on that."

"Fascinating answer," Arjun says. "I appreciate your honesty and candor. Let's do that now, shall we?"

"Heck yeah," I say, waiting for Arjun's reply.

"Heck yeah, indeed," he replies with a laugh. "Let's handle your fear of rejection—by using ESCAPE– a powerful intervention I created to help people reengineer their mind so that they can shift their identity and convert their fear into power."

"Identity shift? Okay…you didn't tell me I was going to be getting a new body. Speaking of which, a new body would be nice, come to think of it. Can you give me a Beyoncé, please?"

"Not exactly how that works, of course," Arjun says with a grin. "Your identity consists of your value and beliefs, especially the beliefs you have about yourself. It translates into wirings in your brain - your brain's unique fingerprint. Neuroscientists call this your connectome. You change your behavior or habit; you change a bit. You change your beliefs; you make progress. You change your values; you make even bigger progress. If you change your identity, you have a new fingerprint, a new connectome. You found the next version of you. Let's continue on our walk, shall we?"

He gets up, stretches, and heads off slowly down the path. I follow him.

"Tell me about a time you felt completely rejected."

I frown. "Arjun, the day you found me, I was standing in the ocean, remember? A big reason for that was because of what Charlie did a couple of months earlier. He left me—and he said I was a failure."

"Yes, I know a bit about that. Do you remember your first experience where you felt completely rejected?" Arjun asks, holding his arms above his head and stretching as he walks.

I take a huge, deep breath and begin. "When I was about thirteen, I was totally in love with this kid, Marlon Turner; I'll never forget his name. I couldn't wait for the school dance, so I could hopefully dance with him. The big day finally arrived, and somehow, I was brave enough to ask him to dance. I was so nervous; I swear I was about to throw up. Well, right in front of his buddies, he said **NO** to me, all the while, laughing. I was so utterly heartbroken, I couldn't even walk away gracefully, so I just stood there. The longer I stood, the more everybody laughed at me. His friends called me, 'ugly,' 'retard,' and a bunch of other names. God, it was a horrible experience."

"Wow. I am sorry about that, Lindsay."

"It's okay," I say, trying to brush it off. "Middle school sucked."

"Let's measure this feeling, shall we? If negative ten is absolute rejection, and zero is neutral, and positive ten means complete acceptance, where do you think you fall in this experience?"

I scoff. Pretty low, that's for sure. "Negative eight."

"I see. Can you think of a time when you felt negative ten?"

Shrugging, I nod. "Oh, I have more, but you asked me for my first experience. Let's see; when I was married to my ex, Jay, he was usually indifferent about most things. We rarely fought. Then again, he acted like he didn't care about me. He ignored me. I was like nobody to him."

"I can see why you are no longer married," Arjun said with an empathetic frown.

"You're not kidding. I cooked for that man and did his dishes. But he was only happy during the thirty seconds he needed me every week. Jay was a salesperson, so he traveled all the time. I felt lonely in my relationship when he was home and when he was gone."

"I know that must have hurt," Arjun says, "but I'm excited you're able to share this. Most people tell their experiences and start crying. And if I cry with you, you know what is going to happen?"

"We're going to be two sobbing hot messes?" I reply.

"Exactly! Though I am the hotter of the two of us," he says with a waggle of his brows.

"Oh, that goes without saying, Arjun." Weird that he already knows how much humor cheers me up.

He goes on. "If I empathize with your tears, it's going to drive negative emotion deeper into your nervous system. My response style is different. **I'm coming from a place of deep caring for you, not for your problems.** Is that okay?"

I paste a mock scowl on my face. "No. I want you to cry with me."

"Not going to happen. Okay, give me a number for this experience…"

"About feeling rejected by Jay? Phew, negative nine, I'd say?"

Arjun laughed. "You trying to disappoint me? You know I'm looking for a negative ten!"

"That's because there's another one—when I dramatically failed in my business. My whole family came to me, blaming me, telling me, 'You don't know anything. I told you, you weren't capable of running a business. We told you becoming an entrepreneur was too risky. We warned you so many times. See, look what happens when you don't listen to us?' They were furious because I'd lost not only my money but their money, too.

"When they all started calling one by one, telling me I was a failure, I wept. Not in front of them, of course, because I had to pretend to be strong. But when I got home, I let it all out and felt so guilty that I stayed in my room for ten days. I was pissed! Pissed at me...pissed at them. But more at me, because I screwed up. That was when I felt the most rejected."

Suddenly, I feel like a huge weight lifts off my shoulders and I heave a shaky sigh of relief.

"Lindsay, what is the level of rejection you feel when you think about your business failure?"

"Negative ten," I say.

Quickest answer ever.

"Look at that. The moment you can identify this, it's easy to fix. These are fearful memories you have about your past. According to Dr. Daniel Siegel, one of the most renowned neuroscientists in the world, 'memory is a way past events affect future function'. In a direct way, experiences thus shape the structure of the brain. Thus, the experiences of rejection you had in the past could activate your fear of rejection in the future. But memory is not a static thing. Remembering is not merely activating the old experience; it is the creation of a new connection based on who you are with and what state of mind you experience today."

Arjun warms to his topic and continues, animatedly.

"In addition to that, you have something called implicit memory that is built up of metaphors. You conceive the meaning of any experience from these metaphors. Ultimately, these metaphors define the idea of who you are, your identity. That is what we are planning to change today. But let's experiment. Take the images of your puppy love, your indifferent husband, and of the business failure, and create one single video of the entire experiences together. Watch it from beginning to end."

Sounds like my own personal hell and I can't help but wonder if there is something more pleasant I could do, like squeeze lemons into my eyes. Still, Arjun hasn't steered me wrong so far...

I close my eyes as I walk, imagining my video. The air smells of industrial cleaner and wax that kept the school's floors overly glossed. Sweaty palms and a heartbeat that pushes through my sweater, I walk toward my boy crush as the eyes of the other middle school kids mock me. The pain of failure floods through me. A creak from the old, oak front door resonates through the kitchen as Jay saunters in from a week on the road. Disheveled hair and a disinterested glance towards me signal that an evening spent in mutual loneliness is on the menu. The smell of wine and sweet, cherry ice cream permeates the bedroom. Tissues are piled next to the drained glass and empty pints of Ben and Jerry's. Another full bottle waits on deck. The phone rings. I don't answer, leaving behind the conversation about my failure to pickle my fears and failures at the bottom of bottles and pints instead.

"This is the crappiest movie ever. Like, relentlessly bleak. Two thumbs down. Zero percent on *Rotten Tomatoes*."

"Okay," he says, trying not to laugh. "Now give your movie a title."

"Lindsay's List of Crappy Experiences, Rated NWI," I say.

"Excellent title."

"Thank you."

"The NWI?"

"Not Worth It."

It doesn't even deserve the accompanying popcorn with SnoCaps and a large Coke. It is a torturing experience to think of all these scenarios at once. I try not to cry from how much I hated myself during these times.

"What are you feeling, Lindsay?"

"How much I hate you for making me think of this. I feel completely rejected, broken, lonely, and torn apart."

"This is normal," he says, his voice slow and kind. "**Most people collect all their experiences when they felt rejected and stack them together.** Then they watch it as an entire movie, placing themselves as the main character." He pries my hands from my face and slowly lowers them. "I want to show you the other side, in contrast, so you will not do this for the rest of your life. Nobody chooses to be depressed, but **about twice as many women experience depression as men.** Depression costs the American economy approximately $210 billion a year."

"Now that's something to be depressed about."

"Yes, and like you told me, our goal is to get you past that fear of rejection. Right?"

I nod.

"It's simple. Let us do power ceremony for three minutes. Now, breathe into your heart for a dozen times, imagining that you do not have a head. And ask the questions, 'What are you thankful for now? Who are you thankful to? Why are you thankful to them? What does that make you feel?' Very good. Now, pause for a second and answer my question. If zero is that you are feeling absolutely horrible and ten means you are in ecstasy, what number are you right now?"

"A nine," I say, in awe.

"Your memory of any experience is saved in your brain sequentially in a timeline. For example, if you ate ice cream from Ben and Jerry's, you save the ordering the ice cream first, then you sitting down and enjoying it, and then you driving back home. When you remember this experience, you start from the beginning, as well. While remembering, if we change the sequence of this experience, the experience itself becomes a new and different one. From then on, your brain can decode it in the new sequence. This is because that is the most recent memory that your brain has about the incident.

"In addition to that, your brain will change the meaning of the experience based on the state of mind you are in right now. If you are in an empowered state of mind, the experience itself can convert to an empowering one. That was why I asked you to do power ceremony first.

"Your mind will also finalize the meaning of the experience based on how the experience ended. If you consciously end the memory with a happy experience, even your trauma can become empowering, while keeping the lesson from it. Numerous research suggests that we can even create memories that did not even exist. When you have gone through extreme trauma, your neurons are deeply connected to create superhighways through a process called myelination. Normally, it takes 10,000 hours of activity to create these superhighways but the trauma speeds it up.

"Myelination means that you are an expert in what you do; whether it is playing tennis or being chronically depressed. Once your cells are myelinated, the communication between those cells are 3,000 times faster. Myelination was considered to be the biggest problem for 'fixing' people with severe trauma. The limiting belief here is, you need to break the myelinations, and it could take years. What I am suggesting is we do not need to break the myelination. Imagine drug dealers from Mexico built a secret-super bridge to Texas to smuggle drugs. If you are the governor of Texas, would you shut down the operation and destroy the bridge that was built or would you shut down the operation and put border security to transport fruits and vegetables from Mexico? The bridge is already built; you might as well use it for good purposes. I call it the Secret Bridge Effect.

"In the same way, we can convert the deepest traumas or the most challenging experiences to the best references of our courage. If you look deeper, you will see that most of the world leaders, including Nelson Mandela and Gandhi, converted their biggest challenges into their greatest opportunites. That is my invitation for you today.

"Finally, deeply emotional experiences are added as first-person experience in your memory. You are inside the experience. For example, when you remembered these experiences, did you see yourself in the picture as first person or are you watching from outside as a second person?"

"Inside as first person," I say.

"Exactly. These experiences are locked into your body as if you are inside of it. Once you change the sequence of memory and change this experience from first person to third person, the experience itself transforms into something even more empowering. It changes from an implicit memory to explicit memory. In other words, these become the conscious memories that you created using your imagination brain – your mid pre-frontal cortex. In a moment, I will ask you to see these experiences in second and third person. You can use your imagination brain to transform your enslaving memories to empowering experiences. Just like Vivekananda, you will make the stick of rejection much smaller than you. I could talk about the science behind this for the next 24 hours, but we need to take care of your rejection.

"Here is what you do, start at the end of the movie and rewind it until the beginning. Start with the business failure and end with the part when you were passionate about starting your business. Watch your lonely life with Jay end with complete happiness on your wedding day. Watch your dance floor rejection end with being head over heels in love with Marlon. End the movie with you feeling romantic about your genuine expression of love and celebrate the beauty of it. Do it now. I'll give you two minutes."

That's one minute and fifty-eight seconds more than Jay deserves, but I've come this far...

I stare off into space, mesmerized. Backward, my movie begins with the day I stood in the Pacific Ocean, and I watch, as it shifts from my terrible fight with Charlie to my boring life with Jay, backward through springs, winters, falls, and summers until I was a blushing June bride. I think about the boys laughing at me on the dance floor, and the reel finally ends with thirteen-year-old Lindsay, sitting at her desk, watching the boy of her dreams, hoping, waiting for the day he'd say he loves her, too—the perfect middle school crush.

And I'm happy again.

"Yes."

"What's the pain level now, Lindsay?" he whispers.

I open my eyes. "Zero. Neither pain nor happiness, just level, even ground."

"Wonderful!" Arjun nods his approval. "Now, let's name that character in the video something other than Lindsay. When you were young, what was a nickname that your family or friends called you that made you feel lesser than who you are?"

"Ugh, you're going to bring me down again, Arjun!"

"Not for long, I promise," he says.

"Fine. They called me Mumu," I say quietly, embarrassed.

"Mumu. An excellent name for the character in your movie. And what is the name of the powerful self within you? Think about a time when you were successful in business. What did they call you?"

"Wishful Thinking," I say with a snort.

Arjun persists. "Come on, Lindsay. Think about a nickname your friends or business partners called you that made you feel really powerful."

"They called me Linds when I was successfully running my business for a short time. Is that what you mean?"

"Linds. That is exactly what I mean. Excellent. Here is what you have, Mumu is your weak self, Linds is your powerful self. Now, imagine you are in a movie theater. The only movie playing is *Mumu's Story*—"

"Then I want my money back."

Arjun smiles. "*Mumu's Story* is the tale of a woman being rejected three times. The first time was over love. The second was indifference from her husband, and the third one was failure in business. Now, sit down as Linds, successful entrepreneur, and watch the entire movie through her eyes. Make sure you don't get too excited and jump into the screen. Stay in the audience, because it is not happening to you. It is happening to Mumu, another person. I'll give you two minutes to watch it. Once you're done, let me know by saying yes again."

As corny as this exercise sounds, I comply. I watch the story of Mumu while thinking of myself as an educated, successful businesswoman. Not in a "looking down on her" way, just feeling sorry for poor Mumu and how I wish I could help lift her out of her hole of depression, make her love herself the way I love myself and feel worthy—I wish she could, too.

"Yes," I say to let Arjun know I'm finished.

"Good. What do you feel?" Arjun asks.

"Sad for her, like I used to know her a long time ago, but I need to get back to my busy, happy life now." And crazily, I do feel like I'm done watching a movie…like I've come out of the dark theater, and now I need to return to reality.

"Do you feel any pain?" Arjun cocks his head.

"No. Not at all."

"Great. So, what's your number now from negative ten to positive ten?"

I consider before responding. "Probably a five now."

"Why?"

"Because I'm not feeling the pain of rejection anymore, and I feel more positive about my life going forward."

"Good to know. Would you have any advice for Mumu? As Linds, I mean?"

"Yes. Well, Mumu's too emotional. She needs to believe in herself more— be stronger, more powerful. She doesn't have to take it so personally when she's rejected. She can choose to see it objectively by realizing that Marlon didn't want to dance, maybe he was embarrassed, too, or maybe he just liked a different girl or even a boy at the dance."

"I see," Arjun says, stroking his cheek as he contemplates my answers. "What else?"

"As for Mumu's marriage, at least she got out of that relationship. That was a smart move, but she focused on the failure of it instead of the success of making the right decision to leave him. Plus, she hung on too long. She should have moved on earlier."

It's interesting—I do feel like I'm talking about someone else, someone not as smart or self-assured as I am.

"Hmm, good perspective, Linds," Arjun compliments the powerful side of me. "What about the business situation?"

"My advice for Mumu there would be, 'Hey, Mumu, you're pretty strong. No matter what happens, you will always find a way. Lots of people with successful businesses failed multiple times before finding what works for them. Use what you learned to rekindle your passion and restart from scratch. You *will* be successful.'"

Arjun claps quietly. "What an inspirational person you are, Linds. And now imagine that someone else was in the theater with you watching Mumu's story. The third person sat in the projection room of the theater, watching from behind the glass. And that person's name is…can you guess?"

I cross my fingers. "Brad Pitt? Ryan Gosling? Please, please, let it be Leo."

"Close. Her name is Lindsay!" Arjun says triumphantly, holding his hands high in the air, as though jubilant.

"Um, how exactly are Leo and Lindsay close?" I laugh at Arjun's reaction.

"Lindsay," he says, brushing my silly question aside, "imagine you were watching *Mumu's Story* from the projection room. Would you watch the movie again?"

"Hell no. That was the most depressing flick I've ever seen. Worse than *Terms of Endearment* and *Pitch Perfect 2* combined."

Arjun shields his eyes and shakes his head in silent laughter. "Well, just for the sake of summarizing, humor me and watch it again. Okay?" Arjun asks.

Ah, I get it. He wants me to watch it again to solidify this experiment.

Fine. After all, I know that girl in the movie. I don't mind looking at her again. She might need more exercise, but she's got a cute face.

"Fine," I say, closing my eyes again in preparation for another round of sad movie-watching.

"Watch *Mumu's Story* again from the beginning to end from the projection room as Lindsay while observing the powerful Linds in the theater. Notice how she reacts. Start now—I'll give you two minutes to finish. Say yes when you finish."

Here goes nothing...

I watch *Mumu's Story* again, except this time, I watch that fine-looking businesswoman sitting alone in the theater. Exuding power, she sits upright, shoulders squared, chest open, with her hands folded in her lap. There's no buttered popcorn leaving crumbs on her suit or grease on her cheeks. Instead, she sips water, a sign of treasuring her own health. From her sad smile, it almost looks like she used to know Mumu long ago, like an old school friend she said goodbye to, but they *might* be close friends again one day *if* Mumu got herself together. When the movie is over, she stands, sighs heavily, as though shedding the negativity from her lungs, then turns and leaves the theater to whatever awesome life she leads.

"Yes," I say, opening my eyes.

Arjun is regarding me with a grin. "Any comments?"

"Well," I sigh, "while Mumu was certainly not in Ananda, Linds was, and the whole time, she seemed to feel sorry for Mumu and wished she would snap out of it. Also, Mumu had pretty low self-confidence. Half of the time, she felt guilt, shame…you name it, and the rest of the time, she was angry. She seemed weak to me. I wanted to tell her that, no matter whatever happens in her life, she needs to take ownership and move on. She's an extremely capable woman. If somebody's mean to her, if somebody doesn't respect her for who she is, then she needs to act on it. She could've resolved a bunch of those issues through dialogue instead of getting mad about it."

Arjun nods his head knowingly, letting me have my moment of catharsis.

"Mumu needs to be mature when handling relationships," I add like I'm suddenly some type of expert. "I feel like Linds has it all together, not masculine, just more like a woman in charge. Wonder Woman!"

"And that is a very important thing to remember," Arjun interrupts. "A woman in charge can and should use her natural feminine maturity. She doesn't need to try to act like a man to be respected. Being a powerful woman will earn respect by itself, but many women adopt men's traits to earn respect, though it is not necessary—women are powerful, too. Go on, Lindsay."

I nod. "That's true, and I found myself wanting Mumu to be proud of her femininity while being assertive at the same time." We come to another bench and I sit down again. It did feel good to walk and stretch my legs.

Smiling to myself, I close my eyes to relax.

Arjun sits beside me and stares out at the towering trees. "As Lindsay, what do you think about Mumu's puppy love?"

Thinking about it a moment, I say, "As far as the first love, I would ask Mumu: 'Why are you even thinking about it now? Look at yourself. Look at who you have become over the years and how successful you are. Look at how much potential and energy you have. You were only thirteen years old at that time. You don't need to pay attention to that. Take control and move on.'"

"How about Mumu's business failure?"

"As Lindsay, I thought that Mumu was too weak in handling her business failure. She should have stood up and said, 'You know what? I will do whatever it takes. I'll use my energy, enthusiasm, abilities, and my skills. I **know I failed, but I'm not a failure.** I'll do whatever it takes to use my energy, my power, and enthusiasm to build this business back again. I will become powerful and inspire people through my example. I will learn from my failure and start my business again, become successful, and pay all your money back.'"

"What is your wish for Mumu?" he asks.

"My wish? Well, she needs to accept who she is. Once upon a time, she used to be daring, willing to go on a new journey. She believed in herself. But circumstances brought her down. Okay…stuff happens, you know? But now, I want her to be that way again. She can do it. She can own herself, be powerful again. She could be that business magnate she always dreamed about being. She could influence and inspire. I want to see her grow and become a multimillionaire, serving thousands of people all over the world. That is my dream for Mumu."

Arjun was silent for a moment, while I digest my own words. "Lindsay, that was incredible. You had your solutions inside of you all this time."

"Better watch out. I might just become the next Arjun, but with better legs and in a power skirt suit."

"Who are you going to live as from now on? Mumu, Linds, or Lindsay? Think about it."

"I want to be Lindsay. She's the most balanced and the most awesome, if I do say so myself." I cross my arms and assume a confident pose, then laugh.

Arjun laughs, too. "Why?"

"Because that's who I am. That's my mission in life. I'm an entrepreneur. No matter whatever obstacles that come my way, I can overcome them. I can walk through fire with no burns. And I know that I'm compassionate and courageous enough to handle anything. And then, when all is said and done, Brad Pitt and Ryan Gosling will come looking for me. They'll duel over me, because they won't be able to resist my charms," I add for good measure. Hey, a girl can dream!

Arjun doubles over laughing. "Wow. What's your number now, Lindsay?"

"A pretty sturdy ten."

He smiles, like his work here is done. He will take his Awesome Mentor Award now, thank you very much.

"If you are interested, we can dig deep into how it worked and more of the science behind it another day. ESCAPE can be used for breaking through a wide range of problems, from overcoming anxiety and depression to converting stress into celebration. For brevity, we did a short version of ESCAPE since that was more than enough for your fear of rejection. If you feel like it is still affecting you in any way, we can do a full intervention on a later day.

"Here is what I want you to walk away with today. **Your limiting identities were not created by you; they were created for you.** Next time, before you feel rejected, I want you to remember everything you just said about Lindsay." He faces me and taps my nose, like a father to his daughter. "And don't…you…forget…who you are."

"I won't," I say, feeling my smile from ear to ear. "I definitely won't."

'Cuz I'm Lindsay, people.

And I'm kind of awesome.

CHAPTER NINE
The Phoenix is Rising

"Great!" Arjun says, clapping once. "Now let's create a recipe for you never to feel rejected again."

"Okay, I'm listening."

"Do you think anybody could reject you, Lindsay?"

"No. Nobody can reject Lindsay," I say emphatically.

"That's excellent," he continues. "How about Mumu?" he teases.

"Yes, she is very vulnerable. You know how to do a sniper attack, don't you?" I say, shooting him the side eye.

"So let's **create our own recipe for rejection, especially for Mumu**. A recipe is a set of step-by-step instructions for preparing a particular dish. Similarly, everyone has a recipe for feeling rejection. Let's find out Mumu's current recipe before we create a new one."

"Sure, that's simple," I say. "Everything! If a cat crossed her eyes at her, she'd feel rejected and turn it into a catastrophe, tuck her tail and hide while licking her wounds. Or just general stuff like somebody's being mean to her, laughs at her, or gives her a certain look. Somebody is disrespectful to her, doesn't listen to her, or doesn't care about what she said. Somebody didn't agree with her."

"Lindsay, this list is huge," Arjun says. "Now, there's no surprise why Mumu felt rejected all the—"

I continue, barely hearing Arjun's words. "I'm not finished yet. If somebody laughed at her looks, or laughed at a joke while she walked by,

117

somebody criticized her clothes or ignored her. It could be as simple as somebody wearing nicer clothes than her or somebody not smiling at her. Her recipe would be called rampant rejection ragu with a side of sappy sorrow. I know, it's a recipe for disaster."

"Oh my gosh!" Arjun holds up his hands to bring me to a halt. "Let's stop, Lindsay. I get it. It's very easy for Mumu to feel rejected, right?"

"Yes. That's precisely what I'm saying."

"That is Mumu's recipe. It is a one-step, simple recipe. For her to access the feeling of rejection, all she needs is somebody to laugh at her, or any other single component in her recipe. Notice that, despite the long list of potential ingredients, only one is necessary for this dish. Lindsay, do you think Mumu is going to be able to run a successful business like this? She needs everyone to like her at all times, agree with her at all times, coddle her and make sure not to laugh when she walks by…it goes on and on! With this recipe, Mumu is subconsciously choosing to live a life of rejection all the time. People who have fear of rejection are in the battle of resisting major rejections. The more they resist rejection, the more it shows up in their life. **Ironically, they have the simplest recipes for rejection.** Let's design a new recipe for her, shall we?"

"I understand that Mumu has a simple recipe, but how could I possibly create a new one?" I ask. "Aren't all these things done already? Mumu has her recipe. Charlie had one. And Arjun, you have a recipe, I'm sure. Different people have different recipes. Isn't that normal?"

"Yes," Arjun says, "that's absolutely true. But you don't need to use the same recipe that was gifted to you by your parents or your caretakers in your formative years. You did not consciously sit down when you were eighteen and choose to have this recipe. It was given to you. Would you keep using the recipe that you created a decade ago when you were a lousy cook even after you became an extraordinary chef? It is your conscious choice. You could just change it today."

"If I improve my recipe, am I allowed a nice bottle of Pinot Noir to go along with it, or…? Ok, ok…How can I change it?"

"It's very simple," Arjun responds. "You create a new one. You design your recipe for rejection. If you say, 'I could **never feel rejected**,' that is not a **recipe. Your mind will not buy it. We need to come up with a recipe complex enough, but achievable, that would make it difficult for you to feel rejected.** Let me give you a practical example. Think about a single mother. Think about all the things she juggles in a day. What might make her feel guilty during the day?"

Even though I'm not a mother, it's easy to imagine. "If she forgot to make her kids' costumes for a school play, or forgets to pack drinks in her kids' lunch boxes…"

"Keep going."

"If the dinner she made was overcooked."

"What else?"

"Maybe if she didn't hear her child crying in the middle of the night from a nightmare, like happened to me one time," I add, remembering how bad my mom felt about it at the time.

"Great. These are good examples of her recipe for guilt. Now put them together in one sentence," Arjun instructs. "What might make her feel guilty?"

I try to remember everything I just said. "Okay… If she forgot to make costumes for the play, *or* if dinner was overcooked, *or* if she didn't hear one of the kids crying in the night, those things might make her feel guilty. Like that?" I ask.

"Yes." Arjun nods. "Now, what word connected all those things? The word 'or,' correct?"

"Uh, I guess so, yes."

"Now, try changing 'or' to 'and.'"

"Ugh, I was terrible in English class."

"Too bad," Arjun says without missing a beat. "I am your new English teacher, the cute one, with the fabulous, shiny, silver hair. Replace 'or' with 'and,' please, Lindsay."

I take a deep breath. I had no idea I would be reciting sentences when I woke up this morning, but Arjun has a way of always surprising me.

"Alright, here goes… A single mom might feel guilty if she forgot to make her kids' costumes for the play, *and* if dinner was overcooked, *and* if she didn't hear one of the kids crying in the middle of the night. There. How's that?"

"Perfect. What is the difference between using '*or*' and '*and*?'"

I think about it aloud. "**In the first situation, any one of those things could make her feel guilty separately.** In the second situation, it's the combination of all those things put together that make her feel guilty. It's a completely different recipe."

"You got it! **We need to change your rejection recipe to make it more complex. Instead of a *or* b *or* c as your recipe, you need to make it a *and* b *and* c.**"

"Now I feel like you've turned into an Algebra teacher."

"But a very handsome Algebra teacher, and smarter than the English teacher. You know why? Because math teachers solve problems." He wiggles his bushy eyebrows at me, and I crack up.

"No doubt. And you get extra credit for all those terrible Dad jokes."

He regains his even tone. "Alright. That was an extreme example to show you how the single mother could feel differently. In the previous example, she could change her recipe to say 'If dinner was inedible *and* I did not make a couple of peanut butter and jelly sandwiches, then I will feel guilty. If I missed a doctor's appointment for my kids *and* I did not schedule another one within a certain time, then I will feel guilty."

"Ah, I see where you're going with this. She's giving herself more leeway, making it harder for herself to feel guilty."

"Precisely. You get what you tolerate. If you declare to your mind that you are not willing to feel guilty unless and until these new rules are met, your mind will comply," Arjun says, giving me a thumb's up.

"That is remarkable. What about you, Arjun? Do you have a recipe for rejection?" I ask.

Ha! Who's asking the questions now, buddy?

Arjun crosses his arms and thinks for a minute. Then, he shifts in his seat and says, "For somebody to reject me, somebody needs to kick my back, **and** push me out of a building, **and** throw me into a garbage can, **and** spit on me. I created this recipe several decades ago."

"Wow, that makes for a delicious dish!" I say with a laugh. But frankly, I'm gobsmacked. That is a serious recipe.

"It does," he agrees. "When somebody does something with the potential to make me feel rejected, I remind myself of my recipe. It's highly unlikely that someone will kick my back, toss me out of a building, *and* throw me into a garbage can all at the same time."

"*And* spit on you," I remind him.

"*And* spit on me. That way, I never feel rejected, because the steps in my recipe are never completed. My recipe is very complicated to achieve but technically still achievable, so my mind is not confused, either. Mumu's recipe was far too simple and easy to achieve, so of course, she felt rejected all the time."

"Of course," I repeat, nodding. "I totally get what you're saying now. Seriously. It's like the sun has come out after a ten-year period of rain."

"Ha, ha. You have a way with words, Lindsay. Now, your recipe for rejection doesn't need to be as complicated as mine. But make it **difficult** for yourself to feel rejection. For you to be financially successful, we need to get rid of this rejection BS. So tell me, what's your recipe, Lindsay?"

I think for a minute. In the past, I was quick to feel rejected. All it took was a stranger who let the grocery store door close in my face, a wary eye from a boy I liked, for Jay or Charlie to tell me they were too busy or tired to talk about work, or for my client to tell me she wasn't happy with the preliminary design of what we came up with. But that's a lot of *or's*. Now I have to add some *and's* and make it harder.

"Hmm. For someone to reject me, they need to pull my hair, *and* body slam me on the floor *and* call me a witch. *And...*" I add for good measure. "These three need to happen within one minute. If all this happens, *then* I will feel rejected." I hold my arms out like *ta-da!*

Arjun nods emphatically. "Incredible recipe, Lindsay! Sounds tastier than rampant rejection ragu. I know you would never let that kind of rejection happen, but if something like that ever happened to you, you'd have every right to feel rejected. Now stand up straight and proud. What is Lindsay proud of right now?"

"Hmm. I'm proud of seeing things in a new way. I'm proud of letting you help me, instead of rejecting help. I'm proud of taking the first steps toward healing rejection." I smile, letting out a breath, and suddenly, I feel lighter, like true weight has lifted off me.

Arjun claps happily. "Yes! You should see your winning smile right now. It's incredible. Repeat your new recipe for rejection…"

"For somebody to reject me," I recite, "that person needs to pull my hair, and slam me into the floor, and call me a witch, all within one minute."

"Good. Now go back to Mumu."

I shake my head. "I'm kind of over Mumu right now. No offense."

"It is important. Trust me, Lindsay," Arjun insists. "Walk the way Mumu would walk. This is how you lived for a long time. Imagine somebody disagreeing with you. Feel what Mumu felt. It's important to lock this new recipe for Mumu physically. Your brain needs to clearly understand the differences between Mumu's and Lindsay's recipes. It should understand that *you don't need to follow* Mumu's recipe anymore."

"Ugh, fine," I say reluctantly.

"Feel what Mumu felt. Walk the way Mumu walked. Slouch like Mumu used to do. Bring your shoulders and head down. Feel the rejection in your entire body."

I do everything he asks and feel kind of silly and also sad that I used to stand this way.

"Now switch back to Lindsay and tell her *she* is in charge. Then, change your physiology to Lindsay's physiology. Head up. Shoulders up. Walk like Lindsay walks. Walk with absolute certainty, chin up, with your shoulders back."

I try it. And the immediate feeling is overwhelming.

I feel like a new woman. Not even kidding.

"Good," he continues to coach me. "With your arms out wider. Great movements for your body. Like Beyoncé." I laugh, but it's true. Beyoncé does have some kickass self-confidence. "Tell Mumu, 'Mumu, you sit back there. I'm in control now.'"

"Mumu, take the back, Jack," I say, imagining myself strutting around town, "because Lindsay's got a brand new bag."

Arjun grins. "Good. Repeat after me. I am the Sara Blakely of Technology, and my recipe for rejection is…"

He asks me to repeat the process all over again, and I comply. I tell Mumu I'm in charge. Through an inner conversation, I tell her she had her chance, but she was ineffective, so now I'm going to show her how it's done. So she can learn. I don't feel silly anymore doing the exercise. I imagine I'm talking to Mumu. I tell her my recipe for rejection, and it sounds good to me.

"How do you feel, Lindsay?"

"Incredible. Incredible."

Once again, he asks me to return to Mumu, and once again, there is resistance from within. But we go through the process all over again, until my stomach rumbles, signaling that it's almost lunchtime.

Arjun says, "Your brain needs to be conditioned multiple times. I'm getting you thoroughly prepared for what you're going to face in the world."

I sigh. "I get it; I get it. Rome wasn't built in one minute."

"Correct. Which is why you're going to repeat this tomorrow, and the next day, and the next thirty days, too. Not as Mumu. Just Lindsay."

"Oh, ok."

"That is right. Let's do it a few more times."

This man is killing me. Or rather, killing what Mumu used to stand for, little by little. In her place, a new Lindsay is slowly taking shape, like the Phoenix rising from the ashes. Head high, I walk proud and tall.

"You wear this new recipe well! Keep doing that," Arjun says. "Keep walking another minute, saying it loudly with confidence and power. Build certainty inside of you. And with this certainty, decide to be Lindsay for the rest of your life."

Something about his words…my eyes sting with tears. Maybe I should have a future in Kleenex commercials instead. But these are tears of happiness. Joy. I'm grateful for this opportunity to start again, to renew, to improve. And isn't that what life is about?

"I feel wonderful, really strong now. Can I hug you?" I laugh.

Arjun smiles and opens his arms. "Of course!"

I give him a huge hug and think about where I was in my life a few weeks ago compared to now. **I get it now, that you should never despair because your life can change at any moment. It was Arjun's wisdom for me, but it could be a new idea, a new distinction that changes everything.**

"Okay," Arjun says, pulling away and looking at me. "Now that you've overcome the fear of rejection, share it and make it social. Call two friends and tell them what you've done. Tell them you overcame your fear of rejection. You can even share your new recipe if you want. True friends will hold you accountable and make sure you stay on the right track."

Right now, I can't even think of two friends I might still have, but I decide on calling my parents when I get back to the apartment.

"Arjun, I'm extremely grateful for what you have done here. It's really powerful. You are a great gift," I say, my tears finally spilling over.

"Thank you," he responds. "I'm so proud of you. The moment I saw you on the beach a few weeks ago, I knew you were someone who wouldn't settle for less. That is why I committed to spending time with you. When I saw the look in your eyes, I knew you would operate from the heart, not from the head. In your deepest despair, there was a spark of confidence inside of you. You didn't realize it until today. So own it, and let's go to the final step for the day."

"Lunch?" I ask hopefully.

"Soon," he replies. "Last week, I gave you steps for reaching Ananda. Now could you add one more? Every morning when you wake up and get ready, when you reach Ananda, you say, 'I am Sara Blakely of Technology, I feel rejuvenated, not rejected. My recipe for rejection calls for somebody to pull my hair, slam me into the floor, and call me a witch.' Declare it with certainty. Walk like Lindsay. And tell Mumu every morning, 'Mumu, today *I'm* in control. I'm Lindsay, and I am in control, no matter what happens today. I will feel inspired, instead of insulted.' Say it with me."

"I am Lindsay," I repeat, echoing Arjun's words. "Instead of feeling rejected, I will feel rejuvenated. Instead of feeling like a failure, I feel successful. Instead of feeling lonely, I will give love. I feel power not uncertainty; I feel excited, not tired. Instead of feeling down, I feel myself growing. I'm Sara Blackly of Technology aka Lindsay. No matter what happens, today's my day. I'll do whatever it takes to protect you, Mumu. If you feel like you are stressed, I am here as a source of power. No matter what happens, I'll be in charge."

"Go on…" Arjun says, which is good because I feel myself on a roll of a lifetime.

"I found my voice inside my business," I continue with excitement, with power. "*I* am the voice of my business. I lead, not follow. I create, not destroy. I innovate, not stagnate. I love, not hate. I care, not judge. I'll always give ten times value to my clients than I receive monetarily. I step up, set a new standard, and lead with love when everyone around me is confused and scared. I'm a *warrior*. Love is my motto. A smile is my weapon. With Faith, I will thrive in storms. I act in kindness. I'm a problem solver. I will own my industry. I will serve my customers with tireless passion. I will compete to be the most customer-focused company in the world. I am a fountain of absolute and unlimited certainty. I am a leader. I am Lindsay. And I lead with love."

Arjun gapes at me like he's seeing me for the first time. Like maybe, all this time, was a woman hiding inside the zippered body of Mumu, and all I had to do was pull that zipper down and let Lindsay out.

She's here to stay.

He shows me how to get rid of the vicious cycle of negative emotions permanently.

"Lindsay, you have come to this world for a mission. You will accomplish this mission. Because no matter what happens, you will take charge. You will be in control. And no matter who challenges you, you will overcome any obstacles you face. Tell me what you learned today," he says, looking around aimlessly.

I summarize everything we talked about from rejecting the old recipe to creating a new one, to internalizing it every morning by repeating it over and over. Arjun yawns.

Loudly.

I look at him, but he won't meet my eyes. Instead, he seems to be most interested in smoothing out a jagged fingernail, using his khakis as a nail file.

Where's my focused Arjun?

I wait patiently for him to turn his attention back to me.

"Oh, I'm sorry," he says sheepishly. "Please go on."

"I'm not sure where I left off."

"Actually, I'm not sure, either."

"So you weren't paying attention?" I ask, a little befuddled by his actions. Maybe I'm learning something new about him here. Maybe he has attention problems, and this is the first time I see it.

"Well…" he trails off, shrugging.

I sit straighter on the wooden bench. "Maybe we should head back to our cars then. I have the distinct impression that you checked out for the day."

"Checked out?" Arjun asks innocently. "What do you mean?"

"You're not paying attention." I stand, taking a deep breath.

"Like I'm ignoring you?"

"Yes!" I say indignantly then realize that I'm being schooled. Again. Everything Arjun says and does has a purpose.

"How does that make you feel to be ignored?" he asks, raising an eyebrow at me.

"Angry…sad…" I say.

"Weepy?" he asks.

"Wait, what?"

The corners of his mouth turn up into that wonderful Arjun grin again. "What about…*rejected*?"

"Rejected? Why would I—" I break off. Understanding sinks in, and I bark out a laugh. "Arjun, that wasn't nice. You were trying to make me feel rejected by ignoring me."

"I wasn't. I was testing your progress," he sings. "You said the old Lindsay would feel rejected at the drop of a hat, right? So, I did that on purpose so that we could test your change immediately. At the same time, I wanted to teach you another lesson, too. I checked out, as you put it, because that is what many men do. They go someplace…no place…to relax. They aren't thinking about anything. You've seen this before, haven't you?"

"Yes, but women do this, too. Hello, ever heard of a spa? Bubble bath? The entire first three seasons of *Orange is the New Black* on Netflix? Still, I know what you mean. It used to make me nuts when Charlie would do that."

"He was going to The Nothing Box, where men go to relax. Think of it as the mental equivalent of white noise."

"Well, whatever it is, it drove me crazy."

"What did you do about it?" Arjun asks.

"I'd ask him what he was thinking."

He continues patiently. "And what did he say?"

"That he wasn't thinking about anything," I say. Even when I am doing something relaxing, like watching TV or hanging in a bubble bath, I am always thinking about something. "But Arjun, how can that be? How can you think about nothing? Nothing doesn't exist!"

"Ah, Lindsay, but it *does* exist in a man's world if only to be the absence of thought. I'm betting that was part of what would make the old Lindsay feel rejected, or frustrated, or angry. But asking a man to explain where his mind is during those times would be as useless as demanding that someone stop hiccupping."

"Wow, I had no idea. How about we stop for lunch?" I ask, looking around and pointing to a picnic table nestled neatly in the smaller pine trees. "That looks like a great place to take a rest and break into the sandwiches I made."

"Sandwiches?" he murmurs with delight, completely forgetting everything we just talked about. "What was I saying again?" Arjun chuckles at his distraction.

"*Pfft*," I say with a smile. "Typical."

I'm relieved and secretly thrilled that there is no anger inside me at his distraction. No feelings of rejection. Arjun just nailed my recipe. Now, Mumu might have felt rejected. But Mumu?

Can't come to the phone right now.

"We shall not cease from exploration, and the end of all our exploring will be to arrive where we started and know the place for the first time."
T.S. Eliot

CHAPTER TEN
Can You Describe Your Customers' Pains Better Than They Can?

"Do you remember when we talked about the three gifts or flairs in business?" Arjun asks, unwrapping his tomato and mozzarella sandwich. "Well, I think you're finally ready to find out your true gift. Will you be the Artist? The technician who does the hands-on part of a job?"

I nod and swallow my bite. "Or will I be the Manager or the Leader?"

"That's right," he says, nodding. "Let's find out a little about each. One great example of this is Vincent van Gogh, the famous Dutch painter. I'm sure you know about how he greatly influenced contemporary art. Several of his paintings are worth more than $100 million today. He produced *more* than nine hundred paintings. Can you guess how many he sold in his lifetime?"

I think for a moment. "Eight."

"Why do you say eight?"

"I don't know." I shrug. "It just felt like a good number."

"In today's dollars, how much do you think he sold his most expensive painting for?" Arjun asks, switching gears again.

"A hundred thousand, maybe?" I venture to guess, with no idea how much paintings went for back then.

"Nope!" Arjun says jovially. "He sold only one painting in his lifetime called Red Vineyard, at a price equivalent to around one thousand dollars today. His brother helped him."

"A thousand bucks, that's it?" My eyeballs bulge at the very thought. "And he became famous *after* he died? Talk about getting the crappy end of the stick. Poor guy. What about the rest of the time?"

"The rest of the time, he was busy producing the two thousand other creations in his repertoire. Why do you think he kept doing that?" Arjun asks.

I shrug. "Because he was a masochist who liked working his rear off for little to no reward?"

"Not exactly. Van Gogh's reward was in the act of painting itself. He loved doing it! So he did it all the time. He **kept on doing what he knew— painting**. In 1890, he died penniless. The reason, he did not know how to market his story. **Marketing is proactively getting customers for your business**, which was **not** his expertise. He was an **artist**, not a **leader**."

"Wow, that sucks for poor van Gogh."

"Seriously sucks," Arjun agrees, taking another bite of his sandwich.

I smile and think about this story and the connections Arjun is undoubtedly going to make. If I had to guess, he's going to tell me I was operating my business as an artist, not as a marketer.

"A lot of artists who break out on their own to run their businesses," Arjun pauses to swallow, "stay away from marketing and sales because of their limited mindset. **When you are stressed, you do more of what you don't need to do at all**. Since many people worked as artists for another company for a long time before they started their business, they mostly have what I call **artist's mindset**. As an employee, they were trained to do things reactively. Someone, a manager most likely, came along and gave them tasks to accomplish, and that's what they did—create an end product."

"So they never learned the business side of things," I throw in.

Arjun nods. "Correct. **They never proactively pursued clients before**. Artists usually start a business out of frustration because someone gets promoted to a management position making more than they do. Sometimes, they start a business because they grow tired of the politics within the company. The repeated tasks bore the heck out of them. They thought they could do everything much better than their employers, or they might feel that others are profiting from the art only they know how to create. Regardless, they have compelling passion for what they do as artists."

I mull it over for a moment.

I remember working for ITS Infosystems, how I used to take complete pride in the social media product I was creating, but it was always Bill Engleman taking credit for everything because he was the owner of the company and therefore making all the money.

Jerk.

At least, that was how I felt at the time. Now I realize what Arjun is saying. He wasn't a jerk. He just wasn't the artist in the trifecta. He was the leader, and he knew how to bring in the clients who were purchasing my product.

Still, where would the CEO and president of the company be if it weren't for **my** idea, **my** execution, **my** artistic talents? Nowhere. On the other hand, I wouldn't have had a job if it weren't for their direction and leadership, either.

It's a team effort.

Too bad I didn't know that at the time. I started Small Business Social LLC because I thought I could position my social media company better than they had.

Arjun had hit the nail on the head with this one.

"You are preaching to the choir on that one," I say, nodding my head slowly.

"You know because you lived it, yes? So let me ask you…who should know the needs and wants of clients the most?"

"I should," I answer, staring at my sandwich. "The entrepreneur."

Hindsight is 20/20.

"And why is that, Lindsay?" he asks.

"So I could serve them the best and make the most money."

"Extraordinary answer, Lindsay. Marketing is understanding the hidden needs and wants of your clients and creating consistent perceived value through an ongoing process."

"English, please," I beg.

Arjun puts down his sandwich and starts using his hands again.

"Shopping is one of our major hobbies today, but sales people almost always struggle to handle objections from potential buyers. Why? We can talk about ethical sales in a moment but note this, **Your clients hate to be sold, but they love to buy.** Through ethical marketing, you tap into the inner conversations your prospective clients have. If you take a close look, you can see that true marketing is having enough empathy to understand the clients' challenges and the compassion to solve them. Marketing is being able to describe your prospective clients' problem better than they could, and explain the reason for it and how it is affecting them now, so they are compelled to check out your solution. It is a spiritual game of giving and caring. **You can fearlessly identify yourself as an ethical marketer.** Marketing is the key moneymaker in your business with almost no downside and unlimited upside. Marketing is influencing people to take action."

I think about what he's saying. It sounds great, but as far as I know, a big downside to marketing can be the time and money it takes to reach people effectively. I don't interrupt, though, because I know that Arjun eventually addresses my worries.

"First of all," Arjun says, "you need to find out who is your ideal client. You get rich serving a niche. You're—"

"Yeah, but how do I find my niche?" I interrupt.

"Good question. You figure out who is searching for your product. Who's motivated to buy your product? Ask yourself the questions: *Who is underserved in my industry? Who has a few or no options other than my product? What are their demographics? How much do they make annually? What are their prime fears? What are their prime frustrations? What are the words they use to describe their pain? Where do they hang out online and offline?*"

"That's a truckload of questions, Arjun."

"It is, and not bothering to find the answers is a big mistake many business owners make. You *must* find these answers. It's imperative. How can you compete in a competitive marketplace where other business owners have bothered to research and do the legwork without doing so yourself? You **must listen actively for emotional needs that are going unmet.**"

I can't say that he's wrong, that's for sure. "What do you recommend? Putting up a survey on surveymonkey.com or asking them in person?"

"Both. The best way to obtain this information is to sit one-on-one with your clients, ask them questions, and listen. Also, do an online survey. Be completely open-minded when you do this testing. Jay Abraham, one of the legendary marketers of this century, famously said, 'Everything is a test. Everything.' Your clients will surprise you. **One of the biggest mistakes you can make is assuming what your clients' needs and wants are.**

Once you have your niche identified, I recommend creating an avatar for your niche. Determine the commonalities of your test group and come up with a single person who represents all of your clients. This is the avatar of your client to whom all your marketing will be directed. Name this person, draw him or her, and stick the image in your heart and office. She is your avatar."

"So I should imagine a cartoon image of my client that encompasses everything about them?"

"That's right. The avatar will represent your average prospective client. Now, I want you to list fourteen fears and frustrations and seven wants and aspirations she has."

"Why twice as many fears than aspirations? Isn't that being negative?"

Arjun nods. "Aha, Lindsay, you are thinking. I like that. I have a completely different take on negative thinking. More about that next week. But people are twice as intrinsically motivated by pain created from their fears compared to pleasure from their wants. People are more motivated to buy to get out of a serious problem. Don't believe just because I said that. Test this idea yourself now. Imagine yourself as your customer. Speak in first person and see if you can feel your client's fears and frustrations. Now speak in first person and feel the wants and aspirations. See if you feel motivated to buy your product if you were in his shoes. If you do, you are integrated to influence them. Now, which one influenced you the most, your fears or wants?"

I imagine myself in my customer's place. "It is fears." I look at my products and try to determine if I want to lay down hard-earned money for branding them. In most cases, I do, but there are a few cases where I'm not so sure.

Arjun continues talking while I think about it. I down my lunch at the same time.

"Build your marketing strategies like you're building a relationship with a new person."

"So, that would be...one boring date at a time? Eventually, there's kissing, romance, maybe even marriage... Gosh, Arjun, it's so sudden, but yes! I'll marry you."

"Lindsay, your sense of humor is what keeps you going; you know that?"

I grin and gesture for him to continue.

"You build relationships **so that you are following direct response marketing, not branding.** Direct response marketing is a type of marketing that evokes a specific response resulting from a consumer's direct response to a marketer. In the small business world, branding is for cowards who are too scared to engage directly with clients. Branding might give you continuation, but it is too pricey for your small businesses. If you need conversion, you need to court your clients."

"That's what I was thinking earlier," I say.

"Yes, branding is selling your ego. Nobody will pay you for it or buy it from you. Response marketing, on the other hand, is educating your clients, listening to them, and selling your product at the same time. You connect with your target client through sharing a truthful story about your product. It is very cheap. Today, you can reach out to your specific audience through Facebook and Instagram advertisements for even five dollars a day.

"Everyone loves stories. Narrate them like a hero's journey with struggles and failures they can relate to. Share your breakthroughs and successes with them, show them how they can meet their wants from it. **Show them what they want and give them what they want and need.**"

"I get this," I say. "I really do. But my number one challenge is getting them to take action."

"Yours and everyone's, Lindsay," Arjun laughs, crumbling up his foil and placing it inside the plastic bag his sandwich came in. "See, your clients think they are taking a big risk when they buy from you. They don't want to look dumb to people around them. Remove their risk with a one-hundred-percent money-back guarantee. Whenever possible, reverse the risk by giving them *more* than one hundred percent. Done intelligently, this could give you additional credibility compared to your competitors. Depending upon your industry, about fifty percent more people buy just because there is a one hundred percent refund guarantee. Always give more than everyone else is giving in your industry. Make your offer irresistible, so that prospective customers cannot possibly reject it. Doing so puts you at an advantage right away."

"Fine, but what if a lot of people return my product? I can't afford another bankruptcy," I say.

Ugh, just thinking of that word again makes my skin crawl.

"It is normal for small business owners to think this when they consider giving more. But the reality is…if clients feel they are getting more value than they paid for, the number of returns reduce significantly. Give them the better end of the deal. Sincerely make them feel that they are stealing from you. Again, depending on your industry, there will always be one to two percent of people who will want to return your product *no matter what.* But if you get fifty percent more business, what do you care?"

"I don't. I would be spinning cartwheels through a field of sunflowers if that happened to me."

These are things I never learned before I opened my own business. I was an artist, not the leader. "So I still get to keep forty-eight percent of additional revenue. That's awesome. But, Arjun, I can't afford to hire a sales force right now. It's just little old me. So how do I even reach my customers?"

"A sales force is great, but you don't need one these days. Use your resources—the internet! Check online to see who's already done the work to find your customers. Constantly hunt for competitors with clients like yours. Negotiate an affiliate partnership agreement with them. Use an efficient affiliate tracking software to pay them automatically as you get paid."

"Okay, but how do I find the best affiliate tracking software?" I ask, shaking my head. I'm starting to feel a little overwhelmed. Maybe I didn't realize that running a business entailed so much, but then again, that's probably why I failed before.

"I just said it…Google!" He chuckles, swigging back his bottle of water.

"Lindsay, I am showing you where to go, pointing you in the right direction. But you will need to do your homework so **you** can own the solutions, not me. Until you work for it, you won't see the real value."

"I know there is a lot to absorb, but I will do it," I say, ready to dig in.

"Now, the last thing I want to touch on regarding marketing is referral."

"You mean like a tip for a job well done?" I ask, collecting all our garbage and getting up to throw it in the trash bin.

"Yes, but for most businesses, this is accidental revenue. If you need strategic referrals, you need to build a system around it and use it. One simple way is to make it part of the relationship. Tell your clients on the first day that you are going to do an incredible job and earn their referral. Ask them in advance, 'If I deliver beyond your expectation, are you willing to share your experience with five of your friends?' When someone gives you referrals, be sure to thank them. If the referral did not work out, don't punish them for it by telling them their referral sucked! **Reward the behavior you want to see in your client.**"

I frown when I think back. "Often, I told my clients their referral didn't work out, and I never got another referral from them after."

"Of course," he says. "That's because they do not want to feel rejected again. That is why you ask for referrals when they are at their heightened state of emotion about your product...when your customers feel the best about your product. **Referrals are the most effective way to get an optimum outcome from your marketing and grow your business geometrically.**"

"That was a mouthful."

But one full of gems, like most everything he'd taught me so far. I was still nervous about putting my all into a new business, but I was also filled with a sweet sensation that I hadn't felt in years.

Anticipation.

Not bad for a sea hag hell-bent on suicide just a couple of weeks before.

I let the feeling flow through me and relish every moment. Like fine wine, only without the hangover.

I can do this, I realize suddenly. I know I can.

Better yet?

I'm *going* to.

CHAPTER ELEVEN
The New ABC of Persuasion

"So what's next?" I ask, rubbing my hands together. I know I should be tired and my brain is filled to bursting, but I'm feeling it now and nothing can stop me.

Arjun considers me for a long moment. "There are three simple ways to grow your business. By growing the number of clients, increasing the number of average purchase values, and by increasing the frequency of repeat purchases. Lindsay, let's say you increase your clients by fifteen percent and increase the average purchase value and repurchase by fifteen percent also—how much will your company grow immediately?"

"Fifty-two percent," I answer with confidence. I mean, after all, math is my strong suit.

"Why fifty-two percent and not forty-five?" he asks.

"Because the growth is exponential."

"Exactly! Is it difficult to grow your clients by fifteen percent in one year in your business?"

"Nope."

"Nope," he mimics me, making me laugh. "The best way to increase your sales by fifteen percent is by building a small sales force starting with yourself. I recommend every entrepreneur and small business owner become the best influencer, the best salesperson in their entire organization."

I ponder this.

"I distinctly remember a time when my company put together a package for a client based on what he told us his needs were. At the time, I had hired a salesman, Guillermo, who supposedly had lots of experience. Listening to him talk to our client, though, was torture. 'Signing the contract today will get your company ahead tomorrow. Plus, if you don't decide today, I can't guarantee this same package later. Waiting isn't in your best interest!' I didn't like his approach, he came across as pushy. I felt sorry for my client, and at times, I even jumped in and took over, because I felt that he cared only about closing the sale. In fact, I think many salespersons are manipulators who don't care about the company, let alone their clients," I say, asserting my point of view.

Arjun nods. "Unfortunately, lots of salespeople are short-term thinkers. That is why you should always act as their trusted consultant when you talk to your prospective clients. **Become a sincere buying consultant who initiates an inner dialogue**, not a pushy used car salesman who shuts others out."

I nod. "Sharks in expensive suits with that extra toothy dangerous smile, untrustworthy, condescending, make-me-feel-like-I-need-a-shower…"

"Hold on, shark hunter! They are just good people with bad skill sets and wrong beliefs," Arjun counters.

"Sorry…caught in my own feeding frenzy. I can't stand that attitude," I grimace.

Arjun goes on, "You should see yourself as an influencer, not even a salesperson. Especially as a woman, your nature is to connect with people. Use that skill to listen to their pain, to tell them your product's story as a solution to their pain. Build rapport with them and **educate** them about the reliefs, solutions, and benefits your product offers. **Build long-term relationships. Our social brains are built to connect.** I disagree with the popular belief that we men and women yearn for attention. **What we crave is emotional connection—intensity.**"

"I usually build rapport with people very quickly. That's always been a strong suit of mine. My problem is with closing a sale," I say, shrugging. I no longer feel uncomfortable talking about my weaknesses. Arjun seems to get it and doesn't judge me. He shows me why it went wrong.

"I touched on this concept the first time we met." Arjun puts his hands on the table and starts explaining, "You might have heard of the traditional ABC's of Sales—Always Be Closing." I nod. "This may have held true several decades ago, but today we need to court our prospects more than ever before. You don't meet a man on the street and expect him to propose to you on the first date. Today, in the online world, some prospects need at least seventeen interactions with you before even considering your product. You need to add consistent value to them before gently asking for a sale. I strongly feel that the **new ABC's of Persuasion is Always Be Caring.** If you convince your prospect that they need your product, they will even close the sale for you.

"Care for them the way you care for your family. Show them results in advance. Give them more than you receive. They will see your sincerity and will reciprocate when you are sincerely invested in fulfilling their needs. But also remember, this doesn't just apply to salespeople or business owners and their customers. This is a concept that should be applied to all relationships in our lives. Husbands should treat their wives as a valued customer and show their committment and care by giving more than they receive. An employee of a company should view their boss as a customer and give their very best, each and every time. And, in return, they will most often receive the very best career growth in return. Sometimes they do get nothing in return. In that case, they will find a place that will reciprocate with them. Needless to say, every company should create a culture where your employees become your internal raving fans. It's a concept that applies in all relationships in our lives."

"That makes total sense to me. When my customers felt I was emotionally invested in their wants and needs, as much as they were, they were more likely to respond."

"There you go. Lindsay, do you know how people make their buying decisions?"

"Flip a coin?"

"Try again."

"Ask their wives?"

"You have a point there."

I laugh. "Okay, from what I understand, people buy emotionally and then justify it logically later."

"Love the way you phrase it! People use their reptilian brain to make emotional decisions. They think like a crocodile and emotionally evaluate their benefits and solutions. Most businesses **try to sell features**, even though most clients are **buying reliefs or benefits**. That's why I recommend you to sit down and write **two dozen reliefs or benefits** your clients will get from buying your product."

"Two dozen?" I nearly fall off the bench I'm on.

"Yes. If you don't know at least twenty-four reliefs or benefits of your product, it is either not good enough or you are not emotionally invested in it.

"Our next job is to find the twelve major objections your **niche** has in association with your product. Eighty percent of the objections will be the same for all of your prospects. Find out the major emotional pains clients face in doing business with you and your competitors. Those are the **key reasons** why people are hesitant to buy. After you do that, I will teach you how to use them to serve them."

I sit there staring at him.

"Well? Open your iPad. Come on, Lindsay!" He claps his hands in rapid succession.

Pulling out my iPad from my backpack, I sigh thinking of the major objections my clients have for buying my product. I also highlight anything that might cause my clients emotional pain. I spend about twenty minutes doing this, while lucky Arjun gets to walk around the forest, touching trees, and staring up their heights.

Cramps in my palm force me to stop. I sigh loudly, audibly, Arjun sees I'm done, and he comes back to the bench to sit across me again. "Finished?"

"Yep. Put a fork in it. I'm done," I say.

"Okay. I'm going to teach you the core philosophy behind the new ABC of Persuasion before we conclude for the day. Sound good?"

"Sounds perfect."

"We'll start by assessing your beliefs about sales," he says, and I know I'm in store for another lesson — no problem. That's why I'm here. "If all salespeople stop selling, what will happen?" he asks.

"The economy will take a crap in a few months."

"We will go into a recession, right? Above seventy-percent of the U.S. economy is comprised of consumer spending. For the most part, that means someone is selling, and someone else is buying to keep an economy out of trouble. Just like money, selling is an enormous positive force. People who sell could be good or bad, but there is nothing wrong with sales. Would you agree with me on that?"

"Yes. That makes perfect sense."

He nods and moves on. "Okay. Now, let us talk about the fundamental idea behind the new ABC of Persuasion. There are seven fundamental questions that people ask themselves when they are making their decision whether or not to buy something." Arjun ticks them off on his fingers as he goes over each one:

1. Can I trust this person?
2. Do they understand my pains and frustrations?
3. What is it I am buying? What is in it for me?
4. Am I being pushed or sold to?
5. What will others feel? Can I justify this with others in my life/business?
6. Is it worth the hassle? Can they prove it?
7. Do I really need it today? Can I postpone this decision?

"The new ABC of Persuasion answers all these questions. Three major phases are involved to address all these—CONNECT, COMPEL and CONVERT."

"That sounds real easy," I say with a light laugh, jotting down those words. Connect, compel, and convert.

"It is," he says. "The purpose of this phase is to build rapport with your prospect. So, how do we connect with people?" he asks.

"We get a large rubber band, wrap it around two or more people, and bind them together," I deadpan, because I am a smartass at heart.

Arjun chuckles. "That's one way to do it. Another way is by learning who they are. **So the first step is to prepare.** Understand as many details about your prospective customers as you can. Use Facebook, LinkedIn, and Twitter to find out more about them. Most salespeople fall in love with their **products. Don't make that mistake.** You need to fall in love with your **clients.** Be vulnerable. Vulnerability earns people's trust immediately. Enjoy connecting with new people. If you are super interested in them, they will be interested in you."

"For once, it is them, and not me. So, make it more about them than about my product," I summarize, jotting that down, too.

"Absolutely. You should be an expert about your product, too. You need to internalize it and, you must believe in it and love it, in your heart. That is why you wrote the two dozen reliefs and benefits your product has to offer. You will need to know who your top three competitors are and understand their product, as well."

"What if, even after doing all this, they still don't want to buy anything?" I ask. It was a problem time and time again.

Arjun sits up straight and stretches. "I will teach you how to qualify your prospects in a moment. For now, let's focus on knowing your clients. Ask yourself: What do I like about this person who may soon be my client? If someone referred this person to me, ask them what is most important for this new prospective client?"

Furiously, my chicken scratch fills the page. Joy leaps in my chest as a feeling of endless possibility abounds. I feel like I'm in college again, which is great since I felt ready to conquer the world back then.

"The next step of connection is to build deep **rapport** with them," Arjun says, and I write the word RAPPORT nice and big. "Building a rapport is the foundation of all persuasion. It's the most important part of the initial phase of sale. For most people, idea of building rapport is talk."

I nod, feeling excited to share my strategy. "The way I build rapport is by asking a question and listening to them."

"That's exactly correct," Arjun agrees. "A salesperson who talks most of the time almost always fails. Asking a question and listening is perfect, also because the new ABC of Persuasion is all about questions. Remember, with words; you only influence about six percent. Fifty-five percent of communication is body language, and thirty-seven percent is voice. People like others who are like them. People who talk fast think that those who talk slow are on drugs. So what do you do when you meet people who talk real fast?"

"Talk at their pace?"

"Yes. This is true with tempo and tonality. If you pick up some of the words they use and use them naturally, rapport will be instant. You build your character to empathize and appreciate this person as if she is a long lost friend. Once you do, they will feel like they found someone like themselves. I cannot emphasize this enough; you do this from the place of absolute caring. It's not trickery, unless it is done with that purpose. Let me ask you a question. If you go to a bar and see two people completely in love, what can you observe?"

"That they should be in a room with each other instead of a bar?" I laugh then quickly regain my composure. We really are on a roll here and I don't want to derail it. "Umm. They're probably facing each other, sitting the same way. When one person moves their hands, the other person will move, too. When one person shakes their head, the other person will shake his head, too. They are mirroring each other. They're in sync."

"In sync. That's right. The pair is synchronized with each other, from their physical movements to their discussion, as if they are dancing together. That is your ideal goal with your prospects."

"So I should look my clients deep in the eyes and tell them how gorgeous they look tonight?" I smile.

Arjun laughs. "Yes. And buy them dinner with extra dessert, piled high with whipped cream and cherries on top if you can."

I'm glad that I have a rapport with Arjun exactly like the one he describes. I make a joke; he makes a joke, too.

Perfect.

"It's all about mirroring physiology. You mirror their speed of movement, posture, gestures, facial expressions, even eye contact. Expert rapport builders can even match another person's breathing."

"Won't some people catch on to what I'm doing, though? Like, won't they think I'm a fake?"

"If you are fake, yes. It has to be natural, Lindsay. It is not the technique that is important; it is the intention. Besides, you think people are paying attention to what you are doing and saying? Almost nobody is listening. They are just hearing what they want to hear. Nobody has ever asked me, 'Hey, Arjun, why are you mirroring my breathing?' Even I am not paying attention as it becomes part of who I am. As for gestures, you do not need do it exactly as they do it. Don't pick your nose if they pick their nose. Be genuinely interested in them, and you will do these automatically. When you sincerely care, you naturally sync with the other person. Okay, the next step in CONNECT is alter the prospect's state of mind. Help them reach Ananda."

"Whoa," I say, holding up a hand. I'm just learning that myself! "How do I do that? Isn't that on them?"

Arjun shakes his head. "You can help the process. Buying is the transference of your inner certainty about your product to the prospect. They are buying new beliefs, not your commodity. First of all, you need to do power ceremony and reach Ananda before you meet any new prospects or clients. That will significantly help alter your prospect's state of mind. You cannot influence anyone else before you influence yourself first. The new ABC of Persuasion will not work if you have a crappy product because you cannot transfer a fake conviction. If you don't sincerely believe in your product, it will not work, either. You will lack the **congruence** needed to convince your prospects and they will pick up on it."

"Pretty darn accurate, actually," I say.

"Yes. And do not give fake compliments. Buyers today are intelligent; they pick up BS very easily. If you sincerely admire something, then by all means, compliment them, but **always** give the reasons why you think it to be true. The best thing is to ask power questions that will alter their state of mind. Ask them questions about their children or vacation if you sincerely care. Or ask a couple of general questions about their business. The key idea is to find something in common and connect with them by asking questions about it and listening deeply. The key word here is *listening.*"

Everything he is saying makes sense and is just part of the framework that goes along with being a sincere, genuine caring person.

"That was all you need to **CONNECT**. Ready for the next phase? It's **COMPEL**."

"Compel…"

"Yes. The purpose of this phase is to help them find a few problems that they have and how they are affecting their business or life. The reasoning behind COMPEL is if your future client perceives the problem they have as bigger than the cost of solving it, it is most likely a sale. That is why COMPEL is the meat in the new ABC of Persuasion.

"In this step, you ask a few strategic questions to find their problems and its implications and **listen**. Do not hesitate to make them feel frustration for one last time. Remember, undisturbed prospects almost never buy. Here are some of the questions you could ask. These are what I call **Troubleshooting Questions**.

'What are their biggest frustrations about the current product/problem?'

'What is not working right now?'

'What are a couple of areas that could be improved?'

'Do you have reliability issues with the current system?'

'Are you satisfied with the current solution?'

"Most of the time they would have already given you a clue on what areas they are frustrated.

"Once they start describing their problems, do not interrupt them. Continue listening to them until they finish. Pay attention to secondary problems that they reveal as they are talking. Make a note of them. Once they finish their conversation, you lead them with **Diagnostic Questions** to find out how it is affecting them.

'How long has this been going on?'

'What is the worst thing about having this problem?'

"And here is the golden diagnostic question. 'How is this affecting you/your business/life right now?' You are listening for things they want to **avoid at any cost**. The top persuaders in the world are those who are masters at this. They ask ten times more diagnostic questions than regular salespeople."

"What if they say that they are extremely happy with their current supplier?" I ask.

"Do you agree with them and leave? Nope! Tell them you admire their loyalty. Now ask them what the one or two things are that they are doing great and carefully listen. Once they finish, agree with them."

"That doesn't seem helpful. Once the prospect is done, can I tell him how horrible our competition is?" I ask.

"You will not disagree with a prospect who loves their current vendor. You will never talk badly about your competitors, either."

"Not even a gum wrapper sized bit of trash talk?"

He shakes his head. "In your mind, always know and believe that you are the best in your industry and you won't need to. You can say things to make them confess that their current supplier is not perfect, though." I raise my eyebrow, and he goes on. "Ask them what three areas their current supplier could improve are? No matter how happy they are, they will have a few things to complain about. And when they give you the details, agree with them again. This time, amplify their emotion with more diagnostic questions like, 'How is that affecting your business?,' or 'What will happen if these issues continue for the next few years?'"

"Ohhh, you little fox, you. And you said there was no trickery." I laugh and start doodling a little fox on my iPad — a little Arjun Fox.

"Well, it might feel like trickery," he admits. "But not really, because they did all the talking and **you cared enough** to inspire them to solve their problem. They told you why they're not happy. You just validated their belief with good intention to serve them. You care about them enough to show them how it is **affecting** them.

"But if you could not find a decent problem they might not be a good fit for you. Don't ever create false scarcity or imaginary problems for the sake of getting a client. You will always regret that later.

"Tell them that you are not a fit for now and stay in touch and ask for referrals.

"If you find them to be a fit, then the next step of COMPEL is Qualifying.

Qualifying is not just checking if they can afford it financially. You qualify the prospects through their diagnoses to see if you can sincerely solve their problems. You need to qualify their needs and wants and lastly—whether they have the money."

"What is the difference between needs and wants?" I ask.

"Think about somebody buying a house. What is the need? Accommodation. They **need** a place to live. They can even live in a van down by the river if basic amenities are available. But what is their **want**? I want a four-bedroom house with three full bathrooms and a swimming pool on a half-acre lot. Lindsay, do people buy for their wants or needs?"

"Their wants, mostly."

"Correct. That is why we cannot sell by talking on and on about the bells and whistles of our product. They just don't care because it does not aspire to their wants. The most effective way to persuade a buyer is by asking strategic questions."

"Then why are we qualifying their needs?" I ask, nervously tapping my iPad.

"Even if they get all they want, their happiness will be shortlived if they don't fulfill their needs. In the example I just gave you, if you bought the four-bedroom house but your toilet is leaking all the time, you might find yourself more irritated than the person living in a van by the river. Because at least the other person has a river view.

"Coming back to compel, let us say you could find those problems. Ask them strategic questions so they can describe how these problems are affecting them. Go back and dig deep into other problems they mentioned as part of their story. Keep repeating this until you find two to three problems that are big enough for them to justify the investment.

"Finally, it is time to focus on solutions. You ask them the Reward Questions to establish the value of solving these problems.

'Why must you solve this right now?'

'Why would you find this solution very effective?'

'How is solving this going to pay off in the long run for you?'

"Keep in mind; you do not ask questions about the problems that you

147

cannot solve. Again, meticulously listen. This time, you are listening for the benefits that they are describing. While answering this question, they are explaining the real reasons why they want to buy your products. These are what they really want.

"The final phase of the new ABC of Persuasion, Lindsay, is CONVERT. The purpose of this step is to summarize your client's problems, how they affect them and invite them to use your solution."

"How do I do that?" I ask.

"You start with problem number one. Describe the problem in your prospect's own words, describe how it is affecting them and what **they said** they will gain by solving it. Do the same for other problems, too. Three problems must be more than enough. Now ask them 'Did I get it right or did I miss something?' They say yes, and you are ready to **tell** them the next steps."

"You mean close the sale?"

"Great persuaders don't close the sales; they recommend the next intelligent actions. You demonstrate the best way to solve their problem, and overcome how it is negatively affecting them today and gain the reward by purchasing your product or service."

"Can you give me an example of the entire process of CONVERT?"

"Sure." He turns to an invisible person to his right and leans in. 'Pamela, you got into this business to help women who work long shifts having to cut bananas. That is why you invented the banana slicer. You also told me that you do not have a system for getting new leads online. It is affecting your business' ability to stay afloat, since most people are purchasing banana slicers online these days. Pamela, you also told me that a pineapple slicing company is very close to figuring out a way to build a new banana slicer. If they accomplish this, you might go out of business. If that happens, according to you, everything you worked for will be gone forever.

"That is why you must have a software system that will help you generate leads online. Once you do that, you will be able to achieve your entrepreneurial dream of automating your business and monitoring it from a beach in Grand Cayman. Your kids can go to Grand Cayman elementary school. Like you said, you can spend money and time shopping in malls while your kids are at school. Did I get it right or did I miss something?

"You also said you are losing out $10,000 a month due to not having enough leads; our social media expert will not only get you qualified leads but also give you an accurate executive summary about their buying habits. In your opinion, do you see our social media expert helping you grow your sales for the banana slicer?

"And Pamela will say, 'Absolutely. It sounds phenomenal!'

"Based on what you told me, I **recommend** you get our Social Media Accelerator premium package so that you have leads coming in starting next week.

"As you can see, Lindsay, I was describing Pamela's problems, how she said it was affecting her and how she will benefit from overcoming the problems she described. Then I recommended the next steps," he finishes with a flourish.

"Very advanced product, indeed. And a banana slicer is literally the best thing since sliced bread. What if Pamela has objections?"

"If you dig deep into the problems and diagnose in advance, you might not even get many objections. Understanding their needs and the pay off they get by solving their problems and then matching your product to meet all those needs is the best way to minimize or eliminate objections. But let us say that your prospect comes up with an objection. Tell them; 'I know you have reasons for saying that. What are those?' Then, listen. The next thing you do is make it the final objection by asking, 'Is that the only question you have or do you have other questions?' Did you notice I smoothly transitioned their objection into questions?"

"Yes, why?" I ask. "Why did you do that?"

"Because people are resentful talking about objections, but they are very comfortable getting their questions answered. You are reframing their objections as questions. This is when they either say, YES or NO. If they say yes, it is their final objection. If they say no, it is *not* their final objection. You say, 'I know you have reasons for saying that. What are those?' Listen to their new reasons and paraphrase them as questions. Ask them again, other than that, is there anything that is stopping you from claiming your social media accelerator package today? You repeat the process until they are out of questions."

"You are very good at this; you know that, Arjun?" I smile and shake my head, jotting it all down.

"Lindsay… you care about them enough to influence them. Once you care enough for prospects and follow these steps, the sale is automatic."

"I do. I care."

"Now answer the question they have in their language. Tell the prospect how your product will solve their problem and how it could benefit them. That is all you need to do about objections."

"How so?" I am intrigued.

"They already told you those are their final objections. So they have no other option but to **decide** to buy."

"Whoa," I say. "So that's it?"

"Almost. The next step of convert is to ask **Readiness Questions**. I did that in the example you just heard. These are questions that you ask that will help you gauge the emotional readiness of your prospect to buy now. Women are naturally good at this. Since these are not commitments, your prospects will give you their most honest opinion about your product. In fact, you do not need to wait until the last stage of sales to do this. Readiness Questions are persuaders' best buddies. You can use them at any time you want."

"Okay, like what?" I ask, getting ready to write a few down. My iPad is filling up with practical ideas I can take back and use.

"Here are three examples: One: In your opinion, how does this potentially meet your needs? Two: Do you think this has the potential to help you lose weight? Three: In your opinion, do you think this new technology has the potential to increase your banana slicer sales? If they don't say yes, you ask them more diagnostic questions and reward questions to get them ready. Then come back and ask the readiness questions again."

"Wow, this is a whole song and dance."

"It is. But most people give up way too early. What if your prospects show a readiness to buy your product even while you are at an early step in the

CONNECT phase. What do you do?"

I think about it a while. "I'll walk them through the process, so he or she understands all the value we are offering?" I don't feel completely sure about my answers.

Arjun shakes his head. "Lindsay, if your prospect is willing to buy, stop convincing and go to the final step of the sale. The only thing you could do by talking more is to confuse them and talk them out of the sale. The final step of CONVERT is to **Facilitate Buying**. If you needed to do a hard close on a prospect, that means you haven't influenced them enough. **The strongest close in the whole world is transference of emotions.**"

"Isn't that a unique way to close?" I ask.

"Yes. At this point, in the new ABC, we simply give them specific direction to buy now. Never assume that your clients know how to buy from you. Give them specifics with simple, direct, bold instructions to buy now. Ask with total verbal and nonverbal congruence. Trust me; they will buy from you."

"Arjun, I trust you know what you're talking about."

"The best influencers who make the top one percent income at any company are successful because they all have something in common."

"I thought it was because of their great closing skills," I say.

"Nope," he shakes his head again, "they all have compelling reasons for achieving their goals. They believe in their product and care enough to prospect and connect with more people than anybody else. They care enough to build **Connection** with their buyers. They care enough to ask and listen to the buyer's problems and **Compel**. They care enough to ask and listen to how they are affecting them and the value of solving them. They care enough to sincerely recommend the best option that fits their buyer's needs and wants and **Convert** them. They care enough to convert objections into questions and authentically answer them. *They always care—Always Be Caring!*"

"Make sense to me."

"Great, and now write down this checklist. It's the new ABC Checklist to use after each sales call to see how good you did. Ready?"

I quickly jot down his questions:

Did they know that I cared? Did they talk eighty percent of the time or more while I only asked questions?

Did I help them reach Ananda? Did I build trust with them?

Did I ask Troubleshooting Questions? Did I ask enough Diagnostic Questions?

Did I ask enough Reward Questions? Did I qualify the buyer through his needs and wants?

Did I authentically recommend the best product/service I could offer? Did I serve them authentically regardless of outcome?

Then, all of a sudden, Arjun folds his hands and smiles.

"Why are you smiling?" I ask, cocking my head to one side.

"That's it."

"That's it?" I ask. "I can go home now and start becoming a millionaire?"

"Exactly. The better influencer you are by mastering the new ABC of Persuasion, the more wealthy you will be."

"I believe you, Arjun."

"Why do you believe me, Lindsay?"

"Because…" I say, packing up my iPad and putting it away. I stand and strap my backpack onto my back. "You're the one with a Ferrari, a great house on the beach, and a spare apartment you can lend a dead broke person. You know something about business I didn't before."

I smile, walking off down the path through the towering trees before calling over my shoulder back to him.

"But I do now!"

CHAPTER TWELVE
Create Your Future in Advance.

I settle into the buttery leather seat of the Gulfstream G550, trying to act nonchalant, taking in the ambiance of the charted jet. The creamy walls complement the rest of the light-hued compartment perfectly. The whine of the engines begin, and thankfully, the air conditioning responds to the plane's firing-up.

Standing in the aisle, Arjun putters around me, grabbing two bottles of Evian before stashing them in his briefcase then finally plunking himself down in the seat across from me.

"Why don't you buy a private jet instead of flying chartered ones. Are you that poor?" I ask playfully.

"Ha ha! Because this plane costs fifty million dollars to purchase. Then I need to hire a pilot, an air steward, and rent a hangar, not to mention manage the maintenance. If you do the math, it's a waste of money, when I can typically go on a domestic trip and come back for a much lower cost. If I were to buy this plane, I would have to fly at least eleven thousand hours to break even. However, I fly less than sixty hours a year. It will take me one hundred eighty-three more years to reach eleven thousand miles."

"Wow. You haven't thought this through at all. You are a foolish, foolish man." I roll my eyes and then smile.

Thankfully, Arjun understands my sense of humor by now and laughs. "Not only that but this way, I can fly different planes. See, most people are too focused on their goals. But I **am focused on creating experiences.**

Others want to buy planes. I just want the freedom to live a quality life without a patdown."

"What's wrong with a patdown?" I ask, hiding a smile. "Oh, you meant by a TSA agent. My bad." I can't help it, and I chuckle under my breath.

"Lindsay, you are as naughty as you are cheeky. I don't know about you, but I am not into cheap massages."

"You got me, Arjun. You so totally figured me out. When I have more month at the end of the money instead of more money at the end of the month, I use the TSA agent's free massage. I am into creating great experiences, too."

He points to me with a raised eyebrow. "Soon I will teach you how to buy experiences rather than buying things. When I lived in India, my father used to say, 'Why buy an ice cream shop just to eat ice cream?'"

"Your father was a smart man," I say, checking my phone for the time. "Wonder when we're getting off the ground." I didn't want to admit it, but I'd always been an anxious flyer.

Arjun seems to know anyway. "Nervous, Lindsay?"

"Just a bit."

"I know it wasn't a planned flight, but I do love a quick hop to Denver. Thanks for coming along."

Not exactly a hardship. Especially in this sort of luxury. Last minute travel plans are a heck of a lot easier when you're not knocking into people at LAX.

"No, thank *you* for this great experience. I'm so looking forward to the trip. Denver's a great place. It's going to be fun seeing the Rockies from my window seat."

Arjun grins. "Ah, another benefit of a chartered jet. Window seats are not a commodity. Airlines are reducing seat size and peanut snacks day by day. In a few years, we might even hear this airline announcement: 'If the cabin pressure is low, oxygen masks will drop from the ceiling. Use Apple Pay or swipe your credit card to activate the oxygen. Activate your oxygen before activating others'. In case of a water landing, our flight crew will be distributing emergency kits at a discounted price of fifty dollars. If you wish, you may use the seat as a floatation device for a much lower price of ten dollars. In case you survive, you may return the floatation device for a 25% refund.'"

I laugh. "You are funny, you know that?"

He bows his head slightly. "Thank you. Do you know why I wanted you to fly with me for this session?"

"Honestly, I have absolutely no idea."

He shifts in his seat and settles in for takeoff. "The first time we met, Lindsay, I coached you about finding compelling reasons. Do you remember?"

"Of course, I do."

"Good. Then I taught you how to live in Ananda. And last week, I taught you how to overcome your obstacles, especially fears of rejection and failure. Once you find your compelling reasons, live in bliss and overcome your obstacles, you are ready to **create** your future in advance. What a better place to talk about a **dream** than thirty-nine thousand feet above ground, right?"

"You are the master of perfect timing, Arjun. Keep talking. I'll listen to you instead of the engines screaming." I grip the armrests tightly.

Arjun continues. "She was feeling excellent, until she felt cramping in her entire body. Her muscles were breaking down into clumps of cells, like a Lego sculpture decomposing into bricks. Her guts quickly changed shape, becoming narrower, shorter, more convoluted. Her tracheal tubes became bigger than before. The breathing tube that delivered oxygen to her muscles had reattached itself to her torso. Everything in her world was turning upside down. Does this sound familiar, Lindsay?"

"Totally," I say. I know that feeling of being turned upside down, like my world is ending. "I'm listening."

"Yet she was blissful and hopeful. At times, she had her doubts, but she trusted with Discipline and 'Ananda.' She believed there is meaning for each and every one of these changes. She intuitively knew that change is the only thing that is certain and it is all part of her emergence. In the ultimate moment of truth, she remembered what her mother had told her. Have a little more Faith. The pain mounted and became unbearable. But she kept imagining being free and beautiful. It was nearly impossible not to give up. And just when the caterpillar thought the world was ending, she turned into a butterfly."

"I had no idea how powerful that transformation was until now," I say, staring straight at him.

"Fools learn nothing from their mistakes, ordinary people learn from their mistakes, extraordinary people learn from other people's mistakes. What did you learn from the butterfly?" Arjun folds his hands, and I realize with a start that we have already taken off.

Thanks to Arjun for the distraction.

"Um...there is no substitute for inner transformation? Dreams cannot be fulfilled without dedicated action," I say, fairly certain this is the answer.

"Yes, you cannot become healthy just by dreaming and walking between the living room couch and the kitchen fridge while binge-watching Netflix. But trust me, I don't recommend killing yourself with hard work, either. I am all for **intelligent actions**. Those twenty percent of actions that yield eighty percent of results or fulfillment. **As a business person, you have only two types of intelligent actions; high-profit activities and high-impact activities.**

"Next week, I am inviting you to visit my office, where I will show you the step-by-step process we use to get fifty to a hundred percent more results. I will also teach you how to take high-profit and high-impact actions to increase your bottom line while being fulfilled."

"I would say I'm in a hundred percent," I agree.

"This is one of the fundamental principles all wealthy individuals have in common. They are very highly productive and sow value to the marketplace first before they reap their harvest. How about you, Lindsay?"

I nod. "Me too. If you want wealth, you have to give back. You don't get something for nothing."

"I agree," he says. "Everything in my life was built using this law of attraction and creating my future in advance. However, you cannot order the universe around as though it is a cosmic restaurant where you eat and then pay. It is like a drive-thru where you pay first. You must give to the universe first. Yes, the Good Book says, 'Ask, and it will be given to you.' But the next sentence is, 'Knock and the door will open for you.' You need to do the **action of knocking**. In the Bhagavad Gita, Krishna says, 'Work is devotional service.' Use common sense. **Don't look for messages and omens from the universe, but look inside and believe in yourself and have Faith in your mission. Trust your gut and your heart. When your purpose and your passion becomes one, you don't need to push anymore, you will be pulled to that goal.** It is like in the movie *Finding Nemo*, when Marlin gets into the East Australian Current. Once you are in the express current of purpose and passion, you will be automatically pulled to your goals. I know I am preaching to the choir here."

Accelerator # 4 - Create Your Future In Advance.

He shares with me how to create my future in advance.

"No, no. Reminding me is good. Sometimes I look for messages from the universe, too, but you used the words 'law of attraction'. What do you mean by that?" I ask.

He nods. "Good question. Law of attraction is a belief that focusing on something brings you closer to that, good or bad. The best way to focus on something is by imagining that it has happened already. Imagination is not better than knowledge. You are either using your imagination brain to create or to destroy, to empower others or to demolish them, to expand joy or suffering in the world."

"So why did Einstein say imagination is better than knowledge?" I ask.

"To paraphrase, what he said was, 'I am an artist and I use a lot of imagination. Imagination is more important than knowledge. Knowledge is limited; imagination encircles the world.' In Einstein's case, imagination indeed was better than knowledge. In Bin Laden's case, imagination was worse than his knowledge. Make sense?"

"Ha. It does. But how do I create my future in advance?"

"Based on my work with millions of people, there are the three simple steps to creating your future in advance. I call this Pre-creation **It is your private victory, where you see your future through your inner eyes.**

"Humans are the only animals who can alter their destiny using vivid imagination. A tiger cannot imagine him being a peaceful animal and practice **ahimsa** or non-violence. A goose migrating from Canada in November does not say 'Gee, this migration thing is killing me. By the time I reach Canada and settle, it is time for me to go back to the United States. It is a terrible idea; I am going to stay back this time.' Every animal other than humans stay pretty much in the same type of habitat for millions of years. We humans moved from caves to tree houses to custom built homes to multi-story luxury apartments, why?"

"We can create anything we want using persistent imagination."

"Exactly. If you were to tell someone in the Middle Ages that humans would fly one day on a 48,000-pound metal box, 39,000 feet above earth, you would have been jailed or stoned to death to get the evil spirit out of you. But that is what we are doing now. Someone else imagined and pre-created this jet plane so we could ride it.

"Bernard Shaw said 'Imagination is the beginning of creation. You imagine what you desire, you will what you imagine, and at last you create what you will.'"

"I am pretty excited to try pre-creation. What do I do?" I say with enthusiasm.

"It is very simple. The first step of pre-creation is **Clarity.**" Arjun continues, pausing to drink a sip of water. "Clarity involves knowing exactly what you want and forming a clear vision of the experiences you want to create. It involves clearly defining what you are going to give first to get back what you want. There are only two types of dreams. Dreams that expand the joy in the world and those dreams that create suffering in the world. Your life on this planet can be very fulfilling and joyful if you left the world around you slightly better than you got it. Please make sure your goals make our world a better place.

"Once you know your goal is making the world a better place, find your compelling reasons why you must achieve this. We talked about this the first day we met. Your reasons must be strong enough to persevere beyond temporary defeats."

"I have that covered," I say.

"Excellent," he explains. "Clarity also involves being able to stop playing the fear induced movies of the past that are disempowering you and start playing the movies of what you want. This also means you are pre-creating the emotions you are going to experience when you reach your destination. The key magnets of wealth are Kindness and Gratitude and Passion. Create those emotions inside of you as you imagine your goals as if it is done already.

"Your mind is like a puppy. You cannot teach a puppy two tricks at the same time. The same way you should take small bites until your mind gets the hang of it. So don't imagine thirteen goals at the same time. Visualize one, achieve that, and move on. Do you have enough clarity on that?"

"Clearly! Ha, ha. Yes," I reply.

"The next step of pre-creation is **Certainty**. Certainty is applied Faith. It comes from knowing and seeing your future in advance. It comes from clearly seeing the next version of you with more clarity than where you are right now. This will eliminate your fear of the unknown.

"The use of Faith here is not from a religious or even spiritual context, but it is perfectly fine to incorporate your current beliefs to create Faith in you as long as you are serving the world.

"Passion and joy are the essential ingredients for creating certainty. You cannot live in frustration or anger or sadness or any other emotions and ask certainty to fill your heart. It is like pouring water into a glass that is upside down. Even if you are depressed or angry most of the time, you can still flip the glass. Once you achieve inner certainty, what other people call miracles would be your daily reality. On a cellular level, your body experiences that you are there already. On a metaphysical level, your mind feels that you have reached your goal. Your spirit is overjoyed that you are living your purpose and passion of expanding joy in the world."

"Wow! That feels amazing."

"The third and the final step of pre-creation is **Completion**. Completion involves seeing yourself finishing the intelligent actions required to claim your victory. In completion, you imagine the people and systems to reach your destination. You would see yourself celebrating your victory with your loved ones and friends to make it even more real for your mind. See yourself growing to the next level as a person with your Super Tribe. Finally, you would see yourself giving back to the universe along with your Super Tribe. **You make the future so real in your imagination so that the reality adapts itself to fit your model of the world.**" He smiles.

I turn and stare out the window at the clouds below, feeling elevated, both physically and emotionally. If we feel our darkest right before our biggest moment of change, then I'm happy knowing I've made it through the hardest part.

"**Emotional clarity, inner certainty, and completion thinking are the primary keys of creating your future in advance.** In pre-creation, you are creating a new internal story and an empowering metaphor of your future. This new metaphor becomes a self-fulfilling prophecy. It is true for all successful entrepreneurs and high performers throughout history," Arjun says, bringing me back to the conversation.

I face him again. "In 1971, a sixteen-year-old boy met a guy named Steve. Steve was very technical and knew more about electronics than the boy, yet they began working on projects together. In *Esquire* magazine, they read about a guy named Captain Crunch who could supposedly make free telephone calls to anywhere in the world. Now, you might be thinking, what is the big deal about making free calls? Well, it cost around forty dollars of today's money per minute at the time.

"They both were captivated, although they thought it might be a hoax. Out of curiosity, the kids began researching libraries for the secret tones that would allow them to make the free calls. Way down, at the last bookshelf on the bottom rack of Stanford Linear Accelerated Center's Library, they found an AT&T technical journal that laid out the whole thing.

"Apparently, AT&T made a fatal flaw in the original design of the digital telephone network. They kept the same frequency of their communication tone as something the human voice could reproduce. If you could replicate the same tone, the entire AT&T network would think that you were a computer. After three weeks, the teenagers finally built a blue box that worked. They put a little logo under the box that said, 'He got the whole world in his hands.'

"Next thing they did, they found the number for the Pope in the Vatican and started calling. They began waking people up, one phone call at a time, claiming Steve was Henry Kissinger. Someone got up to wake the Pope. However, they couldn't talk to the Pope because of how hysterically they were both laughing.

"What they learned was that even though they were young, they could build something that could control billions of dollars' worth of infrastructure in the world. This new metaphor changed this caterpillar into a butterfly. His name was Steve Jobs, and the other guy was Steve Wozniak. In an interview, Steve Jobs later said that there wouldn't have been Apple Computer had there not been a blue box. That became Steve Job's metaphor for his business.

"Successful people see empowering metaphors. They see the miniature activity that they did as the metaphor for what they're going to do on a larger scale. This is not practical thinking—it is optimism in action. Jobs and Wozniak gained their **clarity** from their passion for technology, **certainty** through the blue box, and **completion** by doing consistent actions." Arjun turns to the window and stares out of it thoughtfully, visibly satisfied with what he has preached.

I stare at him. "You're very inspirational." I give Arjun an admiring smile. "You are. Now, I need to pre-create and think positive all the time."

"Can you think positive all the time, Lindsay?"

"I thought that was what you wanted me to do?" I exclaim, suddenly on unsure footing again.

A pretty brunette flight attendant comes by with juice and water for us both, and we thank her. Arjun takes a sip of his water then clears his throat.

"Not exactly."

Apparently, Arjun isn't done blowing my mind yet.

CHAPTER THIRTEEN
The Myth of Practical Thinking

"Let me tell you a personal story. I met Bishnu decades ago in a city called Bangalore in India. He was very impressive and articulate. There was a sense of secrecy in his language. He said he is a doctor and his father was George W. Bush's physician. In his teens, he fought with his father and got out of the house.

"I did not ask, but he voluntarily showed me his dad's picture with the elder Bush and a personal email from Laura Bush. He casually mentioned that he was well connected with American embassy officials all over India if anyone wanted to get a visa to the United States.

"I couldn't believe who I stumbled into. I always believed that I had an alternate destiny although I was making only $90 a month. This seemed like my only chance. Many Indians wanted to move to the U.S. If I helped enough people move for a consulting fee, I could ask Dr. Bishnu to help me to move to the U.S., as well. Finally, it seemed like my dreams were coming true. I brought him to my house, if you can call a sixty square foot room a house. I told my other best friend Titto about the massive opportunity. He was a skeptic. He said 'If Bishnu or whatever his name is can do that kind of magic, why does he need you for it?'

"That was a good point. To avoid making a mistake, I brought him to Ms. Daisy, who was the best Christian clairvoyant in our small town. She saw Dr. Bishnu and me working together to create peace in the world. *Suck it, Titto Thomas*! I said to myself.

"I think you are jealous that I am growing too fast. Gee, I am so lucky.

"Three weeks later, I was in Chennai, another city in south India, which has the nearest U.S. embassy. My friend Benoy and I met Bishnu in a luxuary hotel and handed over around five thousand dollars in a number lock briefcase. He asked us to wait in his room and even ordered food for us. He just needed to meet his contact, and he would arrange an interview the very next day. Bishnu asked me for the combination as I reassured my friend.

"We waited in his room eating the delicious food. This was clearly the beginning of my good life. What an amazing and friendly man, Dr. Bishnu was. Benoy and I were both impressed by his poise and his charisma.

"An hour passed, we did not hear from him yet. Benoy got anxious and I told him not to worry. I would call his cell phone. There must have been a delay in traffic. He did not pick up that call or my next ten calls, either. Minutes turned into hours, and we never heard from Dr. Bishnu again.

"I was embaressed beyond belief. Benoy was furious. I didn't know if I should run away and leave my town, or what to do next.

"Benoy realized that it would be humiliating for him if everyone in our small town found out that he lost that much money to a scam artist, so he suggested that I pay him back and keep this between us.

"I reuluctantly agreed, because I was the one who brought him in.

"My mom had a dream that a tiger was chasing me to kill me the same night I went through this nightmare. My mom and dad both prayed, staying awake and waiting for their son to safely return home, which I did. They never blamed or complained. They supported me all the way. What a gift to have parents like mine.

"I paid off my friend in installments several years later. My biggest loss was not the five thousand dollars. It was becoming too practical to dream big.

"I think 'practical thinking' is the second biggest killer of dreams. Remember the first day we talked about Sophie, the tortoise? You said she was unrealistic to run with a hare."

"Yes, totally. I mean, she was a frickin' tortoise—a boulder on marbles moves faster. But, that's her biology, and nothing is going to change that. Not even positive thinking."

"You are right. She was not realistic, but she was optimistic. She—"

"I don't understand. How could someone be unrealistic and still succeed?"

"Okay, let me give you my definitions for optimism and positive thinking. In my opinion, **optimism is a mental attitude that interprets situations and events as being optimized, even though they don't fully comprehend it at a given moment.** An optimist always sees the most optimized result. If the results are negative, they minimize it in their minds, and if it is positive, they maximize it. Optimists may not necessarily think that everything is positive at a given time."

"And positive thinking?" I prompt him.

"**Positive thinking is an attitude that focuses on only the bright side of people, life, and events, and always expects positive results.** A positive thinker views the world from a positive perspective and often trusts everyone and everything. Let's face it, everyone and everything is not positive. Here is the major complaint pessimists have about optimists. A pessimist says, 'I am an intelligent person who makes realistic and practical decisions.' He thinks all optimists are blind positive thinkers. But all optimists are not like me. They may or may not be positive thinkers."

I narrow my eyes, still not quite getting it. "How can someone be an optimist and not be a positive thinker? I'm lost on this one."

"Let me try explaining it a different way." Arjun shifts around in his seat and leans forward, using his hands again to speak. "At any juncture, we are unconsciously asking two questions. "What does this mean **now**? What does this mean **in the future**?" Positive and negative thinking are the answer to the first question and optimism and pessimism are the answer to the second.

"Here are the four types of people in this world. The first are Positive-Thinking Optimists. Let's say a businesswoman has severe cash flow issues. As a positive-thinking optimist, she might think something like, 'This is part of my journey towards becoming a legend. Everything will be amazing at the end. It is my destiny to be a very successful business woman, and I will get there no matter what.'"

"That's a stretch," I say, rolling my eyes.

"It is a stretch of imagination, Lindsay. **Human beings are meaning**

making machines. With your imagination, you can create any meaning you want and that will become your physical reality. King Midas had a limiting belief that he could create only gold. You can create anything you want through consistent imagination.

"I believe the most successful people in the world are like this. They think of the current challenges as empowering: **positive thinking** and the long-term opportunities are endless: **optimism**. They are uber-positive and optimistic at the same time."

Okay. I don't know if I agree with it, but I listen.

"The next type of people are Positive-Thinking Pessimists. **Pessimism** is the tendency to expect the worst in everything. They focus on the dark side of people, life, and events and always expect negative results. If the same woman is a **Positive-Thinking Pessimist**, she might say to herself, 'Having cash flow issues is good for me. I will spend less money. But I spent my entire savings and my life to build this. I might die broke.' Although she put a *positive* twist on her current state, she is drinking poison by *pessimistically* saying, 'I will die broke.'

"The third type of people are Pragmatic Pessimists. If the same woman is a Pragmatic Pessimist, she will say to herself, 'This is horrible. I am a practical woman. Let me make sure that my children will not suffer financially for my choices and go ahead and pay their college fund before all my money is gone. Unfortunately, I will die broke.' Since she is pessimistic, she won't even try. She has already given up on herself."

I cringe to myself. Maybe I'm pessimistic and negative. After all, I did almost sacrifice myself to the Pacific Ocean and Poseidon.

"The fourth and final type," he continues, "are Pragmatic Optimists. Had the same woman been a Pragmatic Optimist, she would've said, 'It is sad that I have severe cash flow issues. But I am an intelligent woman. I have a mission in life to help others and have fun for myself. I need to serve others and get out of this mess. Through my passion and purpose, I will be pulled to my goals.' Sophie, the tortoise, was a positive-thinking optimist," Arjun concludes. "Lindsay, can you imagine this? A tortoise stepping up to compete with a hare? What are the odds? Why would she possibly go up against an animal that runs around 45 MPH while the fastest tortoise in the planet runs less than 1 MPH? Was it just blind courage?"

"I think I almost get it," I say, tapping my fingers on the armrest.

"That's not overly optimistic," Arjun teases. "You only *think* you get it? How about if I give you another example?"

I nod. "How about the flight attendant bringing some coffee and a snack? That would help, too." I stare out the window again at what looks like the Colorado River snaking through the mountains below.

Arjun's voice has become a permanent fixture in my mind—ever-present, guiding me, even as I rest, looking out the window.

"Let's talk about a garden," his smooth voice says. "As we all know, most gardens have weeds shooting up through the beds of beautiful flowers and vegetables."

"Not mine," I say.

"Oh, your garden didn't have weeds?" Arjun's voice seems dubious.

"No, my garden didn't have flowers or vegetables." I face him and smile. "Only weeds."

"Ha! Lindsay, you crack me up. You are not a pessimist." He eyes me carefully. "No matter what you think. Okay?"

I almost tear up at his words. How does he seem always to know what I am thinking and feeling? But, he's right. I need to forgive myself. I may have had a moment of weakness out on that beach, but for the most part, I am a Pragmatic Optimist.

"Okay."

"A Positive-Thinking Optimist looks at the weeds and sees opportunities, even in them. They take intelligent action to create their ideal vision of their garden. They see goodness in everything and everyone, but they **trust their gut to differentiate good and evil.**

"These are the billionaires who see opportunities even in a depression. Sir John Templeton is a great example of that. When World War II began in Europe in 1939, John borrowed money to buy 100 shares each of 104 companies selling at one dollar or below and realized an enormous profit from it.

"You will attract massive numbers of opportunities in this state of mind. If you choose this path of being a Positive-Thinking Optimist, always trust and listen to your gut feelings to verify things. In my experience with Dr. Bishnu scamming me, I was a Positive-Thinking Optimist, but I did not trust my gut. I became his believer, and everything I did was to prove that he was legit.

I can't help but chuckle wryly at mighty Arjun for being scammed by someone. The man before me seems far too wise for that.

"You enjoying my failures? See, everything **does** have value, even if it's at my expense! Okay, let's move on to the Positive-Thinking Pessimist in their weedy garden. In the grand scheme of things, this is a negative person, but in the immediate future, he is so positive, he can't see the problems in the garden. He is thinking, 'My life sucks, but let me take care of my garden.' But he does not have a long-term plan for that garden. This person is busy rearranging his desk when he needs to be making high-dollar value decisions. There will never be weeds in his garden nor flowers.

"And then the Pragmatic Pessimist is so preoccupied with negative thoughts that she can't see any good whatsoever. She is so focused on the weeds that she can't see the flowers in the garden. 'Weeds in my garden?' she says. 'Of course, there are weeds in my garden! Universe hates me. Why else would He have created weeds in the first place? Why wouldn't He have just given me flowers? Forget it. There are weeds everywhere. I can't deal with this. Let me be practical. There is no way I can have a great garden. It is simply a waste of time. I will buy flowers from a flower shop. My husband left me, I have a nasty boss, and my parents spanked me as a child. And now, there's weeds? Ugh! There's nothing good in my life.'"

"Yeah, I know a few of those," I say, shaking my head.

"The Pragmatic Pessimist," Arjun goes on, "allows these emotions to stack up. She loses control of the situation. Even her high intelligence is clogged by negativity. So what if her boss is a jerk? That's no excuse for cursing the world because her garden has weeds. She was spanked as a child! So? Go pull the weeds out and move on!"

I laugh. "Yeah! Except..." My smile fades. "That sort of sounds like me when we first met, huh?" I hang my head in shame.

Arjun gives me a meaningful smile. "Hey, live and learn. Yes?"

"I guess so."

"That was weeks ago, and you're not going to be focusing on that anymore, right, Lindsay?"

"Of course not! Why would an idiot like me, whom everyone hates, do that?" I ask, hiding a mischievous smile.

Arjun cocks his head at me. "I see that smile. I know you are joking. You cannot hide it from me so easily."

"Bummer. Let me ask you a question. Are you saying negative thinking and pessimism are different, too?"

"Yes. While both negative thinking and pessimism are rooted in dismay, negative thinking is short-term, and pessimism is eternal cancer, though both are destructors of your dreams," Arjun says. "So, let's move on to the Pragmatic Optimist. 'Okay, sure, there are weeds, but I am going to fix them,' the Pragmatic Optimist says."

"That sounds more like me now."

"That's because you see the problem, you acknowledge the problem, and you fix the problem. Trust in God, but tie the camel. There is nothing wrong with staying in that space. You will still attract great opportunities." He points at me like I encapsulate everything he just said.

"If you say so."

"I do. To attract bigger opportunities of life, you need to be **either a Positive-Thinking Optimist or a Pragmatic Optimist. Either way, an optimist!** Bishnu pushed me out of Positive-Thinking Optimism to Pragmatic Optimism for decades. I became reasonably successful being in this space until my pragmatism became my biggest enemy to growth.

"Also, I did not want a scammer controlling the way I think and live my life and the level of success I could have. So I learned my lesson to **trust my gut** and swung right back to being a Positive-Thinking Optimist. That was what shaped my success to the level you see today."

I feel the shift in the plane as it prepares for descent as I feel a shift in my life. What Arjun has talked about today has taught me that I don't need to be super practical all the time, and honestly, that's like taking the weight of the world off my shoulders. I don't need to be positive all the time, either. I can be a Pragmatic Optimist for now. I'm allowed to look at the problem and acknowledge it, as long as I take steps toward fixing it.

The pilot's voice over the intercom confirms our final descent into Denver, and Arjun presses a button, thanking him for a smooth flight.

"So, what should I do now?" I ask in anticipation.

"Well..." Arjun lifts his arms in the air and stretches. "Once you design your outcomes, dedicate seven to ten minutes a day in the morning to do pre-creation as part of your power ceremony. With this process, you celebrate your victory in advance. Let me walk you through the steps firsthand, so you know exactly what to do and what not to do tomorrow."

"Oh, okay. That'll be great for tomorrow. But, I kind of meant like now, when we land." I smile at him.

"Ah. My chauffeur will pick me up from the airport for meetings. Meanwhile, grab your lunch, do whatever you want to do, and think about how you can design your business outcomes using the principles you learned today. I will meet you back at the plane at 3 p.m., and we will discuss exactly that. But before that, let us summarize and integrate these tools into your toolbox, shall we?"

"Here? How?" I ask, looking around.

"Yes, why not?" he asks. "Let us use power ceremony to reach Ananda and pre-create now. I recommend playing music that inspires you for this entire process." With great enthusiasm, I jump up for power ceremony.

Whack!

How quickly the plane's low ceiling reminds me that I'm too tall to do this standing. Sitting slowly and rubbing my head, Arjun chuckles a bit.

"Sit up straight in your seat and passionately state your outcome. If you were not on a plane, however, you would want to stand for this part. But for now, as you just learned, do it sitting down. Go ahead."

"Okay." I sit straight up and close my eyes, taking a deep breath. "I want to feel tremendous relief and hope. I want to feel immense internal power that will help me turn around my financial future."

"Excellent. And what is the goal that will help you reach this outcome?"

"I want to earn fifty thousand dollars in the next ninety days by adding value to small business owners who were part of my social media network, using the software development skills I have. I will help them to automate their business and make more money." Though it feels like rote, and I've repeated this several times already, I'm starting to believe it, and it's become second nature to me.

"Fine. And what are the three compelling reasons why you **must** accomplish this outcome, Lindsay?" Arjun's voice is like smooth honey to me, guiding me through this familiar process.

"I can't continue living my life without shame if I don't achieve this goal. I want to eliminate my debt and be financially free in ten years. I must become a role model for thousands of young entrepreneurs," I say, imagining myself reaching this goal. I sit up straighter.

"Great. Now, let us do Accelerator Breathing for two minutes. If you are feeling lightheaded while you breathe, don't worry about it. That's normal when you are doing it the first few times."

While we do the breathing exercises, I think about reaching my goals. I think about empowering young women everywhere, of standing at the front of a stage while they clap for me and cheer loudly. I have inspired them to start their businesses using my business solutions. They feel strong and powerful and ready to conquer the world because of my story.

"I am going to guide you through some power questions that you may ask yourself each day," Arjun says. "You can choose either to respond in your mind or aloud. Just ask yourself these and answer in your mind. What am I grateful for in my life?"

"I am grateful that this crazy, brilliant man, Arjun, ruined my near attempted self-sacrifice to Poseidon, and came into my life as my mentor," I say aloud unabashedly. I smile and crack open an eye. I see him smiling at me through his fist against his chin. "I am blessed that I could learn from him in a day what I haven't learned in years."

"Why am I grateful for that?" he asks, bowing his head.

"I am grateful because I can see progress in my business and state of mind."

"Ask yourself, how does that make me feel?"

"I feel hopeful and happier."

"What am I excited about?"

"I'm excited that I'm going to grow my business to the next level."

"Why am I excited about it?"

"Because I can get the financial freedom I've long wanted and expected," I reply.

"How does that make me feel?"

"Like Oprah Winfrey giving out free cars to her audience." I giggle to myself, and I hear Arjun chuckle, too.

"Good. Now, think about how you will feel when you achieve your goal. How are you going to celebrate when you accomplish this goal?" Arjun asks just as our plane's wheels touch the ground and the cabin shakes slightly.

"First, I'm going to have an apple martini with Brad Pitt. Then, I'm going to take a two-week long cruise in the Caribbean wearing my new bikini and fancy new cocktail dress, and nobody…I mean, nobody is going to stop me."

"Great! Who are you going to celebrate with?"

"Well, if Brad is available, then definitely him. But since he'll probably have a busy production schedule, let's go with my parents, my cousin Vanessa, and if my fantastic slammin' mentor, Arjun, isn't doing anything, maybe he'll want to tag along, too."

"Haha, I will ask him. He likes the Caribbean. So…how does that make you feel, Lindsay?" He claps in that way he does when something is final, when he is wrapping up a lesson, and just as timely, the airplane grinds to a halt.

"I feel incredible." I open my eyes to a smiling, Indian man who I adore and appreciate.

"Ask yourself, how am I going to grow when I accomplish this goal?"

I sigh. Arjun sure loves his questions.

"I am going to grow my confidence and my inner certainty about business and life. I am going to grow in heart by giving more than I receive to my clients. I am going to grow financially by charging top dollar for my incredible product and service. I am going to grow as an icon of technology entrepreneurs in my circles. How's that?"

"Superb! Who are you going to grow with? How does that make you feel?"

"I am going to grow with Arjun and my family!" I practically shout. "I am going to grow with my friends, who are dreamers like I am. It makes me feel even more excited!" I toss my hands up in the air, exalting in all this happiness.

"And finally ask…How am I going to give back when I reach this goal? Who am I going to give back to?" He says this quietly.

I close my eyes and imagine it. "I am going to give to my clients ten times more value than I financially receive. I will build raving fans out of them. I am also going give back by paying one thousand dollars to Feeding America. They'll provide one meal for at least ten thousand Americans, one-in-six who are struggling to get food on their table. I am going to feed and educate at least one hundred of the hungry children living in poverty with fifteen dollars per child."

"That is a very specific goal. How does that make you feel?"

"Like a financial rock star, baby! Seriously, it's going to make me feel even more important. Since I am giving from my struggle, I'll feel even more proud about myself."

"Wonderful. Walk the way the successful walk—posture, and everything. Think about the three achievements you already have in your life. Give thanks to the God you believe in—or Divine Force or the Universe—for helping you achieve these goals. Feel the joy and excitement in your life because you achieved these goals. Think about the celebration, the growth and giving and the people associated with each of them. Feel the significance of achieving each goal and what it means to you. Notice the inner security you feel. Feel the freedom acheiving these goals brings you, in every cell of your body. Promise yourself to do this every day in seven minutes for the next thirty days."

"Wow, that's easy for me."

"I am sure you will do it. I believe in you, Lindsay. Now ask yourself about the next action. What is the one intelligent action I must take today to achieve my goal?"

"Well, I must start calling my old clients and reconnect with them so that

I can serve them even more with my new ideas."

"And what will your clients say when you call?"

"They might try to reject me, but I have a new recipe for rejection," I say. "I can use the new ABC of Persuasion, too. I will have fun with it. Hell to the yeah!"

"Sounds like you are going to have fun with this, Lindsay," Arjun says, unbuckling his seatbelt and standing to stretch.

I am. I really am. And better than what a new out*fit* will do to make you feel great, it's amazing what a whole new out*look* will do for you. If only I would have known all this just a few months ago. I would say that I might not have lost Charlie, but forget that jerkface! He can just ponder his plumbing problems now, while coloring in the lines of my old Zen coloring books. I'm glad I lost him, because he does not fit my new mindset. The new Lindsay would never have gone out with a loser like Charlie. I'm even sorry that I wasted so much time with him.

All I can do, like Arjun said, is see, acknowledge, and fix the problem and be a Pragmatic Optimist.

And that is exactly what I intend to do. There's no stopping me.

"If one does not know to which port one is sailing, no wind is favorable."
Lucius Annaeus Seneca

CHAPTER FOURTEEN
The Virtual CEO

After Arjun's meetings are said and done for the day, it's time for the return flight to LA. The sun descends over the Rocky Mountains, and Denver glitters below us like a jeweled tapestry. Arjun puts his feet up and orders a tall glass of water.

It's amazing to me how this man could order any drink he wants to get him into the relaxing, unwinding mood, but he goes with the healthiest option on the planet. I order a ginger ale and sit back, closing my eyes. Though I didn't attend any meetings myself, it's been a long day of thinking for me, too, and I'm about to be in for another treat of coaching with Arjun.

Staring out the darkened window at the diminishing city, Arjun begins to tell a story. "A long time ago, there lived four young people, ambitious to become massively rich. They traveled from village to village in search of diamonds until, one day, they heard about an island replete with the precious gemstones. But there was one problem. They had no boat to get them there," Arjun says, looking at me. "So they decided to build a small raft by cutting down a tree."

"Not very environmentally conscious, were they?" I smile.

His shoulders shake silently. "No, they weren't. They only wanted to be rich. So anyway, they built the raft, but the island was difficult to reach. The waters of the lake were rough, there were storms, and the waves were high. Finally, after several grueling days, they reached their destination.

Immediately, they realized what they'd heard about the island was true.

Diamonds sparkled everywhere! The four young folks scattered and began picking them from the ground, traveling deeper and deeper into the island by foot. One young man realized they were leaving behind the raft that had brought them to the island in the first place. 'How can we be this insensitive and ungrateful?' he asked. 'Let us take the raft with us. After all, we only have the diamonds because of the raft.'

"The others agreed, so they decided to carry the raft as they went, each person carrying one corner. After a while, they got so tired that it became difficult to pick up the diamonds—**the reason they had built the raft in the first place.** However, they thought if they were loyal to the raft long enough, the raft would reward them in the end. On and on, they would walk, growing more and more tired, falling, one at a time. In the end, the four travelers did not have the energy to pull the raft off of the island and died with the diamonds in their hands."

For a while, I stare at Arjun, thinking about the story.

"Well, that sucks."

"Indeed, it does," he agrees.

"It doesn't even make sense. Why would they carry the raft around?" I ask. "Why didn't they just leave it where it was and come back to it when they needed it?"

Arjun nods, as though I've touched upon a very good question. "As strange and sad as this story sounds, a lot of businesses today are like this, Lindsay. The raft is the metaphor of a process which the business defined some time in the past, which they're still carrying. It is heavy, and cumbersome, and stopping them from picking up all the diamonds in the marketplace. Every business has its treasures waiting to be discovered, yet business owners remain loyal to the raft, to the process, thinking this will pay off someday. But it won't. **A business needs to anticipate and adapt to grow.** Otherwise, it will die with diamonds still in its hands."

"Wow," I mumble, staring into space. "That sounds like an Indiana Jones movie."

"It is, and you are Indiana Jones. You are the hero. You need to be quicker and smarter than the hundreds of other treasure hunters who have come before you seeking treasure, those who died with the golden idols and sacks of diamonds in their hands."

I can't stop staring at his compelling, storytelling eyes. "You're creeping me out, Arjun."

"Would not be the first time I have been told that, Lindsay." He winks, laughing.

"But does that mean that businesses have to work quickly and randomly with no process? Just run around picking up diamonds. That can't be right, either," I say.

He sets down his glass of water and folds his hands. "Of course not. Let's talk about that for a minute. When I was twenty, I started my first business. I designed and built single family homes. My company, MM Builders, had no process whatsoever. I designed houses, and my junior architect did the estimates. I did not even check if they were accurate or not. I trusted him to do his job. We submitted proposals with estimates that were often twenty percent below the cost of construction, hoping we would make money."

"Wow."

Arjun raises his eyebrows, exasperated. "Yeah. On top of that, some of my workers took turns napping or fooling around while I was gone, since I did not have a system for monitoring their work efficiency. But they sure did have someone monitoring me. They had one person watching to see when I was coming, and while I was there, everybody pretended to work passionately. I could hear the sounds of chisels from a mile away, bricks going up and down. I felt proud to be running a company with these devoted employees. I even hired an assistant who carried my bag—a bag holding important phone numbers—and his last name, coincidentally, was 'Vettickal' which means 'deception' in my native language Malayalam. Like any other twenty-year-old, I thought my company would become a multi-million dollar business one day."

"Sounds like the same mistakes all naïve beginning entrepreneurs make, Arjun. Don't be so hard on yourself," I say.

"Oh, the naïve ones made me look good," he laughs. "I did not have accounting nor bookkeeping. Money came to my account, and money went out of it. I did not know my costs of labor nor materials nor did I know if I was profitable or not, although I thought I was. Everything was guesswork. You can imagine what happened at the end!"

"You became a multi-millionaire with a Ferrari and can afford a chartered plane," I say, because, let's face it, this is how the story ends.

"Okay, not *that* end. Back up. The middle of the story, Lindsay." He laughs a deep, throaty laugh.

"Uhh…you stood in the Pacific, making it saltier and saltier with each tear, crying about the direction your life had taken?"

"Not exactly. I ended up with $30,000 in debt in India. To put things into perspective that was 1.5 million Indian rupees at the time. **A business with no process is guaranteed to fail. Similarly, those obsessed with their processes are setting themselves up for failure. Businesses with an adaptive process will thrive.** You need to build a process-driven business, not a people-dependent one. Not **process-dependent** either, **process-driven.** Without the raft, the young travelers couldn't have crossed the challenging lake to reach the diamond-filled island, but when they did, they needed to redefine a new process for diamond-hunting. Question every process your company uses by asking, 'Why?' That was what Steve Jobs did when he returned to Apple the second time. He asked, 'Why do we do this?' for almost every process Apple undertook. It must have driven everyone crazy—the constant questioning, the extreme analysis—but it was necessary."

"So what you're saying is, I should drive everyone bonkers?"

"In a way, yes but with absolute compassion. Walt Disney was known for pushing his animators, questioning, then pushing and questioning again. People who stay in their comfort zones might find it a bit unnerving, but they are there to succeed by creating something extraordinary. Help them succeed in their career and take your business to the next level," Arjun explains.

"Then, I should have a business process, but I should also be flexible enough to change it as needed." I can't resist using my new wisdom. I feel like the shining star of business smarts.

"Exactly!" Arjun claps for me, and I beam. "Charles Darwin said survival is for the fittest. Well, I say, **survival and excellence is not for the fittest** business anymore. **They are for those who innovate while anticipating change.** Technology disrupts almost every traditional industry in the world and creates new ones, and the speed at which this disruption and creation occurs is increasing, too. From 1950 to 2000, we had more development in technology than in all of four million years of human development on this planet combined."

"What about other planets?" I ask, just to be cheeky. I love putting Arjun on the spot.

"We don't have that information yet," he answers without a hitch. "The technology to communicate with other planets is still being developed. But, back on earth again, in the last ten years alone, we've had more advancement than in the previous fifty years. According to researchers at the Olin School of Business in St. Louis, almost half of today's Fortune 500 companies will be gone in the next decade."

"Holy cannoli!" I mutter.

"Exactly, which means that these companies are not going to adapt quickly enough to changes. Let me give you an example that will bring this idea home. At Kodak, Steve Sasson, an electrical engineer, was tasked with figuring out if a charged coupled device had any practical application. His involvement in this task led him to innovate the first digital camera, and the device to display it."

"What do you consider innovation?" I interrupt, curious to know.

"Innovation?" he asks. "It's creating or improving products or processes, adding more value to meet your clients' wants and/or needs better."

"Well, I want that," I find myself saying. "I want to innovate my business. I remember reading Peter Drucker, something about, 'The business enterprise has two—and only two—basic functions: marketing and innovation. Marketing and innovation produce *results*. All the rest are costs.' Now that I know more about marketing, I would love to learn your take on innovation."

Arjun's eyes sparkled happily. "Lindsay, I didn't know you read Peter Drucker. Love this quote from him. How about if we discuss it next time we meet? I appreciate the way you are taking charge and planning."

"Thanks." I smile, blushing.

"As for Sasson at Kodak, he showed these devices to his bosses in 1975. Do you know what they said? 'No one would ever want to look at their pictures on a television set. Print had been with us for over a hundred years. No one was complaining about prints. They were very inexpensive, so why would anyone **want** to look at their picture on a digital screen?'"

"Pfft, it always happens that way," I say. "Some people just don't have the vision to see past their noses."

"Right. Well, Sasson tried to convince them that, while the image quality wasn't great at the moment, it would improve. He was allowed to keep working on it, even though they thought it was a waste of time. In 1989, Sasson and Robert Hills made the first DSLR camera, similar to the ones on the market today. It used memory cards and compressed the image. Kodak's marketing department, however, resisted it. They told Sasson they **could** sell the camera, but they wouldn't, for fear it would reduce film sales. Kodak had a virtual monopoly on the United States photography market and made money on every step of the photographic process. Why give that up?

"At that time, if you wanted to take photographs of your daughter's wedding, you would likely be using a Kodak Instamatic, Kodak film, and Kodak flash cubes. You'd have it processed either at the corner drugstore or you'd have mailed the film to Kodak and get back prints on Kodak paper weeks later. They considered it an excellent business *process*, so they rejected Sasson's new idea of instantly available digital photos. They basically said, 'That's cute, but don't tell anyone about it.'"

I laugh when Arjun says "it's cute." It's funny to think how many ideas are shot down at the beginning, like Walt Disney's fourth-grade teacher telling him he had no imagination. Another lesson in all this is to keep going, keep believing, and keep innovating until the walls come crashing down.

"Founded in 1888," Arjun continues, "Kodak employed 140,000 workers at one time. In 1996, it was ranked the fourth most valuable brand in the United States. But by the time the company embraced digital technology, it was too late. Kodak management's inability to embrace digital photography made them miss opportunities in a technology they invented."

"That's so sad," I say, shaking my head.

"Indeed, it is. So, Eastman Kodak filed for bankruptcy in 2012. Similar to the four guys who effectively killed themselves with diamonds in their hands."

"Incredible," I say. "Kodak must've been blindsided with their business process."

I'm fairly certain this is an a-ha moment I'm having right here and now.

"They were!" Arjun responds. "Giving the best experience for the customer consistently with constant improvement is the fundamental principle here. In 1888, Kodak started with a slogan: *You press the button— we do the rest.* What were they offering then, Lindsay?"

"Convenience."

"When they rejected Sasson's idea for digital camera, what did they do?"

"They denied the very same convenience to their customers." I was proud to say that.

"Correct. That is why *your* process must be defined based on those core values. Most small businesses in the U.S. are not working, because owners have become operators. The business processes are cemented in their heads. The moment you get the process inside your head onto paper, your creativity is revitalized. **Process must help you to anticipate and innovate, not stagnate.** Processes are foundations for the services, not the ceilings for them. They are the baseline experience your customers **and** employees could springboard from."

"Processes are springboards, I like that," I say, shifting in my seat. I would guess we're about halfway home, and though it's getting kind of late, I'm following his train of thought. "So, my employees are my customers, too?"

Arjun nods. "Yes, employees are your customers, too, but let's discuss that some other time. Process should not turn employees into robots. It must, in fact, become incubators of creativity and innovation. Organizational processes are not for achieving certainty for the business owner but for giving the business stability. Through a process, you can provide a consistent experience for your customers and convert them into raving fans." He pushes a button and calls the air hostess to bring us some snacks.

I'm given a small tray of bite-size ham sandwiches, perfect for a late-night snack.

"Okay, where were we?" he asks.

"You were telling me about process becoming a tool of innovation, not stagnation," I summarize for him.

"Very good. You're an excellent listener and mentee, Lindsay." He points at me and does a silent cheer. I laugh inwardly. "Let us talk about optimization first. Unlike what Peter Drucker said, there are three essential functions in business: innovation, marketing, **and optimization.** Optimization is not only a process but also one of the essential functions of your business. Through optimization, we make all the innovation and marketing efforts more fruitful. **Optimization is a process by which you maximize the desired factors and minimize the undesired ones.** Greater bottom-line can be achieved by optimization of people and process. We'll talk in more depth about this as part of productivity and team building. Are you going to write any of this down?"

"Oh."

Honestly, I'm great at remembering everything, but he's right. I should probably take out my iPad. After all, it's not like he will go over all this again with me one day. I have one shot with Arjun, and I better make the best use of my time. I reach into my bag and pull out my iPad. "Go ahead. Sorry."

"No sorry needed. Here we go…do you remember the three ways you can grow business?" Arjun asks.

"By increasing either number of clients, average purchase value, number of repurchase or doing all the above?" I say, tapping the page with my pen.

"Excellent memory." He picks up a magazine on a coffee table between us, checks it out for about two seconds, then tosses it back on the table. "Now, how can you increase the number of clients?"

"By generating more leads on my website, I can generate more leads for my sales team. A team sounds great, though it's just me right now." I try not to let the bitterness into my voice. So it's just me right now-big deal. I'll build my way back to having a team again.

"Very good. Let us discuss some more ways to optimize your revenue streams starting with your ideas. Here's a list of ways which you can maximize your revenue," Arjun says, reaching into his briefcase and producing a stack of index cards. He rifles through them, examines one, and hands it to me.

I take the card and flip it, reading the following:

1. Increase online and offline leads.
2. Increase effectiveness of your conversion strategy.
3. Increase effectiveness of your customer retention strategy/raving fan service.
4. Increase your transaction value.
5. Increase effectiveness of your upselling strategy.
6. Increase effectiveness of your billing strategy.
7. Increase effectiveness of your anticipation strategy.

"Whoa. That's a lot of 'increases.' What's the difference between increasing transaction value and upselling?" I ask, grabbing a blanket from the seat next to me and wrapping it around my shoulders.

"Well, when increasing transaction value, your customers are either buying the same product for a higher price, or they are buying it multiple times. On upselling, you are selling higher-end products. For example..." He leans forward, pressing his fingertips into a little steeple. "How many iPhones have you bought in your lifetime?"

"Three," I answer quickly. In the last six years, to be exact. And that's not nearly as many as half the people I know.

Arjun nods, as if that was the answer he was expecting. "That is an example of increased transaction value for Apple. However, if you were to be sold a MacBook, that is considered upselling because Apple is promoting a higher end product this time. Now, let's talk about *increasing online leads* by using Facebook, Twitter or other social advertisements."

I breathe out a sigh of relief. "Being in the technology business, that's one I'm familiar with — online strategies to generate leads. What I had a problem with was conversion strategy. I think the ABC of Persuasion will cover that."

"Well, yes, you can use the new ABC of Persuasion as your baseline conversion strategy. Then, customize the new ABC persuasion strategy to fit your team."

"Okay. How do I go about doing that?" I ask.

"While you implement this in a team environment, you see who your best performers are. You train your team to follow the common strategies your top performers use for better conversion. This **one** step itself will take you a long way, Lindsay."

"Okay. Got that." I jot down everything he's saying in a frenzy.

"Now, let's talk about client retention strategy, or building a personalized relationship with your existing clients. **People don't want to break up with companies or people who meet their deeper personal needs.** So, Lindsay, it's your job to consistently make your clients feel significant and special with each interaction you have. If they have issues, fix them immediately. Predict possible problems your customers might have and then solve them in advance. Consistently get feedback from them regarding how they are doing…"

My pen scribbles like mad, punctuating our conversation with its swooshing sounds.

"Ask your clients how you can make their experience with you remarkable. Find out what your competitors are doing and outperform them. If you are giving out coupons for new prospects, try to give coupons to your existing customers, as well. Never punish your clients for being loyal customers. Appreciate them for their long-term loyalty. Call them for the sole purpose of thanking them for their business. Reward the behavior you want to see in your customers. The bottom line here is to deliver a raving fan customer experience. And remember that, if everyone in your life is a customer, this applies to them, too. Your boss, your spouse, your colleagues…even the people working *for* you. If you approach relationships with that same mentality, you will find raving fans across the board."

"Raving. I like that word." I write it down and underline it twice. "The idea is to make them so incredibly happy; you get nothing but 5-star reviews. A hundred stars, if you could."

"Yes. And who doesn't want a hundred star review from their wife or their employees? All of your customers, in your personal life and in business, should be madly in love with your service. Now, with regard to that service, how can you increase your transaction value?" Arjun asks, crossing his legs in the other direction and shifting in his seat.

I think about this a minute. "By increasing the price of my service or by facilitating repurchase." I get it. "But I still need to learn how to **increase effectiveness of my upselling strategy**."

Arjun nods. "The highest probability of a customer converting on an upsell is when they are already buying something from you. Lindsay, look…it's like this…in their minds, they're trying to avoid large decisions, so help them take a series of small decisions leading up to big ones. Offer a high-end version of what they already committed to buying. Look, children are the greatest salespeople in the world, aren't they?"

I laugh because it's so true. "Definitely."

"First, they'll politely ask you if you can take them to the store so they can help you get groceries. On the way to the store, they might upsell and ask you if they can get a candy, too. Once you buy them the candy, what is the first thing they're going to ask you?"

"If I can now buy them a shiny, red toy car." I laugh.

"Exactly. Or the newest Xbox or PS4 game. Right? They'll remind you that you haven't bought them anything good since their last birthday. You don't want them going to therapy in twenty years, saying they've become serial killers, all because their mom did not buy them the red car they so desperately wanted, right? So, you buy it using your credit card that's already near your credit limit. In the meantime, your kids are already looking around for other, more expensive toys to upsell you."

"Wow, masters of deceit." I laugh. "So, in essence, I should keep pestering my clients to buy more and more from me, is what you're saying." I laugh again.

"Exactly! I mean, no!" Arjun shakes his head, rubbing his eyes. "I'm only telling you this to help you genuinely help your client's better experience a product of yours that adds tremendous value. If you are delivering multiple times value than you receive monetarily, why not let them buy more from you? Let us talk about the one simple action that will bring maximum cash flow to your business."

"I am all ears," I reply.

"You must increase effectiveness of your billing strategy. Lindsay, I have worked with companies that get paid less than sixty percent of their delivered service. They spend all their money to deliver the product but don't collect the money. If you don't have an effective billing strategy, building one is the easiest way to optimize your revenue overnight. Use technology to automate your billing process as much as you can and follow through."

"Got it." I put my stylus and iPad down and sigh. As usual, it's a lot to take in in a short time, but I appreciate the crash course. "Finally, what do you mean by effective anticipation strategy?"

"**Anticipation is the business skill by which you will consistently make intelligent predictions about what could be the next paradigm shift in your industry.** So, for example, technology is revolutionizing virtually all industries including advertisement, healthcare, telecommunications, transportation, and many more, making this one of the most important skills in business. In a few years, self-driven cars will be common, right?"

I shrug. "Sounds good to me, because then it will finally be legal to be asleep at the wheel." God only knows what cars will be doing for us. Hopefully flying, making our beds, and brewing coffee, too.

Arjun goes on. "Since the number of accidents for self-driven cars are proven to be significantly less, auto insurance companies need to figure out a new model for their business. Since cars will soon be automated, will auto insurance still be for the car owner or the car manufacturer? If they don't soon have an effective anticipation strategy in place and optimize their marketing and innovation to support this revolution, they could be out of business in no time.

"We all have fears of change, of uncertainty, but **the only thing that is certain is change.** Change in market share, new products—even your industry being disrupted by new technologies. So, how can we be truly confident in an ever-changing marketplace?" Arjun asks.

"I don't know," I reply.

"By using the power of anticipation to study and predict the change well in advance. This way, you are more prepared than most of your competitors **in adapting to the change.** Read futurists like Ray Kurzweil—you do not need to agree with everyone but expand your perspective. Ask new questions no one else is asking in your industry. We'll talk more about this when we discuss innovation next week." Arjun stretches and yawns.

I wonder when his batteries will run out. The man seems to be able to go on forever.

"Okay, what is most important, innovation, marketing or optimization?" I rub my eyes and stick the stylus behind my ear, "Coffee wasn't on the list, so I'll just have to listen and pinch myself."

"Innovation and marketing are the cornerstones of a new business. As the business grows, optimization becomes the most important function. Peter Drucker said marketing and innovation are the only essentials of a business because he believed they were the only revenue drivers. Optimization will help you revitalize your innovation and marketing, thus superseding both. It will help you better retain and upsell to your customers. It will help you make the most effective use of your lead generation and conversion. It increases the transaction value of your customer. Another way to achieve optimization is by defining a process for your business."

"I have to admit; I'm a little lost with all the business vocab right now. It's almost midnight. What do you mean by defining a process?" I ask.

Arjun tries a different approach. "For you to grow your business, you need a system in place to do that for you. If you have a system in place, but no monitoring, you may as well not have any system. With an automated process, you can sit behind the cockpit and watch your business take off."

"So I can enjoy it."

"Exactly. And you won't need to be a slave. It will run itself, relieving you of being the operator. You understand, Lindsay?"

"I think I'm getting it."

"Good. While creating your process, you think of your business as a duplicable entity—a franchise model. So before we define your business goals, do you remember the three gifts or flairs in business?"

"Artists, Managers, and Leaders," I say by rote memory. It's all becoming second nature to me.

"Good. Of the three gifts, who do you think will resist a process the most?"

"Probably the Artists," I say.

"Exactly. Many artists consider systems an insult to their intelligence. Who do you think is most likely to love a defined process?" he asks, and I feel like I'm taking an oral test in fourth grade.

"Leaders," I reply.

"No," he replies to my surprise. "Leaders are free thinkers. They hate systems almost as much as the average artist does. They support the idea only because it can help the company grow its revenue. The correct answer is the Managers. Managers want to keep the paint brushes where they belong, and systems are the very tools that support them. Imagine if you are a solopreneur, and the Leader in you is dreaming, the Manager in you is searching for stability, and the Artist is going crazy wanting to create the product. The Artist in you will kill the Manager, and the Leader in you will be proud of it."

"Arjun, I'm starting to realize why I probably drove myself crazy in my business before. It's no wonder. I had split personalities!" I say, plucking the stylus from behind my ear and tapping it lightly against my iPad. "Seriously. This is crazy. It's no wonder things didn't work out. I was constantly at odds with myself, and I didn't even know it.

"And now you know, Lindsay. Now you know." He touches a finger to his temple and closes his eyes for a minute. I think he's going to fall asleep, and all I hear is the hum of the plane's engine, but then he shakes it off and opens his eyes again. "Any system that we define today must support all the functions of the business, namely marketing, innovation, and optimization. First things first. **A business that is not systemized is a reflection of your inner self.** Which was why I want you to define your purpose or mission in life."

"And how do I do that?"

"I have seen people spend decades doing this. Your life's mission is what *you* think it is, as long as it meets a few criteria. It does not have to change the world or achieve peace in the Middle East." Arjun waves his hands around to impress his point. "The only condition for the mission of your life is that it should serve the greater good. It should benefit something or someone besides you. The more people and things that benefit from your life, the more fulfilled and wealthy you could become."

I lean toward him, shaking my head. "Can you give me some examples, though?"

He nods empathically. "Yes, of course. A great example of a mission-driven person is Elon Musk, the CEO of SpaceX and Tesla, yes? He got into both businesses with the strong desire to help people overcome major obstacles. He founded Tesla, recognizing there would be a huge deficiency of gasoline in the future and then began SpaceX to help humanity move to Mars in the future. If you were to ask him whether he had absolute confidence that he was going to succeed, he would say 'Nope!' But he would also add, 'I saw that this was a goal worth pursuing for humanity.' Is he perfect? No. He went through some major personal challenges recently. Lindsay, I am not suggesting that you should have an ambitious mission like that. Your mission is *your* mission." Arjun stops and takes a deep breath, letting it out slowly.

"So what's *your* mission?" I ask quietly.

He turns a bright smile on me like he's thrilled that I asked. "Here is a personal mission statement I wrote decades ago: 'I am Joy. I am an accelerator of business, career and lifestyle. The purpose of my life is to expand Joy in the world by converting stress and suffering into celebration.' He sits back and waits for me to process.

So what would my mission be? "Your mission is very poetic. I'm an engineer, remember, so sorry if mine sounds a little less creative than yours."

"'We know what we are, but we know not what we may be' Shakespeare's inspiring words. But Lindsay, you're not Shakespeare and nor do you have to be to write out your mission." He pulls out his iPad from under his seat and jots something down on it. "This is a simple structure to follow for your mission statement:

I am _____ (my most important emotional value)_____.

The mission of my life is to serve _____ through _____ and help them to do/achieve _____."

I am... to serve... through... help them to achieve or do.

Suddenly, my thoughts hit a brick wall. "Can you give me some other examples. I mean, other than yours?"

Arjun strokes his chin slowly, then holds up a finger. "I am inspiration.

The mission of my life is to use my talents and skills to build a quality life for me and help others build the same with my business," he offers then continues, "Or this one: I am a caring mother. The mission of my life is to care for my children and help them become the leaders of tomorrow."

And they're all so beautiful and Mother Teresa-ish.

"Got it." I scribble like I've never scribbled before, which I always do with Arjun, and…ouch. Writer's cramp.

It isn't until he chuckles next to me do I realize I've been tapping my iPad over and over rhythmically, creating a beat while lost in thought.

"The purpose of my life is to share my passion with young women in the world through technological innovation so that they can live a life of empowerment." I close the iPad triumphantly. "There."

Arjun finally nods his approval. "Great. I think you've done a fantastic job, Lindsay.

If your business is not aligned with your purpose in life, you are cutting the wrong forest. Let us check it now. What business are you really in?"

I look at him quizzically. "You mean, what business I failed trying to build?"

"No, I mean, what are you selling?"

Oh.

"I'm in the technology sector. I build software for small businesses."

"I was expecting that as your answer. Usually, when somebody asks what business you are in, you talk about the service or the product you are selling." He says this without a single tone of judgment.

"What do you mean?" I ask.

"In your business, software is the product," he says. "Right?"

"Yes. So what should I say instead? That I sell rainbow friendship bracelets?" I scoff in spite of myself.

Luckily, Arjun seems amused. "I bet you would make some great rainbow friendship bracelets if you put your mind to it. But no, what I mean is, most entrepreneurs believe that their customers are buying products. Customers buy emotions. In your current business, once somebody gets something from you, what emotions do they feel?"

Arjun flits from question to question like a hummingbird amidst a multitude of beautiful flowers. "You like your questions, don't you?"

"There is a method to madness, Lindsay. Trust me."

I sigh and sit back. I never considered this before. I mean, I've thought about it in more of a solution-based setting. I've asked myself what problem my product fixes, and I've asked myself if it's valuable, but I've never set it inside of an emotional arena.

"They feel...a huge relief. They feel they're positioned to grow using new technology. They feel a confidence that their business is under control."

Arjun raises an eyebrow approvingly. "Excellent! That is what I wanted to hear. Now, if you were to single out the most powerful emotion from that, what would that be?" He leans in, eagerly awaiting my response.

"Um...I would have to say they feel freedom the most."

"Now, that is the emotion you are selling—freedom. You sell freedom to small businesses. Who wants technology? Bah!" Arjun's eyes are alight with excitement.

"So I sell freedom," I repeat, trying to grasp it all. "I'm going to need a lot of packing peanuts to ship freedom, Arjun."

"Now, what does the emotion of freedom give them? What is the most tangible thing that they get?" he asks.

"They get more revenue."

"What does more revenue give them?"

"They get more cash flow."

"What does cash flow give them?"

"More profit."

"What does more profit give them?" he is relentless.

"The lifestyle of their choice."

"You are selling lifestyle. Lindsay, if you try selling your product, you will talk about all the features of your software that nobody cares about. **If you're selling a tangible experience, you talk about the benefits your clients get.**

"Let us create your company's mission statement now. I'll give you a few examples of mission statements from my clients, based on what tangible experience they are selling, so you can understand what I mean. Here is one.

'I'm in the business of helping entrepreneurs to innovate and make more profit so they can lead the lifestyle they crave. I do it by teaching them strategies to market their product.'"

He pauses briefly then continues more slowly so I can keep up.

"I'm in the business of helping single moms feel financial security. I achieve that by strategically teaching them how to invest. Also this one…I'm in the business of passionately helping my clients have the best possible experience in their new home. I help them by finding their dream homes using my extensive experience in real estate as a real estate agent.'

"Now, tell me what your company's vision is."

I take a deep, steady breath. "I'm in the business of passionately helping female entrepreneurs to create the lifestyle that they love. I do this by serving them through world-class technology that will position them to automate and grow exponentially. There, spoken like a true Arjunian."

Arjun claps his hands. "Arjunian! Lindsay, I may have to start my own country, I like that! You've been paying attention. I'm proud of you. Or do you still want to say, 'I am in the technology sector…' *yada, yada, yada?*" He waves his hands around and makes a goofy face.

"Are you making fun of me? 'Cause if you're making fun of me, I'm just gonna get in my Ferrari and go back to my million dollar mansion. Got that?" I smile at him.

He playfully swats my arm.

"If nothing could stop you, imagine where your company would be twenty-five years from now, in revenue, and write it down. I want you to think big. You have twenty-five years to achieve your goals, so think carefully."

"Hmm…" Tapping my chin, I think about where I would like to be twenty-five years from now. Who knows why, but the number 10 million jumps into my head. If nothing could stop me, my business would be worth 10 million dollars twenty-five years from now. How would this be achieved? I'm not sure, but it would involve a lot of innovation, marketing, and optimization. The role that now fits is to be the Entrepreneur, Innovator, and Leader of my business from now on. I'm ready to give up being the Artist and

Manager if I can help it—it's time to delegate. I'm ready to do what it takes to make my business succeed at the level it deserves to succeed at.

"Well?"

"I want us to do $25 million a year in revenue."

"Fair enough. What about five years from now? How much revenue should you make?" he asks.

"Five million per year," I say. Why these numbers feel right to me, I don't know. They just do, and I feel I can make them happen.

"Okay, Lindsay. A lot of American companies only plan for the next quarter to appease their shareholders, but Japanese companies have hundred-year plans. There are more than 50,000 companies over 100 years old in Japan. Three thousand eight hundred eighty-six of them are over 200 years old.

"Create a simple organization chart for what your business is going to be like five years from now. Document a Strategic Mission for each position. A strategic mission is a fully clarified role for each of your team members, outlining what they're held accountable for. If the key functions of business are innovation, marketing, and optimization, then we need to define each role and how it will support those functions," he says, just as the pilot announces our descent into LAX. "Ah, we'll be home soon. It will be your intelligent action to create the mission for your company over the next few days, okay?"

"Alright, I will do that."

"The more clarity you provide your employees regarding their roles, the better they will perform. Creating a strategic mission for every employee might seem like more work for you, but this is your life, your baby, your business. It's serious. It's your money on the table. Besides, this is a one-time task that you only need to keep updating once a year. Is that too much to ask for something that will pay off in the long run?"

"So why should I update annually?"

"Well, when I speak to different organizations, the biggest challenge I see for employees is that they don't know what they are supposed to be doing on a day-to-day basis. They start their jobs all full of excitement, and then ninety days later, they're sucked in by the urgency and chaos of the organization.

They forget what to do and who they are in the process. Your job as an employer is to give your team the certainty they are looking for by consistently redefining what they are expected to do. **Help them define who they are and what they stand for, and they will help you to build your business empire.**

"Another challenge I often see in many businesses is when someone leaves. When Joe Smith decides to up and leave the organization one fine morning, nobody knows the specific skill set required for the new person. Nobody knows how to train the new person, because everything Joe Smith did was in his head. Newbie Mary Ann needs to study from scratch what she is going to do for the first six months of her career. This is why, as entrepreneurs, we all must monitor what each employee does and annually update their strategic missions.

"Finally, optimization involves creating and following operations manuals for day-to-day activities. Your operation manual is the entire recipe for all the activities in your business. It will have steps to be followed by each employee to achieve their daily goals."

"In case I up and die," I say with a nod.

"In case you up and die, that's right."

A little morbid, but sensible. I like it.

"The manual must reflect the habitual way of running your business if you are not there to supervise. A process will help business owners step out of the nitty-gritty of daily firefighting and focus on the big picture. **In other words, they will start owning the business instead of operating it from their heads.**"

"Got it."

"And operations manuals with clear strategic missions provide both new and existing employees the well-deserved clarity on day-to-day business operations."

"But why have both a strategic mission and operations manual?" I ask. "Why not just one?"

"Strategic mission is the map towards the destination. Each person might be starting from a different place, but their shared destination is the same, which is the mission or purpose of the business. The operations manual is the signage that shows roads, bridges, and intersections they collectively or individually need to take to reach that destination."

Gazing out the window with this bird's eye view, the nighttime lights of Los Angeles dazzle and twinkle, like a blanket of diamonds laid out along the ebony ground below. The plane whines in its descent as Arjun and I prepare for landing. The tires screech down, and a moment later, we've landed.

Hello, LA, nice to see you again.

Upon walking into the apartment a short while later, I set my keys down in the bowl by the door, throw my bags onto the couch, and toss my body into bed. It feels nice to sink into the downy comforter and breathe in the silence. Arjun always leaves me with a lot to think about, but all good things. Things to move my life forward, definitely things to take to heart.

As usual, I find myself thanking the universe for blessing me with his presence.

Noticing a voicemail I hadn't seen since we'd landed, I press the button and hit speaker. What I hear next sends my heart plummeting into my stomach. Charlie's voice.

"Hey, Lindsay, long time no hear. Just wanted to say hi and see how you were doing. Also, just wanted to share the good news about my new job— they hired me over at Deene & Kellerman. Remember the law firm I was always after? Yeah, well, they finally got me!"

His voice sounds ecstatic, and I can't help but notice the concrete butterflies sinking to the pit of my stomach. Have I learned nothing?

"Anyway, just wanted to say...I'm sorry about how we ended. Give me a call. Maybe...I don't know..." he hesitates. "Maybe we can go out for dinner or something. You know...catch up. Anyway. Here I am, talking to a voicemail, right? Silly of me. Call me back, Linds. Love Ya."

Beep.

Love ya?

Linds?

Who does he think he is...all like, "Oh, so sorry about the fact that I kicked you out of the house and left you destitute. No worries that I've treated dogs better, hey, no biggie, right. No hard feelings. Let's just be pals and all that again, right, Linds. Forgive and forget."

What in all of holy hell?

Mouth agape, I can't stop staring out the window at the beautiful view of the city spread before me.

Charlie called.

He finally called after three months. Three months! I could have been dead, was almost dead, and he wouldn't even know it. But he got that job he always wanted, and now he wants to talk. No, better yet—he wants to see me for dinner.

So what do I do now??

PART II

MY JOURNEY

"There is nothing so useless as doing efficiently that which should not be done at all."
Peter Drucker

CHAPTER FIFTEEN
The Email Myth

Jello…

Jello is that substance that falls somewhere between liquid and solid. It doesn't completely fall apart into goo, nor does it work as a support structure like bones do, but that is what my legs feel like as I make my way to the lunch date I still can't quite believe I agreed to.

"Sorry," I quickly apologize as my uncontrollable legs run me into a woman seated at the table next to mine.

Here at a sidewalk table at Siam Bistro, with those butterflies playing rugby in my gut, and legs that won't stop quaking, I nervously wait for the man who broke my heart.

I know I shouldn't be here. Shouldn't have called him back, even if I *did* make him wait three days before doing so. It's taken me months to purge him from my system—mostly—and seeing him could reopen all my wounds.

Then again, there's nothing wrong with hearing what he has to say, is there?

What if he only wants to apologize? I would be a total jerk if I didn't at least listen.

Glancing at the time, a surge of energy shoots through my Jello legs and my inner gazelle instincts urge me to flee the predator. I still have time to go before he arrives. He's late, as usual, this was a bad decision, and I could chalk my absence up to anything—getting sick, getting tired of waiting, anything. After all, he's used to giving himself excuses. But I have no time to make a break for it, since he suddenly appears from around the corner, spots me, and smiles.

Get down! I tell those gut butterflies that have launched into my throat, even though I want to duck down out of sight, too.

Charlie doesn't deserve them, and I don't deserve to feel anything less than peace.

"There you are," he says, reaching across the railing and signaling to the hostess that he's with the lame woman sitting at the bistro table. Then, like some hugely egotistical, loser ex-lover in a romantic comedy, he hops over the barricade and plops himself right into the chair across from me. Part of me imagines him mid-air leaping over the barricade and catching his pant leg, landing with a crashing thud face first at my feet. I stifle my smile.

I can't believe it's him, same green eyes, same brown hair, same angular face, and full lips. I hate him; I hate him, I hate him…

"Hey, you." He hugs me hard.

Don't like it! Don't you dare like it, I coach my body.

I try not to breathe in the familiar, woodsy scent of him. That's all I would need is a physical trigger to send my brain into a nostalgic tizzy.

"You look great! Look at you! Wow!"

He's blowing smoke up my rear, even though he's right—I do look the best I've looked in a while. It's amazing what dropping an extra hundred and ninety pounds in the form of a crummy ex can do for a girl.

We make small talk, and, of course, he excuses himself for being late, blaming it on the traffic. Has his tardiness ever been because of him and his poor choices? The thought makes me happy that I can finally see his faults.

After we share an appetizer and make mindless sort of chatter, Charlie folds his hands and gets a good look at me. Like those gazelle instincts from earlier, the little girl inside of me wants to run far, far away before this man can start saying things that will render me stupid and useless.

"I'm really sorry for the way I treated you, Linds. You didn't deserve it."

That, for example.

"No, it's fine. You taught me a lot about myself, and in retrospect, I wasn't ready for a relationship when I had so much growing still to do."

"Well, maybe it was both of us."

"Maybe," I say.

"The thing is, Linds…" he begins, and I know I'm in trouble right away. "I want to try again. Don't you? I have a new job at the law firm. I can take care of you now. I wasn't in the position to before, but now there's no need to live a life of misery. What do you say?"

How can I say anything when my jaw just shattered the tabletop?

"Umm…"

"It's a lot to take in. I know. I'm sorry. I shouldn't have ambushed you like this. I'm sure you were starting to get your life back in order without me there to mess it all up again, huh?" He smiles sheepishly, and part of me wants to knock his teeth in. The other part of me is still thinking about his words— *"there's no need to live a life of misery."*

"Charlie," I begin, clearing my throat. "Money wasn't our only problem. There was also that pesky matter of my feeling pretty darn insignificant around you. I honestly don't know why you'd even want me back."

"What?" He reaches out and holds both my hands, looking genuinely shocked. "Linds, my life wasn't complete without you. I realized this. I thought you would be happy."

"I don't know what to feel, quite honestly, Charlie. Can I take some time to think about this?" I ask. The next words are harder to say. "I've been through a lot. You have no idea how much."

Could it be that he has had a turnaround? He seems so different, so passionate now. So invested in my feelings. Where was that Charlie when I needed him? Maybe in a bad place, like me. Shouldn't I give him the benefit of the doubt?

"Of course, Linds. Of course. I just want to say; you don't need all these risks running a failed business when I could help you transition into a great job as a software engineer. You could make comfortable money in Silicon Valley, and we could live happily ever after." His smile is bright and hopeful, and I wish, so wish I could believe his words.

Is he right? Would working for someone else be better? Less stressful and scary? My paycheck would be steady, and hey, it is a lot more than what I'm making now, which is nothing.

The Jello is back, only, this time, it's in my belly. I don't know what to do or say. Thankfully, the food comes, and two steaming plates are set down between us.

For the rest of our meal, we just eat and talk about the weather.

But the other kind of "whether" is my internal conversation...

Whether to dive into coupledom and give Charlie another chance? Or whether to stay the course and remain single.

3 Days Later—

I'm sitting in Arjun's office, waiting for him to finish a phone meeting in an adjoining room. His desk is oversized and made of mahogany, and the sounds of Vivaldi's "Four Seasons" play softly in the background.

Which season are we in?

I listen for the tell-tale notes that easily identify the textured notes in the Summer concerto. I wander over to the large window and draw in a breath at the beauty of the LA skyline.

Charlie's proposition still weighs heavily on my mind. Should I accept it? Would it go the way he described, where I make decent money post-bankruptcy while he pulls the majority of our weight? What should I do?

I hear the sounds of someone clearing their throat and I jump away from the glass.

It's Arjun. "I'm sorry if I scared you," he says with a smile. "Thank you for your patience while I wrapped up that call."

"Of course," I say. "The view and Vivaldi were keeping me company."

"I love Vivaldi concertos."

"I agree," I say, taking a seat in his leather wingback chair. "Then again, I'm a sucker for anything from the Baroque period. So relaxing and stimulating at the same time."

"And it's that harmony we are always striving for, isn't it?" Arjun takes a seat at his desk, and I'm struck by how he looks. I usually see him at a beach, a park, the woods...but today, he's every bit the businessman. "Lindsay, today, let's talk about the number one reason for failure in business, career, and life. Let me start with a story."

"Naturally," I say with a grin and a sweep of my hand.

"One day, a complex machine in a manufacturing plant broke down. The company was losing $25,000 every day. This machine was offline, but nobody could seem to fix it. Finally, the company that manufactures the machine tracked down the design engineer, who now runs a consulting company.

"When the consultant's assistant explained to him that the machine could be fixed for $75,000, all expenses to fly out there, the president didn't hesitate. He was elated. And, he told them, if they could fix it within a week, he would pay a $25,000 bonus."

"Wow," I scoff. "I'm in the wrong business."

"You don't want to fix machines, Lindsay. Listen."

"Yes, I do. $100,000 for just one week?"

"Can I continue now?" He arches one eyebrow.

"Yes, of course."

He smiles. "So, the engineer flew to the company the very next day. She arrived, checked into her five-star hotel suite, had a delicious lobster dinner, and rested for her meeting the next morning. Everybody was anxious and in awe of her expertise. Carefully, she studied the machine. 'You're a woman. Are you sure you can fix it?' the president asked."

"Oh, no, he did not," I say, shaking my head.

"'Not only can I fix it,' the woman said, 'but I bet you called me because too many men tried this but failed. But first, do you have my fee?' she asked. The president nodded. 'Of course, but...' The young woman cut him off. 'I'd like to see the check, first.' 'Okay, okay...' Frustrated, the man pulled out his $75,000 check for her. 'And the bonus?' the engineer asked. 'But you haven't even fixed anything yet!' the president cried. 'Yes, but do you have the bonus you offered?' she insisted. 'Yes, yes.' 'Good. Can somebody get me a hammer?' the engineer asked."

"Uh, oh..." I say.

"'A hammer? Whatever for?' The president was confused. But before she could explain, somebody produced a hammer, and she calmly walked over to the machine, studied the side one final time, and struck the machine with the hammer. Amazingly, the machine started purring as it went back to work. 'If you have any related issues for the next year, I will repair it for free. I'll take my check for $75,000 now. You can keep the bonus,' the engineer said."

I giggle under my breath. "Smart woman."

Arjun continues with his story. "The president said, 'All you did was whack the machine with a hammer! You want $75,000 for that? Anybody could have hit the machine for ten dollars,' he argued as he handed the payment over. 'Yes, anybody could have hit the machine,' she said, admiring then folding her check. 'My fee for hitting the machine is only eight dollars. The rest is for knowing WHERE to hit it.'"

"Ha, ha, love it." I do a slow clap for his story.

"This is what I call most intelligent actions," Arjun explains. "Since we are on the topic of hammers, with enough use of a hammer, we start to think everything is a nail. Abraham Maslow, the popular American psychologist, famously said, 'If all you have is a hammer, everything looks like a nail.' That is why just hitting somewhere is not enough. A lot of action is not enough; we need strategic actions. There are only two types of intelligent actions in business and life. High-Profit Actions and High Impact Actions."

"Okay…" I shift around in my seat. "Now, I've read plenty of books, attended many workshops on high performance, productivity, and time management. Most of them didn't work at all; some helped a little for a short time. What do you consider time management, Arjun?"

To my surprise, Arjun shrugs. "There is nothing called time management. You cannot manage time. It is a fixed entity."

"Okay… boss. What do I manage then?" I ask.

"Ha! I teach businesses and professionals how to get that edge they need to succeed and how to produce great results. Our system is called C³ — Pronounced C Cubed. C³ is a set of skills to **direct your emotions and take intelligent actions** and get the best use of the only fixed resource in life called time." Arjun says all this while staring at the thunderstorm rolling in outside. He has it all memorized.

"So, time management is emotion management?" I ask.

"Basically. Yes."

"How come? That doesn't make sense to me."

"Okay. Let me ask you a few questions. When you are with your most favorite person in life, does time fly faster than lightning?"

I haven't been with a favorite person in ages, but time with Arjun seems to go quickly. "I guess so," I say.

"Right. When you're with a person you hate, does time move like a snail?" Arjun asks.

"In the beginning, when Charlie and I were together, it was like a sugar rush, sweet, delicious and the good time just flew by. Later, it wasn't like a snail, more like dragging the dead weight of a mobile home on my back...through a river of molasses," I say as I nod fervently. "Plus, I don't even have to hate someone I'm with to feel time dragging. I may find them boring as all hell. Once, on a date, a guy asked me if I could date anyone, dead or alive, who would I date. I answered William Shakespeare. He said it has to be a real person, not a character in a play. What do you even say to that?"

Arjun shakes his head, suppressing a laugh. "Ay, ay, ay, Lindsay. Did you tell him that William Shakespeare was a real person who lived? That must've been one hell of a date. What is the difference between these two situations?"

"The difference is in the emotions I felt. With my friend, or when Charlie and I were all ga-ga, I felt connected. With my not-too-smart date, I felt like a dead fish."

"You got it. **The difference is in the intensity of emotions.** Spending time with another human being for a certain period can be perceived completely differently based on your level of emotions. So, how does your mind measure time?"

I venture a guess. "Time is measured through emotional intensity?"

"Correct." Arjun continues. "Stephen Hawking, one of the greatest scientists of this century, said the direction of time is set by the level of disorder we perceive in the world. In other words, **as we move towards the future, the level of disorder in your inner world increases.** The activities you were passionate about ten years ago do not give you any intensity today,

205

so your brain requires a high-adrenaline video game instead. We allow technology to quicken our inner chaos."

"So, Candy Crush is killing the love and contentment with my own life, and my productivity, too," I say.

"You got it."

"Darn. I knew it."

"That is why, even though we now have the best technological tools at our disposal, productivity has dramatically dropped. Are we still hitting with the hammer for ten dollars? Yes. We are hitting day and night on iPhones and Androids and other smartphones. Do we know where to hit? We have no clue, maybe Facebook and Twitter?"

"Or Instagram. I'd put my money on Instagram."

Arjun laughs and continues, "Many productivity coaches say that email is the fundamental productivity killer in modern society. It is not. Although, I agree, emails are the 'To-Do List' for other people."

"What do you think is the killer of productivity, Arjun?" I ask.

"I think it's the level of disorder inside of us—entropy. **When your entropy increases, passion decreases. When your passion decreases, productivity diminishes.**" He pulls a sticky note off a stack on his desk and writes that down like he likes the way it sounds.

"For me, email takes up lots of valuable time. From everyone I know, too. I'll have to disagree on this one."

"Lindsay, when do you check your email?" Arjun asks, folding his hands, and I feel another story or lesson coming.

"When don't I check it? I refresh pretty much all day long."

"All right. Why do you check your email all day long?"

"I want to be responsive to my clients. I feel good when I check it, like I'm scratching things off my to-do list. I almost feel like I'm living in an emotional prison, though, like the next email or Facebook status update is going to make me feel different."

"Good observation, Lindsay. Are you saying you need to feel emotional intensity and you get it by checking emails or Facebook updates?"

"I guess so," I say. "I mean, I can't be doing nothing at all. I need to be doing something. I'm distracted and can't focus most of the time."

I always knew Facebook was a time-suck, but it also makes me feel connected to people I'd otherwise never see.

"Does that sound like something we talked about just now?" he asks.

"Entropy? Level of disorder?" I nod slowly. Ugh, I walked right into that trap, didn't I?

"Let me ask you this. Do you postpone?"

"I do it only for one day at a time. I even created the new tagline for Nike, 'Just Do it, tomorrow. If there is no rain.' I am also the president of a meet up called procrastinators unite - tomorrow."

"Haha. Nice tagline and idea. So you do have some experience in this field of procrastination. When you do, is it because you are not physically capable of doing something or you are not emotionally ready?"

"Not emotionally ready," I say.

"When people say they do not have time, what they are really saying is they do not have the energy to manage their emotions. We only have twenty-four hours a day. In this country, some people make $1,000 an hour while others make less than ten dollars an hour. If you are not able to **manage your emotions** when you are making $8 an hour, how could we make you the chairman of Apple?"

"'Whoever can be trusted with very little can also be trusted with much.'" I get it.

"Lindsay…" He shifts around in his seat, preparing to say the same thing in different words. I've seen him do this before. "If you do not remember anything else I am saying today, remember this: **Results are achieved through managing emotions.** To defy your entropy, first, you need to reach your peak state of mind called Ananda. Does this sound familiar?"

"Ah, Ananda. It all boils down to Ananda for you," I say with a teasing groan.

He chuckles. "That's right, and I already taught you how to do this. If you don't manage your emotions, your brain goes to autopilot mode and feels the intensity by worrying about your projects instead. That's why, before you start working on your business, you must reach Ananda all the time. Do two minutes of Accelerator Breathing in your car to reach that peak state if you are in a real hurry."

I pull out my iPad and say aloud, as I write, "Two minutes…breathing…peak state for optimum Lindsay."

"Tell me why you need to master productivity?" He nods his head, clearly tickled at giving me this pop quiz.

"Okay…well…productivity is important for several reasons, the main one being that my time is fixed. I don't have more time than anyone else I meet in the street. If I lose money or even relationships, I might be able to get those back. But if time is wasted, poof—it's gone forever. Time's a fundamental resource I can use for building wealth and creating many fun experiences for me and my loved ones. I want to spend quality time with my family and friends. The better I can manage time to do what *I* want to do, the more fulfilled I will be in life."

I take a huge breath and let it out. *Whoa—I sound like an infomercial.*

"Excellent, Lindsay, excellent," Arjun says, giving me a quiet clap. "We all have more things to do than we could possibly handle. We want to spend time watching the news, playing games on the computer or internet… It's enough to keep us occupied for months. Add to that two to three email accounts, plus three social media accounts that keep alerting us to new, exciting things every three seconds. Our inner world has become a high traffic information highway. We are sociologically and psychologically preconditioned to instantly respond to this overload of information."

"It's true. Why do I have that compulsion to look at every notification or to answer everything right away?"

"One, because you're a nice person, and two, because your brain wants to deal with the more fun, exciting items with less impact first. **Our brains are addicted to mediocre actions.**"

"So my brain is doing mediocre, half-arsed work and it's time for the whole arse. Well, yeah, and in my experience, it's easy to confuse actions with achievements. Just because I responded to hundreds of emails doesn't mean that I achieved anything significant. Random actions are not achievements!"

"Exactly right, Lindsay. That is where C^3 comes in handy. It will help you eliminate stress, filter out useless actions, and FOCUS only on the *intelligent actions* that will give you the most return on your investment of time. It helps you to focus on what is most important for you while passionately completing the project."

Arjun, unable to sit for very long, gets up and begins walking around his large office. "If you study the last hundred years of productivity literature, you will see that they are all rooted on four major systems. I've read hundreds of books on the subject, because I was frustrated, like you. Some were great, others…"

"Meh?" I offer.

"Yes, I never used that word before, but I like it. *Meh* pretty much describes them. Okay, let's take a very brief look at how it all started. Four major productivity philosophies encompass the evolution of hundreds of time management systems we have developed over the last century. Let us jump in, shall we?"

"Yes. I'm excited. Let's do this!"

CHAPTER SIXTEEN
Productivity Revolution

"The earliest practical productivity system I know of started about a hundred years ago. **Charles Schwab** was the chief executive officer for Bethlehem Steel Company. One day, a man named **Ivy Lee** came to him with the following claim: 'I can increase your people's efficiency and your sales if you will allow me to spend fifteen minutes with you.' He did not charge Schwab any upfront fee. He simply wanted him to try the idea for a month or so, then pay Lee what he thought the information was worth. After only three weeks, Schwab sent Mr. Lee a check for $25,000 (worth around $750,000 today)."

Arjun pauses at the window to stare out, hands clasped behind his back.

"So, what was Ivy Lee's golden advice?" I ask, turning in my seat to face him, a little bowled over by the number.

"Every evening, make a list of all the things that are on your mind which you need to work on the following day. Don't leave anything out. The order does not matter. Then decide which are the first three things you will work on, and write the numbers 1, 2, 3 against them. Don't go any further than that. On the next day, start **on number one. Do not start on number two until you have finished number one!**"

"Seems reasonable."

"This is a To-Do list with a decent priority system. The concept of today's To-Do lists are modified versions of this advice."

"Believe me; I'm the Queen of To-Do lists. I've tried every single kind, and no matter how organized my lists are, my life is as complex as ever. My

To-Do lists end up more like a Doo-Doo list. Useless."

"It is not you, Lindsay!" Arjun turns to look at me, hands in his pockets. "Working from a To-Do list is not enough for today's fast-paced entrepreneurs. I could see how this worked for managing time in the 1920s but not for today. This lack of efficiency gave birth to the three other major approaches of productivity."

I get ready to jot them down.

"Towards the 1980s, the need for fulfillment and meaning in life became vitally important in our work-life-relationship trifecta. This gave birth to a new paradigm of productivity that I call **Purpose Driven Productivity.** The productivity gurus in this category believed that they needed to begin any project with the end in mind. According to this school of thought, seeing the end outcome before you start your day or project is the best way to FOCUS on the most important things. This is a proactive and intrinsic approach. You should have the right map towards your end goal. According to this philosophy, if you are using a map of New York to travel to Manhattan, great. Using that same map to travel in London, you will not reach your destination. One of the major thought leaders of this philosophy compiled four quadrants of productivity to convey the idea that most people use today." Arjun goes over to his desk, grabs his iPad, and lays it on my armrest. I peer down at the diagram filling the screen:

	Urgent	Not Urgent
Important	I	II
Not Important	III	IV

"Now, let me ask you, Lindsay, which quadrant should you be spending most of your time in?"

I examine the diagram. "Quadrant I, because I should be working on things that are important and urgent." At least, that's what makes the most sense to me.

"Interestingly, many of my seminar attendees invariably say Quadrant I, but that is a perfect recipe for a stress breakdown! We have been conditioned to work on important and urgent actions our entire lives, so we think those are the most pressing ones. We unconsciously assume most pressing must mean most important. The correct answer is Quadrant II. You need to work on the important – not urgent – actions to take your business to the next level. Working **in** your business as we discussed before is a Quadrant I activity. Mastering your business is a Quadrant II activity.

"Since this philosophy is aligned with your purpose, you are inherently motivated. They ask you to define your life's purpose and clarify the major categories/roles in your life. Once you find the major categories, find your ultimate vision or outcome for each of them. They recommended capturing the ideas and actions into corresponding roles. Most of them suggested that we must find purpose for every outcome before taking action."

"Does it work?" I ask.

"It caused big problems for me," Arjun says. "Whenever my wife asked me to clean the house since she is washing all the dishes, I asked her what the purpose for it is? I don't see the need."

"Holy crap, Arjun. And you're still with us? I would've taken a frying pan to your head for that." I laugh.

"Why do you think people like me quit using these systems? They're very complex, not to mention impractical. Writing down the reasons for all the actions one takes in his or her entire life? Let's assume you are an overachiever; you'll be writing ninety reasons per week. In addition to that, managing major roles adds one more layer of complexity and takes up a significant chunk of your time. How about doing laundry, cleaning your kitchen, or changing the oil in your car? What categories do those belong to? How about checking email? Do I find purpose for all the emails with this system? How do I use my calendar? How do you manage the ideas that come to you while you are taking a bath?"

"Oh, my God! That one happens to me all the time!" I groan.

"Isn't it funny you get the best ideas when you bathe?" he asks. "These could be overwhelming to most people. Does it have to be that difficult? Most importantly, how could I be productive at my highly demanding place of business or work?"

I'm tired just considering all these questions. I shrug.

"That is why the next philosophy evolved," he says, wagging his finger at me. "As always in evolution, it went the extreme opposite direction. Towards early 2000, demands on employees to get stuff done quickly raised dramatically. This led to wide acceptance of what I call **Project Driven Productivity**. This was the first philosophy to come up with a decent framework for getting project-based things done. Thus, this philosophy was accepted as extrinsic—-meaning, getting the externally focused stuff done. It created efficient project workflows that help people perform better for customers or employers. But their personal lives and energy level sucked. They did not have the concept of priority or roles or even a concept of what was important or urgent. This philosophy used control, context, and perspective as the guiding principles.

"In the current world, where almost everyone lacks control, people were blind to everything else. So these systems naturally evolved into reactive systems that help you manage things by controlling them. The steps they suggested were of effective planning, including capture, clarify, organize, review and do. They kept you free by using capture as a constant tool. Actions were scheduled based on contexts, such as office, home, or wherever. Context means you schedule your actions based on where you are physically located. Sounds pretty complex already, right?"

"I'm going to need a drink to process that. Got any vodka?"

"I'm fresh out of vodka, Lindsay. How about some water?"

"H_2O.k. That'll do."

Arjun pulls open a small refrigerator blending in with the wall and removes an ice-cold bottle of water, handing it to me. "There you go."

"Thanks. One more thing I can scratch off my To-Do list!" I smile.

"For perspective, this model uses an airplane taking off as a metaphor. You review your projects from the runway, at 10,000 feet, at 20,000 feet, and so on. This is an excellent **project management system**. To be fair, to each of these giants of which I speak, they all agreed that we needed a productivity system that integrated intrinsic—- meaning internally focused and extrinsic—- meaning external outcomes. But most people's limited perception about these systems based on their current **need** became their system."

Arjun shifts around the room like a light ghost. Sometimes I wonder where he goes when he's talking, but I do my best to keep up and listen.

"Then, there's the famous two-minute rule, which says if something can be done in two minutes or less, do it right away. Great idea, but it has its challenges, too. For example, did you know that around fifteen percent of Americans take cell phone calls while they are making love?"

"Really?" I ask. "How does that go? 'Hey, honey, can you please hold your position while I take this super important business call? Should only take two minutes.' 'Baby, we can be done before that!' I crack me up, Arjun." I laugh at my stupid joke.

"Nice one, Lindsay."

"Thank you. I'll be here all week," I say. "Don't forget to tip your waitress."

But jokes don't sway Arjun from making his point. "The problem with this system is it has no concept of priority. It is a reactive system, which assumes if your mind is clear and free, you will automatically be focused on the most creative things. In an ideal world, that would be true. We need drive, motivation, and reasons to focus on the most important things.

"This philosophy needs a lot of time investment just to be on track because of the many steps involved. So people either got fed up and quit, or they went to the superficial implementation mode. In the long run, if you didn't quit, you could still be working hard, but you are stressed and might not be fulfilled. Even worse, when you drop this system, which is highly likely, your mind becomes even more clogged and closed to new ideas. You might start to think there is something wrong with you personally, which is why these don't work for you. Or even worse, your work life will be great, but your personal life could be terrible. This phenomenon gave birth to the next evolution of productivity. I call it the **Power Driven Productivity.**"

"Power...Driven...Productivity." I write it all down, trying to keep up with Arjun's brain.

"Yes, leaders of this philosophy believe that the ultimate measure of life is not the time we spend, but rather how much energy we invest. They believe the more energy we bring to the workplace, the more empowered and productive we become. Since energy capacity diminishes with use, or lack thereof, they recommended we balance energy with intermittent renewal. They also recommended taking multiple small vacations a year, so you can rejuvenate and become more productive."

"Yeah, that's a dream come true," I say with a wistful sigh.

"Your brain needs time off, Lindsay. They talked about drawing energy from physical, emotional, mental and spiritual areas of our lives. This philosophy taught us to demand more from each area, so we build strength on each. Leaders of this system taught us to incorporate daily rituals that catapult your energy. They ask you to find your deepest values and greatest strengths and find your personal and business vision. They help you find barriers that stop you from fulfilling your vision and help you build habits to strengthen each of the four areas, including physical, emotional, mental and spiritual, so you are better prepared to overcome those barriers."

"Information overload," I say, shaking my head. "This sounds like an incredible system, though, and I'd be happy to build strength on each of these areas. But what do I do when things hit my fan at a hundred miles per hour?" I tap the stylus against the armrest, thinking of all the times "things" have hit the fan.

"Ah," Arjun says, pointing at me. "You are thinking. That was exactly what they missed. This philosophy did not have an essential framework to get results. These systems are not useless. Each approach has its own benefits, although it's hard to implement any of these as a comprehensive system. If you look historically at productivity literature, in a hundred years, we evolved from To-Do list, at least some of us, to Purpose Driven Productivity to Power

Driven systems. The emphasis changes based on the relevant need at the time, level of entropy, or what we lacked in that period. Many smart people tried all or some of the systems and failed, starting with me. It reduced their stress for one week, then the second week, they were back on the stress roller coaster again. They gave up all the systems and went back to, you guessed it…"

"To-Do lists in their head?"

"That's right." He laughs his bubbly, happy laugh. "We are creatures of habit, Lindsay. Effective systems must be simple and powerful enough to crush our inner resistance. They should also help you to identify and integrate the intrinsic and extrinsic actions and help you lead a stress-free life. Too many external actions will suck the life out of you. Too many internal actions will make you not want to do anything. **Integrating the duality of internal and external actions is the key to be an effective person.** The bottom line is that none of these systems are comprehensive enough to help you align with your purpose while being productive at the same time. We needed a completely new way of thinking to do that. For years, I asked why can't we have a system that encompass all these? Why can't we come up with a system that will align you more towards your purpose while driving your projects to completion at lightning speed? How can we do both with high levels of energy most of the time? What vital productivity principles did all of these systems miss that I can integrate into my life and business?"

"I don't know, but I can't wait to find out!"

CHAPTER SEVENTEEN
The Three Missing Gems

"And I will tell you! But first, here are three principles of productivity that most of them missed. I touched on this on the first day we met but did not give you any background information. In 1906, Italian economist Vilfredo Pareto created a mathematical formula to describe the unequal distribution of wealth in his country, observing that **twenty percent of the people owned eighty percent of the wealth**. After Pareto created his formula, others observed similar phenomena in their areas of expertise, including sales, marketing and productivity.

"In productivity literature, Pareto's principle can be rephrased as the following: **Principle #1 80% of your results will come from 20% of your action.** At any given time, you need to identify and work on those 20% actions for maximum effectiveness."

"Yes, I've been thinking about this a lot since you last mentioned it. How do I find out my 20% intelligent actions?" I ask. "Because I am *all* about only doing 20% of the work, trust me."

"Find the ten important actions that you can do to grow your business. Ask the question: What are the two out of ten actions that would give the biggest result for my business? The results can be two types. Profit for the company or impact for the customer. Those are your 20% actions."

"I can spend most of my time on those 20% actions that are intelligent," I reply.

"Excellent!" Arjun comes around and lightly punches my shoulder. He's no different from any other kind of coach—football, swimming, gymnastics…small business. "Finally, 80% of your results come from 20% of your time. I call it Flow Time. But here, first, write this all down. Ready?

"**Principle #2 Parkinson's Law states that the demand upon a resource tends to expand to match the supply of the resource.** Let me ask you this, what was the lowest annual income you had in a full-time career? What was the highest?"

I have to think back a bit to all the jobs I ever worked. "The lowest was $15,000 a year, and the highest was $120,000."

"Very good. How much did you spend when you made $15,000?"

"Probably around $17,000." I laugh ruefully.

"I figure you had used a credit card for the rest. How about when you made $120,000?"

"Like a kid in the candy store, I spent it all," I say. "I guess it was just a higher level of poverty, because I still had nothing at the end of the day."

"Very well. The same person who lived at $17,000 spent $120,000 when the supply of money was abundant. Correct?"

"Yes. But how is this related to getting results?" I ask. "No offense, Arjun, but remembering all the money I've wasted is really bringing me down."

"I'm sorry, Lindsay. That is not my intent. Let me explain. Time is the same way. The more time you allocate to a project, the more time it will take to finish it. For productivity, you could rephrase this law as—**Work expands to fill the time available for its completion.**

If you don't challenge yourself and set a higher standard for yourself, you could fall into this trap.

"A classic example is SpaceX. SpaceX, with its limited resources, was about to build and launch a rocket in six years, when NASA, with its unlimited resources, took several decades to do the same."

"**Principle #3, Flow Time,**" he says in almost the same breath. "According to Mihály Csíkszentmihályi, **flow** is the mental state in which a person is fully immersed in a feeling of energized focus, involvement, and enjoyment in the activity. This positive psychology has been widely referenced across a variety of fields. In business, you can experience Ananda and the suspension of time, the freedom of complete absorption in activity. Flow is one of the most valuable experiences an entrepreneur or a professional can have, even more than making money. Flow time is done not just for a future result but also because being in flow itself is a reward. The best experiences usually occur when your mind expands its limits in a passionate endeavor to accomplish something challenging and meaningful. Flow is when time disappears altogether, and you are in **complete control of emotions** in the service of performance."

"The zone."

"Say it again?" he asks.

"The zone. You know, when people say they're in the zone? They're totally absorbed by the joy of what they're doing."

"Ah, yes. Good, Lindsay. Remember I told you, time is measured in emotion. Most successful entrepreneurs always focus on and do the next intelligent actions and do them as soon as they can."

Accelerator # 5 - Focus on Intelligent Actions.

"This is not just a business concept. There are business flow times, personal flow times, relationship flow times, and celebration flow times."

"I see."

"What are the most productive hours of your typical day? For some people, it is between 7:00 a.m. to 10:00 a.m. For others, it may be 10:00 p.m. to 1:00 a.m. What are yours?"

"Definitely 9:00 a.m. to 12:00 noon, thanks to my nine-to-five work life before," I explain.

"Yes, that makes sense. Now, tell me the three things you value most in your life?"

"Relationship, wealth, and health," I say, confident about my choices.

"Good. What is your ultimate vision about wealth?"

"I must have at least two million dollars in net asset with $100,000 in passive income."

"Very well. What is a word or phrase that will describe your personal identity once you reach that kind of financial success?"

"Uhhh…" I struggled to think of one. "Lindsay Big Bucks. Or maybe Rich Chick?" I ask with a chuckle.

"I like it, sounds excellent. Good, you have defined one of the power roles (PR) in your *personal life*. When you go home tonight, do the same for relationship and health. Now, what do you value most in your business?"

"More Benjamin Franklins! Make it rain! Make it rain!" I laughed, pretending to be throwing dollar bills high into the sky.

"Great, so positive cash flow is one of them."

"Heck to the yeah! I mean, yes." I smile politely, reining myself in. "Also, revenue growth and using my full throttle creativity."

"Of course. Now, tell me what is your ultimate vision about cash flow."

"Let's see…I should be able to have ample money to invest in my product development. I should have surplus money to take care of my extraordinary team and enough reserve for a rainy day."

This sounds about right and reasonable.

"That sounds like a plan. What is a word or phrase to describe your business identity once you reach that kind of cash flow?" he asks.

"Benjamin Franklin is my buddy!" Goofy, but it does sum up my feelings. I want to make money work for me, not have me working for money. "Just kidding. Let's go with Queen of Cash."

Luckily, Arjun is laughing his salt-and-peppered head off.

And I can't help but feel like I've already succeeded somehow…

CHAPTER EIGHTEEN
Time to Profit

"Ready to keep going?" he asks, once he's done laughing.

"Yup. Hit me with it."

"All right. So, C³ not only integrates all these philosophies and gives you a three-step framework, but it also helps you achieve the intrinsic as well as the extrinsic outcomes.

"C³ has only three simple steps:

1. CAPTURE
2. CLARIFY
3. COMPLETE

"**Capture** is the elimination of unresolved actions from your mind. It's getting rid of your inner hullaballoo. Too many mental lists are robbing your energy like junk food. Your mind just needs to know that you will act on it. If you have too many things going on in your head, you are constantly dragging your energy down by unconsciously planning for 24 hours a day. The technical term for this type of planning is **worrying**. If you get good enough at worrying, you can be promoted to **anxiety**."

"I'm already the V.P. of that department and on the fast-track to making partner!" I raise my stylus up high in solidarity. "I could run an anxiety ashram with daily activities like working out on a human hamster wheel, spinning the same anxieties around and over and over, and over…"

"Are you sure you're an expert?" He raises an eyebrow and chuckles.

"Exactly when was the last time you were worried about an earthquake killing fifty thousand people, or a tsunami taking 230,000 lives, or even 3.1 million kids dying from starvation every year?"

"Man, Arjun. Why do you have to be such a killjoy? Here I was, thinking I was an expert worrier. I mean, I do care about these things, but I don't think about them all the time. But now I am. Thanks. I think…"

"I know you care, and that is why I am investing in you. But when was the last time you were so worried about those things, you couldn't sleep?"

"Never."

"You know why?"

"Because I'm a selfish monster who only thinks of my misfortune?"

"No, it's because it's out of your head. **Out of head, out of mind.** It feels like someone else's problem, doesn't it? **Getting something out of your head transforms the experience from subjectively stressful to objectively delightful.** Capture is your ticket to a stress-free life. This is what Archimedes did when he ran naked through the streets of Rome."

"Are you implying that I need to run naked through my neighborhood to get things out of my head and be stress-free? Maybe there's something better like Evernote.com to capture ideas? Would you recommend that?" I ask.

"Jerry Seinfeld captured all the jokes he ever thought of on paper. Getting your ideas and actions out of your head is the number one way to unleash the genius in you. This, I believe, is one of the major reasons Jerry became the first, self-made comedian billionaire. To answer your question, Evernote is very good for capturing ideas that do not need immediate actions. If you use Microsoft Word, you can use OneNote, a free tool that ships with Microsoft's office product. Trello.com or Asana.com are great tools to capture your ideas, too. These tools are examples of what is available today. Every 1-3 years, I recommend shopping for better tools. I recommend you keep two Capture lists, one for business and one for your personal life. Capture all ideas, actions, projects, communications and all the other things you want to do."

"I kind of do this already," I say.

"Good, then let's go to the next step, which is **Clarify**. Clarify is the backbone of C³. In clarify, you are refining the ideas and actions you have captured and identifying the next intelligent actions to take. I will give you a step by step process to do this. Without clarifying, you are depending on your willpower to get things done. Clarifying lets you use less of your willpower, so it does not wear out. Some people tell me they do not have time for clarifying. I tell them that is exactly why they must do it. If they are not spending thirty minutes clarifying the outcomes, they are clarifying and worrying 24/7."

"Then they definitely don't have time to do that." I laugh.

"If you haven't captured anything in the last 24 hours, there is nothing to clarify. Here is how you clarify. You take the first idea you have captured and ask the following question. **Is there an important result?**"

"What are the results for you?" I ask.

"Results are outcomes that will generate more profit or more impact or at least move things in that direction. If there is no profit or impact, there are no results. If there is no result, move this idea to trash." Arjun reaches for his iPad again and then flips it back toward me.

C³ Productivity Flow

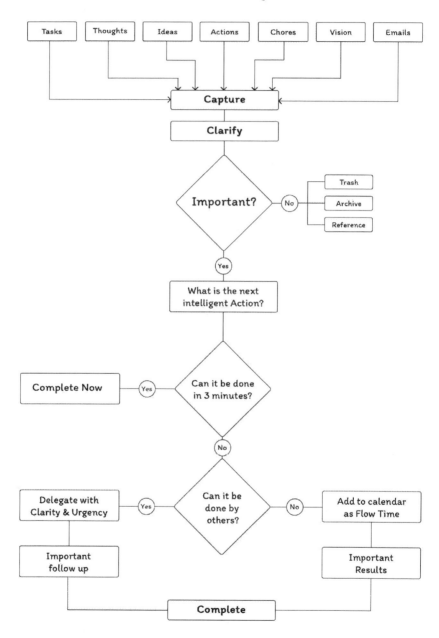

I pull it close and examine the diagram displayed there.

"What this question does is," he says, "it takes away all the Captures that are not result driven. It takes away the low priority weeds off your mental garden. You will be working only on result driven actions at this point. **It is prioritized for you already.** Once you know that you are working on an important outcome, what do you think is the next thing to do?" Arjun asks.

"I need to find the most efficient way to do it."

"Exactly. You do this by asking the next question, **'What is the next intelligent action on this?'** Can you tell me what this question does?"

"It weeds out unintelligent and least productive actions to get to the results?" I ask, hoping I've absorbed any info that Arjun has imparted to me today.

"That is correct. **You automatically apply Pareto's principle,** the idea of 80% of results come from 20% actions, by weeding out the lousy actions. Remember, there are only two types of intelligent actions; High-Profit or High Impact. What if you can finish this action in three minutes or less? For some people, by the time they add it to their system, it will be five minutes. That is why you ask, **'Can this be done in 3 minutes?'** If it can be done in three minutes or less, do it right away and mark it as complete. If there is an intelligent action with an important result, and it can be done in three minutes or less, do it right then and there as you are Clarifying."

"Why three minutes? What's so special about three minutes?"

"Great question. Here's why—the cost of a single interruption is around thirty minutes. If you were interrupted while focused on something, depending on who you are, it takes you between fifteen to thirty minutes to get back to full attention. I have observed that for most people, about three minutes is the period that they could be interrupted and still not lose focus. At this point, you know the idea you have has an important result, you figured the next intelligent action, and you know it cannot be done in three minutes. The question then is to ask is—**Can this be done by others?**" If it can be done by others, this will give you leverage to work on your most important results. As you delegate, make sure that you communicate with absolute clarity about the end result. Let them get to the result in their own ways, you only care about the result. Keep in mind, if there is urgency or deadline associated with the result, make sure that they are clearly conveyed."

"What if the building is on fire?"

"If there is a fire, don't sit down to Clarify. You or your team must put it out by finding the deadline and giving yourself enough alerts for it. If urgency is a ten out of ten, you might need to leave everything you are doing to put out that fire. **The beautiful thing about Clarify is that it's an urgency killer.**"

"What do you mean?" I ask.

"If you're used to doing only urgent things all the time, you could become addicted to it. You might be feeling an adrenaline rush or a false sense of engagement when you do urgent things at the last minute. You might be telling yourself and others, 'No one could put out these fires, except me.' The more clarifying you do, the less urgencies will pop up unannounced. Since you are on top of things, the number of urgencies will diminish a lot over time."

"So urgency is like holding the match in one hand, igniting adrenaline, while trying to play firefighter with the other. OMG! That's an over-inflated, bouncy castle-sized ego."

"Exactly because you've become so good at handling urgencies. Remember, one who is good at hammer…"

"…thinks everything is a nail, and I don't want to run around playing whack-a-mole or whack-a-nail. And I definitely don't want to create more work for myself."

These mini emergencies had always popped up for me to solve, who knew I was part of their creation?

"Back to delegation. Once you do, mark the action as Important Follow-up (#IF). If it cannot be delegated, we will move to my favorite part. Schedule them as Important Results (#IR) on your next available flow time with clearly defined next intelligent actions."

"Sounds good. Time to step it up? Get it? I know you've got steps for this," I say teasingly.

"Yes, this might sound like many steps, but keep in mind, after a week, these questions become second nature to you. You will reach a point where you look at the captured idea and ask these questions simultaneously and Clarify in seconds.

"Once you finish the first idea, go to the next idea that is captured until you finish all of them. I recommend spending 30 minutes clarifying every working day.

"The next and final step is **Complete**. Complete involves finishing the next intelligent actions (#NIA) and following through on the important follow-ups (#IF). Before you start your flow time to kill all unnecessary alerts that hinder your productivity, get rid of all the email and social media alerts, put your cell phone on silent, and commit yourself not to take any phone calls during that period. Check your voice and text messages to see if the building is on fire. Do not respond to either unless it is an emergency. Communicate to everyone in your office and home about when your flow time is. Tell them you don't check your email until the afternoon, but they can text you or call anytime in case of an emergency. This trains them not to interrupt you every three seconds. If someone wants to talk to you, ask if it can wait until the afternoon. If it can't, tell them you are working on something, and you will be available in forty-five minutes or less. If they say it cannot wait, it is either an emergency or they don't know how to manage their priorities. Time-box your actions to 45 minutes starting at 9:00 a.m. with 15 minute renewals."

"What does that mean, exactly?" I ask, a little confused.

"Start your flow time at 9:00 a.m. and set a timer for 45 minutes and work on the next intelligent action on your business and only that. In this case, you are time-boxing for 45 minutes. At the end of 45 minutes, renew yourself for 15 minutes by taking a short walk inside the office, a water break or stretching or doing something that relaxes you. You can even check your phone and text messages for emergencies at this time. Use a timer to keep you accountable. Repeat this from 10:00 a.m. to 10:45 a.m. and so on. After the third flow time, take more time for renewal, if needed."

"So I focus for 45 minutes, renew for 15 minutes and repeat."

"That is it. It works," Arjun says again. "This is what separates ineffective people from highly effective people."

"Got it," I say.

"The other steps are not valuable if you don't effectively complete your next intelligent actions and attain results. Don't mix up the times and do renewal for 45 minutes and flow time for 15." I can't help but notice Arjun's playful smile when he says that.

"Thank you for clarifying," I say. "I definitely would've done that."

"One key thing that you need to remember as you complete your task is to abandon perfection and finish it on time with excellence. You can always come back and fix the defects from initial result and make it outstanding, so don't focus on that right now, either. Let us jump into and finish the final step, shall we?"

"Let's," I agree. It's getting pretty late in the afternoon, and I still need to go by the gym before going to the apartment.

Yes, I go to the gym everyday after Arjun's teased me about my shortness of breath. Something about these lessons make me want to get started on things right away, and health and fitness feel suddenly very important to my overall success.

"Here are a few best practices that help you leverage your time even more. Best practice number one is Envision. For Envision, see your ultimate vision of your life and simply answer these three questions at the end of each day. 'What is the one most important result for my business tomorrow? Why is it important for my business? What is the next intelligent action to reach to that outcome?' Once you identify those intelligent actions, schedule them in your calendar in your flow time the very next day.

"Ask the same for your personal life, as well.

'What could be the biggest breakthrough in my personal life tomorrow? What is the most important result I am looking to achieve by end of the day tomorrow? What is the next intelligent action to reach to that outcome?' Once you get the answers, you schedule that in your calendar and visualize yourself enjoying and completing it. I recommend you spend between 5 minutes to 15 minutes time-boxed for envisioning but not more than that."

"Can I spend less time than I've allotted?"

"Yes. I recommend **envisioning at least five minutes every day towards** the end of the day. **Time-box your planning and bias actions over heavy planning.** Envisioning can be done daily, weekly and quarterly or yearly, all time-boxed to fifteen minutes with similar questions. You can do it by asking a very simple question. 'Ten years from now, when I look back at this day/week/quarter/year, what would be one result for my business/life I would be most proud of?'"

"Seems pretty simple but very powerful."

"Here is best practice number two, **Reflection**. The purpose of reflection is to help you feel fulfilled by integrating the progress. I time-boxed my reflections to 5 minutes a day, although you can do more. Reflection involves only one set of questions—'What remarkable result did I accomplish in my business/personal life today? How does that make me feel?' I believe that success or failure is a collection of daily actions. These questions will help you integrate your day's success into your nervous system. The next question is: 'How can I be more effective with people and more efficient with systems tomorrow?' This is a perennial optimization question that I designed for coaching clients years ago."

"Why did you say effective with people and more efficient with systems?" I ask.

"That might be a discussion for another day, Lindsay. Here is best practice number three. I sleep for an average of seven hours a day. For at least two decades, I used every opportunity to get a power nap during the day. Research shows that a twenty-minute power nap will fully energize pilots who fly internationally. It can also boost your memory, cognitive skills, and creativity, as well. Inarguably one of the the smartest men who ever lived on this planet, Leonardo da Vinci, the greatest American inventor of all time, Thomas Edison, world leaders like John F. Kennedy, Ronald Reagan, and Winston Churchill all took power naps almost daily. So can you."

"Yes! I knew I was onto something! I'm gonna take a nap right now. Sorry, Arjun." I settle into his wingback chair and pretend I'm snoozing.

"Wake up, Lindsay. Do you have any questions about what you learned today?" Arjun asks with a laugh. I hear him going through his desk drawer.

I pretend to be startled awake. "What? Hmm? Oh, yes I do. Are you suggesting that I should work only on forty-five minute intervals?"

"No. There is no hard and fast rule that you should work only in forty-five minute intervals. At this point in my life, I do two hours flow time with thirty minutes renewal."

"As I use flow time, how do I handle interruptions?" I ask. Not that anyone is going to interrupt me at this point, except for maybe my mom to see how I'm doing.

"Set the expectations with each and everyone you work with. Long ago, I started asking everyone who came to me the following fun question with a poker face—'Can this wait until next Thursday afternoon at 3:00 p.m.?' At that point, everyone typically laughed and gave the latest time they could have the result. Often, people just wanted to off-load the action from their head. They are unknowingly trying to use you as their capture system. They just want to know that it will be taken care of. Show them if you commit to something, it *will* be done. They might not even have a deadline. Practice saying NO with a smile or a sexy voice. The first time, it might feel weird, but you will master this skill in no time. Let the other person's chimp belong where it belongs, not on your shoulder."

"Chimp." I laugh. Such silly metaphors. "How about priorities? I haven't heard you talk about priorities."

"And you won't right now, because my mouth is tired from talking, and you, dear lady, need a break. But I will say, priorities are automated in C^3. The moment you ask the question, 'Is there an important result?' You automatically eliminate all unimportant ones. Now it's a matter of urgency. When you ask yourself, 'What is the urgency for this result?' You know what is urgent, and you handle them by scheduling on your calendar. This is another reason why you will clarify every working day."

"I think eliminating checking for emails will be the hardest for me."

"We apply the same rules for emails, as well. Emails are already **captured** into your inbox. So you can skip that step and move on to the next step, Clarify. The question is, 'Is there an important result?' If it is no, then Archive it. If the answer is yes, ask the next question: 'Can it be done in 3 minutes?' If yes, then do it right then and there. Other than this, never work from your inbox."

"And how do I do that?" I ask, curious.

"If you see it cannot be done in three minutes, ask the question—Can it be delegated? If so, delegate and move it to a folder or mark it as important follow-up (#IF). There is only one final category. It is important, cannot be done in three minutes, and cannot be delegated. Move those into a folder or label them as important results (#IR). Constantly review these folders and see what the next intelligent action on each of these is."

I peak at his iPad and review the steps to manage my emails efficiently.

C³ Email Mastery

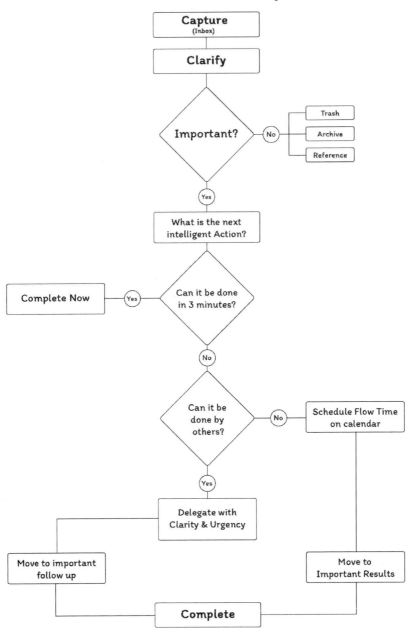

He demonstrates how to manage my email in half the time.

"I have a laundry list of unfinished actions in my head. What about those?" I ask. My brain is on fire, and I need to do this right.

"Dedicate three flow times for this. Start a free account on Trello or Asana and create two boards—one for personal and one for business. Capture all open loops you have about your personal life one at a time in the personal board for 45 minutes straight. Write everything that comes to your mind. You might even repeat stuff, don't worry, keep writing. Take 15 minutes break and write all your tasks, ideas, or actions in your head for your business. Keep writing for 45 minutes or until you do not have anything more to write. If you are familiar with Trello or Asana, use it. If you're too scared of technology, use paper."

"Scared of technology? I love it. Remember, I'm an engineer." I waggle my brows at him.

"In the next flow time, clarify each of these using the same steps above. Abandon or archive ideas that are not productive. Delete the duplicates. In fact, do it this week. I am curious to see how you feel after you dump all the stress from your body."

"Wow, you have just given me a tsunami of information. I don't even know where to begin processing it," I say, but when Arjun looks like he's going to tell me how to do that, as well, I hold up a hand. "No, I got this. Seriously. Thank you so much."

"You are very welcome. Don't forget to finish your homework and free up your head before the next session this afternoon at 2:00 pm."

"Got it." Putting all my things away in my bag, I nod and shake Arjun's smooth hand. I walk out of his office with enough energy to light a village.

I'm so excited. I will do all the new lessons, but I still have a nagging little voice in my head asking if the risk is worth it?

What if I fail again? Charlie promised that he'll get me through my mess but, if I remember correctly, he was good at overpromising and under-delivering. Honestly, I can't trust him anymore.

But then again, why did he come back into my life? Because the universe has things in store for us? Because we have unfinished business, or because I'm going to be tested on my new resilience? I could always decide to give it another try, and if it doesn't work again, it doesn't work.

Then again, I kind of love my new autonomy and could so totally flip Charlie the bird and walk away right now. I don't need him. I have control of this situation.

But just when I think I've got the matter settled, the thought of all the work ahead of me versus the ease of sliding back into something familiar...back into Charlie, is more appealing than I care to admit. Especially if he's willing to help take care of me and find me a cushy job, and learns to be more understanding and kind.

Don't call him, call him, don't call him, call him...

With trembling fingers, I dial his number and wait.

"Innovation is the specific instrument of entrepreneurship…the act that endows resources with a new capacity to create wealth."
Peter F. Drucker

CHAPTER NINETEEN
The Difference That Makes The Difference

"All recharged after your break and ready to continue?" Arjun asks with a grin an hour later.

I nod, but can't deny the guilt spreading through me like a cancer.

I feel like a total fraud. Granted, I haven't technically done anything wrong yet. But that might be because Charlie hadn't answered his phone and I'd been forced to leave a message.

I can still change my mind…which means there's no real point in sharing this little internal crisis with Arjun, is there?

No harm, no foul, Lindsay.

Still, as Arjun pours his tea methodically, it feels a little like his dark eyes are peering into my soul.

Like the Telltale Heart, only worse, because it's happening to me.

"How about another story?" Arjun asks.

"Yes! Please." Anything to take the attention off my flaming cheeks. Plus, the idea of sitting and drinking herbal tea while listening to a tale in Arjun's comforting voice would definitely take this edge off.

"Great," he says, handing over my cup then taking a seat in his favorite leather chair. "Now pay attention closely."

I salute Arjun, and cup my hand around one ear, emphasizing my attention. "I'm listening…"

"One national consumer product company had a unique issue when manufacturing their toothpastes. When the tubes were filled with toothpaste, two percent of the tubes remained empty. The faulty empty tubes were causing many distributors to complain, and as a result, they began threatening not to carry this company's products. As expected, the CEO was upset about the lost revenue, lost resources, and lost credibility in front of their partners."

"Well, that sure would cause decay in the company," I interject, taking another sip from my tea.

"To say the least," Arjun adds, and then continues, "'I have budgeted one million dollars to fix this problem, now get me ideas' the CEO announced one day during a senior management meeting. After much discussion, many engineers suggested great ideas. One suggestion stood out from the rest— design a machine to weigh the tubes of toothpaste. 'If the weight isn't the standard twenty-one ounces, the machine will buzz loudly to notify the technician. That person will then physically remove the faulty tube to ensure it does not go into the cases. We will build custom-designed software to monitor the machine and its reporting.'"

Arjun takes a calm breath of air when he is telling a long story, a lot like meditating, and it puts a smile on my face. Suddenly, I'm at ease again for the first time since I called Charlie.

"Everybody agreed this was the best solution. It would cost less than a million dollars, so they built the elaborate machine and software that supported the monitoring. However, the project got delayed and went over budget to 1.3 million dollars. Naturally, management was concerned about the cost, but they were also happy that the big problem was getting resolved.

"Soon, the warehouse filled with obnoxious buzzing every time a tube was determined to be underweight. No one could've expected so many empty tubes. After a month, the CEO was so satisfied that the complaints had stopped, he decided to go to the office and give that engineer a ten thousand dollar bonus for coming up with his marvelous solution. 'I want to see this machine in action!' he said gleefully.

"He set off to visit the plant so that he could experience the magnificent buzzing of the detection machine first-hand. Except...the plant was silent. Except for the normal machine noises, of course. But there was no buzzing, no excitement upon workers discovering a bad egg on the conveyor belt.

When the CEO investigated further, he found the machine in a separate storage room. It wasn't even running. There it sat, alone and forsaken and dusty, as employees dried their wet clothes on it.

"The CEO was furious. 'We spent 1.3 million dollars on this machine! It's supposed to be saving us millions, yet you shut it down and move it to storage? How dare you! You all will ruin this business!' he yelled at the plant manager and anyone who would listen.

"The plant manager waited until the CEO stopped ranting then calmly explained, 'One of our technicians was annoyed by the buzzing sound—'

"'Oh!' the CEO interrupted sarcastically. 'So, this is a voluntary organization where you make decisions for the comfort of every other Joe. I see.' He seethed with fury at this point.

"'Sorry, sir,' the plant manager said. 'What I was *going* to say was that one of our technicians was so annoyed by the buzzing sound, he installed a fan above the conveyer belt to blow the underweight tubes off before they got to the machine. Works like a charm. I promise, we didn't spend any of the company's money. The technician was perfectly happy spending his twenty-five dollars for the fan if I allowed him to stand under the fan and work in cooler conditions.'"

Arjun smiles and folds his hands. This is his teacher stance, which means he's going to ask me to assess, and I'll have to come up with a witty, ready response.

"You're going to ask me what I learned from this story, aren't you?" I say, laughing softly to myself.

"Quite astute you are, Lindsay. A+ student. So…what did you learn from this?" His bright smile stretches across his sun-weathered face.

Closing my iPad, I say, "Innovation mostly comes from ground up, not the other way around. It's organic and simple at its best."

"Yes. Do you remember my definition of innovation, speaking of simple?" he presses.

"Innovation is creating or improving my products or its fulfillment to meet my clients' wants and needs better," I say by rote memory. I'd studied my notes every night for the last several weeks.

Arjun nods. The Old Wise One is pleased. "Excellent memory," he says. "So, if your business is cutting trees to make paper, and your tree supply is waning, then you need to abandon cutting down the current forest, right? You innovate by simply replanting, or finding a new forest or making paper without even using trees. Innovate means to change the current methodology. To make changes to the established ways of thinking."

"The leader looks at the forest and might say, 'You know what? This doesn't feel right. It looks like we don't see a lot of beautiful trees anymore – I don't know, but something's got to change. Do you want to check the other forests to make sure that we have a long-term revenue stream?' Managers or operators do not see forests; they only see the trees in front of them. They all reply, 'Oh, no. You are being too picky. Let's focus on the performance and efficiency. How could you possibly say that our thirty-year-old system doesn't work? That's why we became a several-million-dollar company.' But change is inevitable. It's the only thing that keeps us moving, or else we become stagnant," I say, staring at the wall of flower paintings behind Arjun.

Maybe I needed to change things up in my company. Maybe I let it become too stagnant, and that's why it failed.

"That's true, Lindsay. And to make matters worse," Arjun says, "anyone who questioned the system was shot down. Many said, 'These people are too negative. Let's give them a training on positive thinking.'"

"That's hilarious." I shake my head and nearly erupt in laughter. "Positive thinking should always embrace intelligence, shouldn't it?"

Arjun's shoulders shake in that silent laughter of his. "A classic example is Blockbuster. You remember Blockbuster, don't you, Lindsay?"

"Arjun, you flatter me," I say deadpan. "You know darn well I'm forty, and looking younger every day! I remember Blockbuster when it was born, baptized, went on its first prom, got married, got divorced. I've seen all of Blockbuster's biggest days..."

He flips up his hands in admission. "Okay, okay...so you remember the $10 billion company. They had an excellent system for fulfilling their product. First, they provided their customers with the convenience of renting movies from their brick-and-mortar stores. People filled their cars with gasoline, drove to Blockbuster, and rented a movie. And if they didn't return the movie on time, they had to pay a late fee. Simple, right?"

"The best. I miss those Blockbuster days, the perfect night out when you only had ten bucks to spend."

"Indeed. But Blockbuster never saw the trees being eliminated from their forest. They were working *in the business*."

"Ahh…I know where this story is going…" I say gleefully.

"So, one day…" he ignores me, as he should, and continues, "a man came to his local Blockbuster store and returned a late copy of *Apollo 13*. He was charged a forty-dollar fee! He was so embarrassed about this incident that, later on, on his way to his gym he realized there's a much better business model to be used out there. What if…you could pay a movie rental company about thirty dollars a month to rent movies for as long as you wanted? He imagined a movie rental business by mail with a fixed cost like a gym.

"And just like that, for changing the status quo way of thinking, this man began a small company two years later that would mail unlimited DVDs using a subscription model. In 2000, this man, Reed Hastings, went to Blockbuster and asked for $50 million to sell them his successful DVD mailing business. Not only did Blockbuster not purchase this small, innovative company, but also did not even jump on the successful DVD mailing business until four years later. Starting in 2004, Blockbuster spent $500 million over the next four years to compete with Hastings' company and failed. Pretty miserable when you consider they could've bought it for $50 million. In 2007, Hastings' company started streaming movies over the internet. In September 2010, Blockbuster filed for bankruptcy. By 2019, Hastings converted his $40 late fee embarrassment into a 150 billion dollar company. And that little company Reed Hastings started is called Netflix." Arjun beams.

I have to do the slow clap. "Bravo."

"Thank you, thank you. Wait, what am I thanking you for? I wish that had been my idea," Arjun says, continuing, "so you see…Blockbuster could not see the trees being eliminated from their forest. That's what happens when people don't master their businesses—someone else comes along, innovates, and you're done. So, what did you understand from this, Lindsay?"

"That hindsight is twenty-twenty." I shake my head. "And if you snooze, you lose."

"Both are true. What else?"

"That Netflix innovated the fulfillment side of DVDs by creating the mail order subscription, and then later innovated the **product and its fulfillment** by creating the streaming model."

"Exactly." Arjun stretches in his seat. "Innovation is not necessarily having a new idea. It is providing a different, better experience for your customers. Creativity is a skill that can be learned through strategic imagination and practice. Once you are creative, you can innovate something different and better that can impact the world. Innovation is about finding and bringing a new perspective to your industry, so you can integrate multiple points of view that are valuable for you and others."

"Is that all? So easy peasy!"

"I know, easier said than done, but it can be done. Just takes practice. You do it using imagination. Imagination is running our mind in reverse. It is creating something that does not exist yet. Since that can be completely new to our minds, novel experiences trigger the imagination. The path to innovation is not obvious but counter-instinctive. When I was in high school several decades ago, I thought, 'Newton discovered gravity, Einstein discovered relativity, and Edison invented electricity. They left nothing for me.' In 10 A.D., a Roman engineer, Julius Sextus Frontinus said, 'Inventions have long since reached their limit, and I see no hope for further developments.' In 1898, the U.S. Commissioner of Patents at the time was believed to have said, 'Everything that can be invented has been invented.'"

"Little did he know..."

"Exactly! And to think that was around a hundred years before Google, the internet, and the iPhone. We need to have the right mindset to innovate. You can either think it might not work, so why try and fail? Or...it might not work, but I will have fun trying anyway."

"I agree," I say, reflecting in a moment of silence. "I remember the story of Dr. Spencer Silver of 3M accidentally discovering a new adhesive in 1968. For close to a decade, it was a weak adhesive with hardly any use. Then, boom—Post-It notes were born," I add excitedly.

"An amazing example." Arjun applauds me. "We must open up our minds and ask new questions that no one has yet asked in your industry. Growth happens outside of your comfort zone, which in turn creates innovations. The key elements of innovation are…"

1. Perspective
2. Integration
3. Implementation

Flipping open my iPad again, I jot those down.

"Let us take Netflix's journey as an example. When Reed was charged the $40 late fee by Blockbuster, the first thing he experienced was embarrassment. He was scared to tell his wife how much he'd paid in late fees. That is called the instinctive response. But later that day, he went to the gym and contemplated the gym's revenue model. He must have asked himself a question very similar to this: If I pay $30 for working out an entire month at the gym, why can't I start a movie rental business using the same monthly subscription model?

"This is the seed of counter-instinctive thinking. Reed zoomed out and introduced a new **perspective** into the business model. He asked a question no one in his industry was asking. You can do the same by asking the following question: 'What is an innovation that could completely disrupt or change the landscape of my industry?'"

Arjun is on a roll, and I'm quite the attentive student jotting down everything he says.

"Here is another question: 'What are the five top innovations in my industry over the last twenty-five years, and how can I take my business to the next level? What is a new perspective about my product or its fulfillment that I can bring to my industry?' Asking these same questions is exactly how Reed came up with the fixed-cost model of Netflix."

Scribbling down the questions as fast as I can, I liken learning from Arjun to wrapping your lips around a fire hose, taking a drink and not being blown away from everything that's being blasted at you. It takes stamina, but if you put in the effort, a deep thirst is quenched.

Geez, listen to me now. I'm starting to sound like him with the metaphors!

This time, he stands before continuing, and I know I'm in for it. If Arjun is standing, I'm in big trouble—it means he's just winding up.

"The second aspect of innovation," he says, "is **integration**. The greatest discoverer to ever live on this planet was Leonardo da Vinci, who famously said, 'To develop a complete mind, study the art of science; study the science of art. Learn how to see. Realize that everything connects to everything else.' In integration, you are connecting and comparing current solutions or ideas available inside or outside of your industry.

"Let us take the example of Netflix again. When it first launched, Netflix was only rental by mail, not subscription-based and worked more like Blockbuster. It wasn't popular. But then Hastings must have asked the question: If one could pay $30 a month and work out at the gym **as little or as much as** one wanted, then why can't we start a subscription-based movie rental business by mail following the same principle? See, the question itself has evolved, connecting not only two industries but also an existing solution from a different industry. Questions are the sources of creativity. Find and ask those questions that no one else is asking in your industry. Great questions will create great innovations. Combining two great questions like Hastings did will make you a genius in your industry. This is the ultimate integration."

Arjun stands at his large, sunny glass wall, staring out at his patio garden.

"I'm guessing you're going to give me questions for helping me integrate now," I say.

He turns to smile at me. "You know me so well, Lindsay. Start by asking yourself 'What are three major customer frustrations in my industry? How are they already solved in three other industries?'"

"I've never thought of that before. That's a good starting point." Thinking out of your industry-box is key.

"Yes, and this is how Hastings came up with the subscription model—by finding the solution from another industry. Another question to ask yourself is: 'What is a trend that I can derive from the last five major innovations in my industry? How are these trends related to each other? How can I use them to predict the next trend in my industry?'"

"See, and that's where I get stuck a lot of the time," I say. "I have great ideas, but how do I put those ideas into motion?"

"And that is where the final step of innovation comes into play, Lindsay. This is **implementation**," Arjun explains. "Great entrepreneurs are great implementers. They're great at shortening the time between idea and prototype. As you know, a lot of ideas might not work, but how do we know which ones will until we test them? We don't. We need to get customer input first. Promise yourself that you will not put large sums of money into any product development based on a hunch. Most of the time, what you think customers need is not what they need. Never assume you know what they need better than they do. Always ask your loyal customers what their frustrations are. Then build the bare minimum and test it with the same people. If the response is positive, great. If not, move on to the next idea."

I hate to admit it, even to just myself, but I never did that with my company. I always assumed I knew a good idea when I had one and never bothered to ask for any feedback. I'll try this from now on. Certainly can't hurt.

"As you implement, the factors that make the biggest difference are your perspective and the people around you. Even your perspective could be controlled by people who influence you. So, choose your influencers wisely!" he concludes happily. "Well, Lindsay, how do you feel about all this?"

I sigh loudly, closing my iPad. "Really good, but I'd never thought of doing some of these things, so I feel a little like a business failure now."

"On the contrary, you are here learning what you need to learn. That is the first step in improving. Think of how many people are making these mistakes without anyone to guide them. You are collecting the tools you need to succeed. So, congratulations." Arjun smiles warmly, takes my empty tea mug, and taps the wall before disappearing into the office kitchen. "See you again next week?"

"Definitely. Wouldn't miss it for the world," I say, collecting my purse and heading for the door. Arjun knows I'll find my way out these days. The way I am part of his inner circle, I sometimes feel like his daughter. "See you next week, Dad," I murmur.

From his break room, I hear him murmur back with a chuckle in his voice, "Okay, daughter. Be amazing."

Be amazing. Not bad advice. Because now comes my personal life, which needs more help than any business teachings I could ever receive from Arjun.

That evening, I feel good as I walk into my apartment, high on the events of the day, despite the Charlie issue weighing on me.

"Life is never boring with Arjun around," I muse, recalling my mentor's effervescent personality. Slipping off my shoes and plopping myself on the couch, I throw my arms back on the headrest and sigh. This is usually the time of day when I'd head into the kitchen and pour myself a glass of Merlot to celebrate for making it through another busy day. The urge is still there—how could it not be after twenty years?—but as I walk barefoot into the kitchen, this time, I open a bottle of flavored seltzer water.

Strawberry, I think enthusiastically, pouring the bubbly beverage into my glass. It's been ten weeks since my last alcoholic drink. Time to celebrate with my new bubbly.

My phone rings. I slip it out of my pocket, answering the call before I have the chance to glance at the name on the screen.

"Linds?" a familiar voice purrs over the line.

My fingers tighten around my glass, but I force them to loosen and set it down on the counter.

"Charlie," I say, my voice as chilly as I feel inside.

"Hello to you, too, babe. I was really glad you called earlier. I didn't think you would."

"Yeah, neither did I." And right now, I'm mostly regretting it. "How's the new job?" I ask, desperate for something to say.

"Really great, thanks for asking. Hey, do you think we could get together and talk some more?"

"Look, I'm actually super busy. I've got some new clients, and am doing some consulting for a friend. I don't have a whole lot of time for my social life right now. I just called to check and see how the new job was going and to say hello."

I twist a loose curl around my finger as he goes on to say how sorry he is for having lost me, how he's learned quite a bit and is in a much better place, and how we should start all over. At the very least, he says, we should talk it all through one more time, face to face.

People did change, I remind myself. And something, no matter how fleeting, had made me call him earlier today. Maybe I needed to see him one last time to finally put him behind me once and for all. I'll give him thirty minutes and then get a good night's sleep for the work I have ahead of me tomorrow.

Relinquishing anger, ready to forgive and move on with my life, I give him the address to my new apartment and nervously wait. No matter what, I will not get involved with him again. No matter how long I've been alone. No matter how he smells. No matter how charming he is. No matter…I think my will is already waning, just thinking of all those things I didn't want to think about.

That's not what this is going to be about. I will simply listen. *LISTEN.* Nothing else.

An hour and a half later, he still hasn't arrived, and I'm on my fourth glass of strawberry seltzer water. *At least I'm still in control,* I congratulate myself.

He probably regretted calling me back and gave up on coming by. Probably better this way. I start getting ready for bed when I hear a rap at the door. With a frustrated sigh, I go to answer it.

"Nothing changes, does it?" I say as he stands there, looking pretty much the same as when I last saw him. The fact that he didn't dress any nicer or make any attempts to look presentable tells me a lot.

He's holding a paper bag, which he supports with one hand.

"Babe," he says, walking in and pecking my cheek with a kiss.

The familiar scent of his skin grazes my nose, stirring up all sorts of old emotions. I hold it together.

No matter what.

"I stopped to get some wine." He holds up a bag weighted by four bottles. "I didn't know what you're drinking these days—red or whi—"

"I'm not drinking at all, Charlie." I walk away as he puts the bag down. "A lot has changed, in fact…"

"In ten weeks?" His furrowed eyebrows say he doesn't believe me, as usual. He saunters into the kitchen as though he's been here a thousand times and starts fishing through drawers.

"I mean it," I insist, even though I don't feel the gravitas behind my words. I've realized through my work with Arjun that I'm actually a recovering alcoholic, and it won't take much to crumble under the pressure. Already, I can feel the weight of an ox sitting on my chest from the anxiety.

"You don't have to have any, but I'm having a glass with my meal. You can join me if you like. Now, where's the bottle opener?"

The next morning, Charlie sits on the edge of the bed. His naked back is quickly covered as he pulls his shirt over his head. Untidy hair flops on top of his head. Watching him, I can't pinpoint what I'm feeling.

Inside my stomach, ropes of emotion twist and knot together, then pull at each other, and knot up once again —nauseating.

On one hand, I felt I could handle it last night. I convinced myself it would be "just this once," and I do still feel that way.

But on the other, the thought of him coming by again later? Of not being alone every day? Of having someone to talk to?

It's overpowering.

Charlie drops a kiss on my cheek. "I'll see you tonight," he says cheerfully, slipping into his jacket.

I wince, rubbing my throbbing temples and battling the other half of my brain. "Charlie, I don't know if this is a good idea."

"Of course it is," he insists. "Didn't I prove to you last night how much we belong together?"

Despite the Pinot Noir Band playing the maracas in my head, I think back to the night we spent together. We were always good together in the short-term. It was the long-term that sucked.

"I guess."

"And tonight is going to be even more special," he promises with a wink before leaving.

Once the painkillers kick in, I grab my phone and start making calls for my getting my hair and nails done. I convince myself that this is all just a simple bump in the road, a temporary distraction. Deep down, I know Charlie isn't the right one for me, but a few days, what's the harm in pretending all is normal again? Just to give my brain a little break...

It's a day to unwind, I think, pulling out the credit card I swore I'd never use again.

I've worked hard enough. I deserve another night of happiness. Even Arjun believes in the benefits of some time off.

At the grocery store, my cell phone rings. It's one of my top clients. I wince at the screen, realizing I was supposed to meet him for lunch.

"Dang it," I blurt right as a woman is pushing her grocery cart with a toddler in tow past me. She gives me an awful look, and I feel bad shouting in front of a child. "Sorry." I give them both my best apologetic smile.

I'll make it up to him tomorrow, I decide, letting the call roll into voicemail. He's very easygoing anyway. Instead, I search the wine shelf for the same brand Charlie brought last night. Finding it, I slip two bottles into my cart. Tonight will be a temporary sabbatical from the rigorous life re-training I've put myself through.

Hours later, tendrils of perfectly done hair frame my face, while the makeup is light and perfect. An alluring, deep-red polish perfectly finishes my freshly manicured nails. I honestly can't remember the last time I dolled up like this.

Pop!

The cork springs from the bottle of wine. The maroon liquid slides into my glass as I wait for Charlie. The tangy sweetness slides down my throat, and I revel in the flavor once again. Strangely, an image of Arjun pops into my head, smirk on his face. I make that image into a little photo and jam it into the mental garbage can. Just as soon as I do, Arjun's voice pops into my head.

That's not helping! I can't think of him or anyone who might disapprove right now.

I have to do this for me. It's a part of my letting-go process...

My stomach growls, but I won't snack on any appetizers before Charlie gets here with dinner. In the meantime, my phone rings. My client is calling again. I forgot to return his call from this afternoon and give an explanation, I was so wrapped up in getting ready for tonight. Dropping the phone back onto the counter, I take another hearty pull on my wine before refilling it.

Two hours later, I'm beyond starving and decide on a few crackers and olives. Admittedly, I'm also beyond annoyed that Charlie isn't here yet, but I know him, and he'll come through eventually. Popping the cork on the second bottle, I decide to call and see what's keeping him. It rings three times and I slam the phone down on a kitchen towel. Had it been on the counter, I would've cracked the screen — the phone rings. I answer quickly. "Where the hell are you?" I demand.

"Lindsay?" I hear a voice on the line, but it's not Charlie.

Quickly, I glance down at my phone screen and wince. It's Smith, another client of mine. I was supposed to talk to him this evening to go over solutions for his new business venture. For some reason, my head has been mostly up my rear since yesterday. I chastise myself for falling for Charlie's BS once again.

"Smith?" I ask, hearing the confusion and drunk bewilderment in my voice. "What's up? I haven't been feeling well. Can I call you back tomorrow?" I slur.

"Sure, no problem. Get better, okay?" Smith replies. From his deadpan tone of voice, I'm sure he can tell I'm tipsy, not sick, but I'm too inebriated to dwell on it.

I just want Charlie to get here so I can string him up by his toenails and yell at him. I should bill him for my hair and nails to recoup some of my losses. *Jerk.* Whatever—the loser used me again. I hate him. No matter what, I hate him for good this time.

The next time I call, his voicemail picks up and, with the maturity and clarity only a couple of bottles of wine can provide, I babble into the receiver.

"Hey, a-hole, thanks for nothing. Charlie the chicken of the sea—chicken of me. If they made a movie about you it would be called, 'Charlie and the Chicken Factory' and the critics would pan it, fry pan it, and drowned it in hot sauce. Or how about 'It's the Great Dumpkin Charlie Drown' and instead of it ending up it theaters, it would be dumped like a sack of dog poop. Speaking of dumped, I'm dumping you, you limp biscuit. You could've had it all, you fool. I gave you my best, and you threw it away. Now do me a favor…don't call me ever again."

I don't remember much of what happens after that, because I pass out. Waking up in the morning, it feels like someone built the Empire State building on my head.

I squint at my phone. It's past nine.

Past the time I'm supposed to meet Arjun.

This sickly self-disgust and disappointment that sweeps over me feels far too familiar. That yucky kind of familiar that I wish would just disappear, just like Charlie had.

Again.

Who's the fool now, Lindsay?

CHAPTER TWENTY
Convert Stress and Suffering to Celebration

Oh, shoot.

If I'm too irresponsible to get up on time, then I'm too irresponsible to succeed in life and business. At this point, I shouldn't even go. I don't want to waste Arjun's time, and the idea of facing him like this makes me sick with shame.

But I can't just stay in bed, either.

Arjun has done way too much for me, I've come such a long way and I cannot—no matter what, no matter how hungover I am right now, or close to migraine status I'm teetering—give him a BS excuse. I didn't come all this way with my training just to screw it up irrevocably now. I can still fix this, can't I?

I grab my phone and call him.

"Good morning." I try to sound chipper and fail miserably. "I am *so* sorry I'm running late. I have a good reason, though. Personal problems, and—"

"Lindsay!" he interrupts. A seagull caws in the background. "Where are you? We are waiting for you at the marina."

"We?"

"My executive team and me. We are going fishing this morning, remember? Are you lost?"

"No." Part of me wants to lie, but making excuses *must* become part of my past, just like Charlie. "I totally screwed up, Arjun. I woke up late. Just go if you have to go. I'll catch up with you later."

"No. No, no, no, Lindsay. We will wait for you. Hungover or not, get ready and come down to the marina. We have much to go over."

"Oh. Okay, then. I guess…"

Wait, did he say I was hungover? How did he know that?

Man, Arjun is *good.*

"I'll get dressed now and be on my way." I sound like a little girl talking to her father. He's right to pressure me. I'll never get anywhere in life if I fall behind and make others wait for me in the process. Getting a good kick in the butt is what I need. What I've needed for a long time.

"Good girl, Lindsay. See you in a bit."

I could see the smile on Arjun's face even through the phone and, suddenly, I feel a whole lot better.

As if seeing Arjun's luxurious office, condo, and car weren't enough, forty minutes later, I have the pleasure of getting on his fifty-foot super yacht. No big deal, just a kind billionaire out for a stroll on the high seas with his senior team of a dozen successful men and women, all taking advantage of a lovely Wednesday morning to go fishing. Nothing different or amazing about that at all.

Who am I kidding? Me, a successful business owner? Just *working* for Arjun would be a dream come true.

"There she is!" He's as happy as ever to see me, with arms open wide, and for a moment, I think I'm going to break down and cry.

He waited for me. Arjun waited. He believed in me enough to pause his day until I dragged my rear out of bed and schlepped over here.

"You didn't have to wait for me," I say, hugging him. "But, thank you. I appreciate it."

"And you didn't have to get out of bed." He pats my back, giving me that all-knowing Arjun look. "But you did. And as a bonus, you've brushed your teeth and hair, even after that hangover," he chides.

A small smile breaks out on my pathetic face, and I hold it together.

"Come, Lindsay." He rests his hand on my shoulder and leads us down the dock. "Let us have some breakfast while my team prepares the tackle."

We approach his yacht, and I'm stunned by how beautiful the vessel is—

gleaming white with gorgeous polished wood railings and decks. Part of me feels like I'll never get to this level, like I should just quit right this second. Another part of me says to suck it up and learn from the master.

We board the yacht. On a table underneath the deck awning, a small breakfast buffet awaits us. Arjun and I take seats in two, white Adirondack chairs. It's a beautiful, clear day filled with gleaming sunlight, cawing gulls, and choppy waves dotted with diamond highlights. As the yacht pulls away from the marina and glides into the Pacific, I enjoy coffee and vanilla yogurt with berries, drizzled with honey while Arjun makes a mint tea and angles his seat to watch his team temporarily turn into fishermen.

"So…" He adjusts his sunglasses, and today he reminds me of a movie star.

"You're going to tell me a story, aren't you?" I ask and sip my coffee.

"What do you think?"

"I think yes."

"You are quite the astute observer," he says. "Now let's begin."

A laugh settles in my chest as he settles into his seat, and I open my notes to prepare for another Arjun story, profoundly grateful to be receiving it, even after my missteps.

Chin tipped to the sun, he begins, "It was a bright sunny morning in a mountain village—"

"Why's it always a village?" I ask. "Why not a city? Or a theme park? Or, I don't know…a dark Chicago alleyway?" I suppress a smart-ass smile.

He glances at me. "There are rose bushes less thorny than you, Lindsay."

"A rose by any other name would still smell as sweet, thorns and all," I volley back, knowing that Arjun truly appreciates me, thorns and all.

"Shakespeare. Nice one. As I was saying…in a mountain village, an old man and his grandson were headed to the valley market to sell a beautifully groomed donkey. They set off happily down the steep path, and after a while, they passed some travelers lounging off to one side.

"'Look at that silly pair!' said one of the travelers. 'There they go, scrambling and stumbling down the path when they could be riding comfortably on the back of that sure-footed beast.'" Arjun pauses to take a sip of his tea before continuing. "The old man heard this and thought it was true that he and his grandson should be riding the donkey, so they mounted it and continued on their descent.

"Soon, they passed another group of people lounging by the wayside. 'Look at that lazy pair, breaking the back of that poor donkey!' The old man thought they were right, and since he was heavier than his grandson, he decided to walk while the boy rode on the donkey's back."

I smile, because I know where this is going.

"A while passed," Arjun continues, "and they heard more comments. 'Look at that disrespectful child. He rides while the old man walks!' The old man thought they were right, and it was only proper that he should ride while the boy walked. Otherwise, it would be disrespectful. Sure enough, the villagers continued to give their opinions. 'What a mean old man, riding at ease while the poor child has to keep up on foot!'

"By this time, the old man had grown bewildered. When he heard criticism that the donkey would be too worn out to sell, that no one would want to buy him after the long walk to the market, they sat dejected by the side of the road.

"After the donkey had been allowed to rest for a while, they continued on their journey, this time employing a completely new method. When they finally arrived in the late afternoon, the old man and boy were gasping breathlessly into the marketplace. Slung on a pole between them, hung by his tied feet, was the donkey."

I chuckle and write in big letters in my notepad: IT'S YOUR LIFE. ENJOY THE JOURNEY AND THE DESTINATION, underlining it twice.

"That sounds like an Aesop fable that says, 'You can't please everyone. If you try, you lose yourself.' Or something like that."

"Something like that, indeed," Arjun agrees. "Being your **true self** is the greatest gift you can give back to the universe. But being your true self doesn't mean following every instinct you have or declaring, 'This is who I am—deal with it. I am an angry person, and you should know that by know.' That shows resistance toward growing and is actually very irresponsible."

"I agree." And I almost did that this morning when I didn't want to get out of bed. I nearly gave in to my old habits as I had the night before. Like Arjun said, getting out of bed and getting my big girl pants on was a huge step.

"Like the grandfather in the story," Arjun says, "his true self was not the person he changed into every time the onlookers gave their opinions. His true self, his true identity, was what he began with—the dance he was destined to perform. Anxiety and suffering is a byproduct of performing someone else's dance."

"So, we should stick to our own style of dance," I say. "No matter how awkward or nerdy it might be or how much the teens at the club laugh at us." I smile.

"Lindsay, you have a unique way of seeing the world…" He chuckles and folds his hands in his lap. "But I like it. Here's another way of seeing it… Imagine a zebra grazing the savannas of Africa. In the blink of an eye, a lion appears three feet from her. The fight-or-flight response kicks in, and the zebra starts running for her life, fleeing as quickly as her muscles can move. A very long four minutes later, she narrowly escapes the lion. But her survival means that a different animal fell victim to the predator, and the zebra suddenly sees her best friend being eaten alive by the fierce lion."

"Boo. Why'd you have to use a zebra as an example? Why not a rat or something less beautiful and majestic?"

"Because you wouldn't care about my story unless it was something more palatable than a rat," Arjun replies, his tone matter of fact. "Let me ask you now, do you think our zebra will have PTSD the next day?"

"Of course not."

Arjun leans forward, his bushy eyebrow cocked. "How about anxiety? Depression? Is she going to sit around feeling victimized, saying, 'My life is ruined because I nearly became lion food?'"

I shrug. "Actually, no one knows what a zebra is feeling, but I don't think so. I think she'll go about her day grazing in the savanna."

"Why will she do that?"

"I don't know," I respond. "You're the Animal Planet expert."

"Oh, Lindsay, you are too much. But you are right—the zebra goes on about her day, because animals automatically turn off the stress response as soon as the threat is over. It's different for us humans. Instead, we move the lion from outside to inside our minds and memories."

At a triumphant shout, both Arjun and I look over to see one of his employees furiously reeling in a fish. For a few minutes, we watch the fight then shake our heads sympathetically as the fish is lost and the line goes limp.

"Aww, too bad. You will get him next time." Arjun gives his team members a thumb's up. "Plus," he chuckles and looks towards me, "there's always more fish in the sea."

"So, about the lion," I turn to him, refusing to dwell on that thought now that Charlie is in my rearview mirror. "What does that mean?"

His pensive eyes turn to me again. "It means we recreate the lion inside our heads using our imagination. Humans hold on to memories. We respond to that lion, not just at the moment of threat, but for the rest of our lives."

My brow furrows. "Are you saying memories or imagination are bad things? Didn't Einstein say imagination is better than knowledge?"

Arjun sits back in his chair, props his elbows onto the arm rests, and tents his fingers together. "Here is what Einstein said: 'I am enough of the artist to draw freely upon imagination. Imagination is more important than knowledge. Knowledge is limited. Imagination encircles the world.'"

"Right, that's what I meant."

Arjun smiles. "Einstein's imagination expanded the world. Michelangelo's imagination inspired generations. Da Vinci's imagination fascinated the modern world. Stalin's imagination killed twenty million people. Hitler's imagination wiped out six million Jews. Bin Laden's imagination took three thousand lives on 9/11. Does this make sense?"

I nod slowly. "I think so."

"In other words, imagination is not *better* than knowledge—it is more important."

"I see. So imagination is important, for good or bad?"

Arjun raises his hand in triumph. "Exactly my point. The zebra in the savanna doesn't have the faculty of imagination to recreate the lion. But we humans do. As I told you before, that goose from Canada does not have the imagination to say, 'Meh! I don't feel like going to Florida through the Atlantic Flyway.'"

I think about a goose checking out Google Maps, trying to decide which route to take, and a laugh bubbles from my lips. "So, what I think you're saying, Arjun, is that we can use our imaginations to create our own realities?"

"Yes, and beyond," Arjun responds. He stands and walks to the railing of the yacht to look out at the vast ocean. "**Stress is your imagination working against you. Anxiety is over-preparation against stress. Anger is a misdirected response to stress. Depression is anger directed inward. And suffering is all the above.**"

I get up and move next to Arjun. "Are you saying that stress is the mother of all suffering?"

"Absolutely." His head nods, bobbing up and down emphatically. "And most people stress themselves out over just about everything—ironically, including stress."

I prop my arms up on the railing and lean on the varnished balustrade. "That's true, but how can we **manage stress** when we know so much, think so much, and live such active lives?" I ask.

He looks at me out of the corner of his eye. "That's the wrong question. Lindsay, if you are managing stress, you are already enslaved by it. Here is the right question: 'How can I convert my stress, anxiety, and suffering into celebration?'"

Suffering to celebration? Okay, he's going to give me some mind-over-matter advice. *Easier said than done.* "All right, boss," I say dryly. "How do I do that? Do I use Maslow's hierarchy to create security, first?"

"Absolutely not. Maslow's hierarchy of needs—namely, security, safety, love, esteem, and self-actualization—are the needs for the mind. The moment we see ourselves as minds, we have lost the game already. The mind is simply a process that **we** create to regulate information and energy. **You are not your mind.** Thoughts are simply **the** by-products. You are not your thoughts, either. You can consciously change them at any time."

"But isn't that like lying to ourselves?"

"Not at all. Your thoughts form your perception; your perception creates your reality, Lindsay. If you are a poor man who goes around believing you are the King of England, well, who's to say you are not the King of England?"

"But that's delusional."

"But that's all life is, Lindsay—a consistent imagination we create for ourselves with passion and purpose and taking intelligent actions to fulfill that imagination. And the sooner you see yourself as a successful woman, and take vigorus actions towards it, the sooner you will become one."

Okay, that hits home. What he's basically saying is that I am in control. I manifest my own destiny. Fake it 'til I make it. Believe in me, and it shall be. So, if I'm at a terrible point of my life, it's because I put myself here.

Staring out to sea, I ask, "Who am I, then?"

"You are God's authentic art. You are divine perfection." There is beauty in Arjun's smile that lifts my spirit. "You are the child of God or whatever you honor as your higher being…God, or Allah, or Brahma, or Jehovah, or 'the Universe,'."

I love where he's coming from, but I still want to get to the bottom line. "You said we should convert stress and suffering into celebration, but how do we do that?" I ask anxiously.

"You may use any or all the tools I have given you so far. Or you may call upon Faith to help you, whether you are religious or not. Everything I have taught you are the building blocks leading to Faith. If Faith is the Ph.D., I am just a kindergarten teacher explaining the alphabet letters of Faith. Absolute Faith is the Ph.D. of life." When he reaches over and squeezes my shoulder, I know I really need to listen. "Even if you haven't learned anything from me yet, learn this. Through Faith, you can move mountains, part the sea, create harmony in the world, or choose your future. Whatever you consistently have Faith in, and take action towards, becomes true."

I have heard this same sentiment a hundred different times interpreted a hundred different ways by a hundred different people, but it always sounds impossible.

How am I supposed to make myself successful simply by believing I am?

"It's too good to be true." I look down at my hands, not wanting to look him in the eye. While I admire his passion, I'm not sure I believe this idea a hundred percent.

Arjun bangs his hand lightly on the deck railing. "It **does** sound too good to be true. But that is the simple truth. The human mind wants to go through the hero's journey to justify its existence. Drama is the mind's playground. All of art and most of literature is written for the mind. Look at all the epic stories. The poor village is attacked by a dragon. The dragon takes the princess captive. Villagers are scared. A timid young boy steps up and inspires everyone to go kill the dragon. They laugh at him initially. When they see his determination, they become willing to give him a chance."

"Sounds like every movie I've ever seen," I tell him.

Arjun chuckles. "Because every movie has its hero, and you are the hero of your own journey, Lindsay. When you reach the end of your movie, do you want the dragon to kill you, or will you slay the dragon and go home a hero?"

"I will let the dragon take me and wait for Jason Momoa to rescue me."

He smirks. "Come on, now, Lindsay."

"I'm serious. Have you seen that man's muscles? Good Lord."

"You don't need Jason Moo-moo-a to rescue you."

I laugh. "You're right. Who wants to live with that guy? I'd spend my whole life fighting off throngs of women, and that is not the way to convert stress to celebration."

"That is true. But consider the boy in the story. When the villagers reach the boy to watch him take on the dragon, they find two dragons instead of one. The dragons almost kill the boy, but…he slays one and then narrowly escapes with the princess as he slays the other. He marries the princess and becomes the king."

"Yayyy, The End. And then we all walk out of the movie theater and into reality again."

He turns toward me. "Yes. **Every** culture has a version of this story. David and Goliath from the Jewish Faith, Ramayana and Mahabharata from Hindus, and you can't forget Greek mythology, which is all based on these basic story tropes. Even Christ who came as the messenger of Love was forced to be looked upon as the symbol of sacrifice and suffering. Mythologies, the stories we tell ourselves time and again, are more powerful to the mind than the facts themselves. The modern definition of it is 'alternative facts.'

Oftentimes, our mind believes whatever it wants to believe."

For once, I have nothing to say.

I simply look at his eyes above the sunglasses and know that he is telling the truth. It's all about perception. I can choose to have joy and celebration in my life right now.

Arjun pushes away from the railing and retrieves his tea before coming back to my side. "The story excites our minds because of conflict," he continues. "Conflict is the underdog winning against the frontrunner. Our hero needs to fight the demon, kill the dragon, and save the world. The human mind needs this conflict, or else we'd have nothing to fight for."

Oh, snap. He's right. Without conflict, our minds would have no drive or motivation.

I stop and pose some tough questions to myself this time.

Do I live my life as if I am fighting a dragon full time? Is he saying that the dragon is in my mind? Am I creating this dragon through my imagination to satisfy my mind? How easy my life would be if all I needed was Faith…

Arjun takes a deep breath while I become transfixed on the ocean waves. After a while, we silently walk back to our seats, and he points at my iPad. "May I see?" Reluctantly, I hand him my iPad. He starts writing something on my notepad. When he hands it back, I see what he's written:

Accelerator # 6 – Convert Stress and Suffering to Celebrations.

"So, if it all boils down to Faith, how do I practice that? I'm not much of a religious person, Arjun. Does that make me doomed?"

"Faith can be inside or outside of religion. **When Faith is celebrated, all conflicts disappear.** Everything I taught you so far is to prepare you to fight and slay the dragon. **With applied Faith, dragons shrink into lizards. Faith will connect you with the fearless side of yourself.** Life becomes a celebration. If you believe in God, you can practice Faith through the tradition of your spiritual practice."

"I would say I'm more spiritual than religious."

"Well, then, I can work with that, too…Think of the dragon in our story as your financial crisis, depression, or psychological insecurity. That dragon is chasing you. Now, you can use visualization techniques to align yourself to what you want, or you can keep running from or fight the dragon." Arjun sets aside me and looks at me directly once more. "You ask for Grace from the Universe to stay aligned to financial freedom, which is what you consider happiness. Remember, happiness means different things to different people. Thus, applied Faith is imagination combined with grace."

I nod slowly. I think I'm starting to get it, but I have more questions. "Do I **need** Faith to be successful, though?"

"Let me ask you a different question," he counters, looking over at the execs eagerly watching another attempt to reel in another fish. The rod bows under the heavy burden, and I begin to see the parallels to real life in a way that nearly blows me out of the water.

"Do we need this fancy yacht to go fishing?" Arjun asks. "Can't we just get a fishing rod and stand on the beach and catch fish just the same?"

I grin. "We could, but it would be different fish, I would imagine. Smaller ones."

"Right." He shrugs lightly. "Then, why do we go on the boat?"

"To catch the bigger ones. The ones we want," I reply. Again, I watch that rod arch under the weight and ferocity of the fighting fish.

"Exactly why we practice Faith, too. Remember what Steve Jobs said, simplicity is the ultimate sophistication. I say, **Faith is the ultimate simplicity and sophistication.** With Faith, you create bigger impact in the world. The more Faith, the bigger the impact."

I'm not sure how I'll manage it, because I'm still not sure how it works, but I'm going to do my best to practice Faith in my life.

Why?

Because I have Faith in Arjun, and he has shown Faith in me.

He shares a video on how to convert suffering into celebration.

CHAPTER TWENTY-ONE
Your Inside Out Raving Fans Strategy

"Come on, Lindsay. It's getting hot out here."

Arjun and I retreat downstairs to start putting together refreshments for the crew. I begin slicing up cheese, still thinking about all the things Arjun has said this morning when, lo and behold, he begins to spin another story.

The man is a bottomless pit of anecdotes.

"Tony Hsieh was great at building customer care with his company."

"Tony Hsieh...sounds familiar. Which company?"

"Zappos," he replies, as I place the company name in my memory. "One time, he took a number of his clients out for drinks, and afterwards, they returned to their hotel. As they were saying goodnight, Tony heard that one of his clients wanted pizza but the hotel's room service was closed for the night. Tony suggested to his client that he call Zappos."

"But Zappos is a shoe company." I chuckle.

"True," Arjun responds, opening a box of crackers. "But he insisted, even though his company sold shoes, that the client should give them a call, so he did. The team member who took the call at 2:00 a.m. not only found three pizza parlors that were still open near the hotel but also ordered it for the client." Arjun's eyes glow with excitement.

"That's some pretty great customer service, I agree."

He arranges the cheese slices on the plate. "Yes. So, tell me, Lindsay, who are your clients?"

"Anyone who buys my products or services."

"Yes," he says. "But don't forget your team, your vendors, your partners, and your loved ones. Your team members create a world-class experience for your clients, your vendors and suppliers facilitate your business to flourish, and your loved ones receive you back home at the end of the day. They are *all* your customers."

I imagine any future husband I might have thinking that he's my customer. "Yeah, but you can't tell men that, Arjun, or they'll never leave us alone. Babe, make me a sandwich. Babe, order me pizza. Babe, wear that little black thing you know I like...I mean, I *am* your customer." I laugh at my own joke.

He holds up a finger, wagging it at me in a teasing reprimand. "In that example, you are his customer, too. We all want something from the people in our relationships, Lindsay. In essence, we are all customers. Think about it—Zappos was able to deliver world-class experience because they selected and treated the internal clients and their team with extraordinary care. They invited only A-players to join the team. Any team member who was hired had three months to decide whether they were a cultural fit. They still pay $5,000 to quit their jobs if they feel they are not a fit. My policy is to hire slow and fire fast."

"What do you mean?" I ask.

"Once we have the right team in place, we manage them effectively. Management is empowerment. You empower people through continuous leadership development." He takes a sip of his tea and leans against the table of snacks.

"Leadership development." I begin slicing apples for the snack tray. "I love that."

Arjun reaches over and pops an apple slice in his mouth, munching before he continues. "The first step of management is to help your team meet their social needs. For most people, social needs are feeling significant, connection, and growth. Sincerely treat them with respect. As human beings."

"That seems like a no-brainer."

"You would think so, but you'd be surprised by how many people fail at this very simple step. They believe that being a boss means looking down at their team from their higher-up position. My father once told me and my sister, 'You guys can make mistakes, but be up-front. Come to me when you do, and you will be fine. Hide it from me, however, and you will have the greatest of consequences.' I still love this strategy to this day. When I was young, I would literally run home to tell my day about my mistakes just to share them with him."

"Sounds like a great dad." I smile.

"Oh, he was."

I could see a little Arjun in my mind, racing home to tattle on himself. It was funny, but his father's wisdom tugged at my soul a little. I never had that kind of experience with my father.

"So, what happens if I give my employees free rein to make mistakes, and they start making a bunch of them due to this honesty policy?" I ask, playing devil's advocate.

Arjun smiles. "That is why you are hiring A+ players, the best of the best. Given the freedom, A+ players will make fewer mistakes and take more ownership if you empower them with freedom."

I set aside the fruit tray and accept a tall glass of iced tea that Arjun offers me. "That makes sense," I say before taking a long drink. "Choose your family carefully."

"Exactly." Arjun sips his iced tea before continuing. "The second step of empowerment is helping your team meet their psychological needs: security, creativity, and contribution. They need to feel secure knowing they can count on you to cut their paychecks and keep them employed. They also need to feel that their creativity is encouraged and that they're contributing to the organization."

"So, it's not just the physical security of a paycheck," I say, picking up a slice of cheese. "It's also security that they're cherished as individuals."

"Exactly," Arjun says. "Once their social needs and psychological needs are both met, they will feel truly fulfilled and ready to serve your clients."

"So," I conclude, "world-class customer service starts at home."

"Exactly right. If your internal clients, your team, do not feel fulfilled, it is as if you are building a five-hundred-story building with no foundation. This is what most companies miss. They think they can fake a great customer experience by recording their customer care. Not going to happen in a million years. Humans are creatures with subconscious minds, and they will pick up others' emotions and intentions. You cannot fake a world-class customer experience. You need a world-class team first to do that.

"Lincoln said it right, 'You can fool all people some of the time, and some people all of the time, but you cannot fool all people all the time.'"

I nod, "I pity the fool who tries to fool everyone else." Pausing, I digest Lincoln's quote. It's always been one of my favorites. "So, Arjun, once I have a world-class team, how do I deliver a world-class customer experience? No fooling around. This is the million-dollar question, isn't it?"

We head back to the deck, and Arjun tells his staff that snacks are ready. Some retreat immediately, while others continue fishing with fierce determination.

Now, in the shade, Arjun leans back in his chair with a sigh. "That part is easy. Let me ask you a question, though. What do you think is better? Giving a very good customer experience all of the time, or a world-class customer experience half the time?"

Hmm, that's a good question, but I feel like no matter what I say, Arjun will tell me I'm wrong. I venture a guess. "A world-class customer experience half the time?" As soon as the words leave my lips, I know that wasn't right.

Arjun raises an eyebrow at me. "Giving a world-class customer experience half the time is a recipe for disaster. Imagine someone's dad or mom caring only fifty percent of the time and indifferent the rest?"

I wince. The man knows how to get to the point, and quickly. "Yeah, I guess you're right. Also, I suppose getting world-class service all the time raises my expectations, which would make me frustrated when the experience isn't perfect every time."

"Which happens," Arjun says with a shrug. "For example, what if Apple comes up with a product that reviews say is very good, but not excellent. Will you be interested in it?"

"No," I respond. "I expect world-class products from Apple."

"Right. Speaking of Apple, having a world-class product is in and of itself the best customer care."

"Sure, a stellar reputation helps, of course."

"Of course," he agrees, waiting a minute before continuing. "Once you have a world-class product, the first step to a world-class experience is predictability. People who go to Chick-Fil-A or Starbucks know what they will get no matter where they are in the world. That is why you need to **DEFINE** the experience you are providing. For Zappos, it is 'Deliver WOW' by providing the best customer service possible. What is it for you, Lindsay?"

Without blinking, I have a good one ready. "My definition of world-class customer experience is to create clients who rave about working with us."

"Nice! Let us call it the Raving Fan Experience," Arjun decides. "When you go back home today, define all the things that need to happen in order for you to convert satisfied customers into raving fans."

"Will do." I trail my fingers across the condensation of my frosty glass.

Arjun squints at the sky and watches a cawing gull for a few minutes. I wonder what is going on in the water to excite the bird, but Arjun doesn't give me much time to mull over it.

"The next step of Raving Fan Experience is to **OVER-DELIVER**. Promise high and deliver even more. This is a critical piece. Humans are conditioned to respond to those who go the extra inch."

I laugh. He finally tripped up with his analogies. "You mean extra mile?"

"No." He grins and demonstrates with his own thumb and forefinger. "Just an extra inch. We are not looking for a drastic change, but a tiny percent better than last time. Delivering beyond expectations all the time creates trust and credibility, even if it is very small."

"That sounds simple enough."

"Absolutely," he confirms. "And the key is to never stop improving. Always deliver a tiny percent better than last time. Just like your team members, these are people with the same needs. They also want their respect and connection. Build rapport with them, listen to them. They also need to feel secure that you will deliver a *predictable* service *all* the time. You do that by creating a system that can be improved over time. Everyone in the company must be trained on these systems before they even start working."

"So, you mean create a step-by-step process. Meet the exceptional standard of customer experience to be used as a baseline?"

He nods. "That's right. Systems are just baselines upon which one can improvise."

"Baselines," I say, folding and unfolding a paper napkin. "I like that. It gives room for improvement."

"Exactly," Arjun confirms. "And the final step to your Raving Fan Strategy is **ADAPT**. You need to test your strategies, ask your client if what you are providing is what they want. If their expectations and your standards don't match, you adapt to their needs. Also, your customer's needs change over time, as well. When they do, adapt to their newer expectations."

"Got it."

"So, what are the three steps of your Raving Fan Strategy again?" Arjun asks.

Yay, a test. I love being put on the spot!

Not.

Luckily, I got this. "DEFINE, OVER-DELIVER, and ADAPT. Did I pass with flying colors? Am I not the most attentive of all the students you've ever had? Am I ready to rebuild my brand in the world of business?"

He chuckles and sips from his tea.

"Almost, Lindsay. Almost."

PART III

MY DESTINATION

"It is the ultimate luxury to combine passion and contribution.
It's also a very clear path to happiness."
Sheryl Sandberg

CHAPTER TWENTY-TWO
This Life is a Gift

A week later, we are back at the same beach where we first met.

The one where Arjun found me at rock bottom. Pummeled, pushed to the sandy bottom, pathetically afraid of dying by the ocean's force, I was more than a mess with the seaweed dreadlocks to prove it.

I eye the water, which seems to be waving at me.

Ocean, I'm never turning my back on you, or me, again. So glad you didn't toss me to Davy Jones' Locker, and that I was a spectacular failure at ending it all.

Gratitude bubbles up that, for once in my life, there's a failure that makes me happy.

It's high heat of a bright summer day, and my sandals dangle from my fingertips. Walking beside Arjun, I dig my toes in the cool, wet sand near the surf. We've been walking for a while now without talking, something that doesn't happen often, but when it does, it's delightful. Like sliding into comfortable slippers, the ease of being with my mentor is astounding.

Turning my face to the blue sky, I watch the gulls dipping and gliding over head. "You know, Arjun, silence suits you."

His lips stretch into a smile. "Sometimes silence just drops in."

Just then, I feel something hit my shoulder.

Arjun laughs, "And seagull poop, too! Here take this tissue." Quickly, with a minimum of eye rolls, I wipe the bird bomb off, and point the tissue at Arjun.

"Do you want this back?" Arjun shakes his head no and I giggle a bit.

But silence doesn't last long around us, thus, Arjun begins a new story. I've come to love these stories, and I realize that I'll miss them terribly when they're gone.

"A long time ago in India," he begins, "there was a tradition called Swayamvar, where princesses chose their husbands from a group of princes who lined up in front of her. One princess, from the time she was sixteenteen years old, her parents, the king and queen, would introduce her to many handsome, intelligent prospects. She turned them all down, to the frustration of many."

"At sixteen all I was turning down was the top of my ankle socks, let alone marriage proposals," I added.

"Finally, in frustration, the princess publicly announced she would select the first man to swim across the lake which their castle overlooked. The king and queen were overjoyed but worried at the same time. The lake was teeming with man-eating crocodiles, terrifying fish, and other mysterious water creatures."

Speaking of water creatures, I jump a little when my toe feels the bite of what turns out to be nothing but a small rock. I pick it up and toss it into the water.

Arjun looks back at me. "Terrifying fish?"

"Toe-eating crocodiles."

"Ouch. I should stay away from the surf then." He smiles and continues his story. "Anyway, suddenly, the king, queen, and princess all heard a *splash*! To their surprise, a young man from a local village had jumped into the lake and was valiantly swimming across the water. The royal family watched anxiously as this brave man challenged the waves. With great fanfare, the valiant villager accomplished the task, and, wet and shaking from exertion...met the woman he was to marry."

"The princess?" I ask, just checking. Can't be too sure these days.

"No, the queen," Arjun replies with a side eye.

"Ha! Two can play the sarcasm game, huh?" I love Arjun for returning my serves. "Oh, to have so many men after me."

Arjun stops for a moment and looks at me knowingly. "When it's the right one, it only takes one person," he says softly. "Who needs scores of admirers?"

The man has a point, I think, before he clears his throat and continues with his story.

"All were impressed with the valiant swimmer and began celebrating, but it was the king who voiced the question on everyone's minds. 'I can't believe this!' the king exclaimed. 'How did you find the courage to jump into our dangerous lake?'

"'I will tell you,' the man panted. 'But first, I need to find the person who pushed me in!'" Arjun beams with squinted eyes at the punchline of his cute story, and I laugh heartily.

Last time we were here, I wasn't laughing, I was gasping. I was gnashing my teeth, fighting with the ocean, fighting bad hair, and fighting looking like sixty going on forty.

Ah, I don't miss that at all. I marvel at how far I've come in just ninety days.

We arrive at the spot.

The spot. The notorious place where we met for the first time. This is my last day with Arjun. I am moving out of his guest apartment next week, and I'm going to miss these talks.

Arjun knows that my being on this beach weighs heavily on me. He knows I face my biggest fear just by being here: That I won't have learned a thing and will hit rock bottom again and find myself back here one day.

But it won't happen. I won't let it.

I won't let the time I've spent with him pass in vain.

"What did you learn from this story, Lindsay?" he asks.

"That nobody wants to marry a picky princess?" I joke. Hey, I have to break the tension of our time together ending somehow.

"That's one way of looking at it," he responds quite seriously. "What else?"

I sigh. "Sometimes, you just need a push."

Arjun smiles, hands in his pants' pockets.

As silly as the story was, there was great moral truth to it. I go on. "If I truly want to succeed, I need to burn my ship. I need to put everything I have into doing so. I need to take the risk."

Arjun adds, "For the prince in the story, someone pushed him into unsafe water, leading him to his kingship. Who will push *you* from the burning ship toward *your* destiny, Lindsay?"

"Captain Jack Sparrow?" I venture.

"Come on, Lindsay... I know you can do it."

I think carefully before I continue. For some people, it might be outside influences, like job-related issues, relationship issues, health issues, or whatever. But I know, in my case, it was none of those things. Even hitting rock bottom wasn't enough to push me off the burning ship.

"Me," I conclude with pride. "I will."

Sparkling brown eyes study me. "Indeed. Burning your sinking ship will help you accelerate your journey. But true victory comes from **Grace** alone, Lindsay. If you do your part, Grace is always available to assist when you practice your Faith."

"I think I've found my Faith now," I tell him. I've realized that believing is seeing, and whatever I envision will become true.

"Good. Because Faith lets you clearly see the things that are not yet created. **Faith is visualization, the highest form of imagination, the most powerful force in the entire Universe.**" He waves his hand to the iPad I'm clutching.

But at some point, I have to put it down. Stop being afraid. Just do it. I hand over the notepad, and he writes:

Accelerator # 7 - Create, Celebrate and Contribute.

"Yep." I nod. "I know it's time. Maybe I'm just scared of taking that first step." As though the ocean agrees, a large wave washes in and surrounds my feet in cold water.

"Don't be. You are on the cusp of being successful," Arjun says, handing me back my iPad. "But once successful, do celebrate your victory strategically."

"What do you mean?"

"What I mean is, have a party when you achieve something big. Get high-fives from your friends, but that's not enough. Create a strategic plan to make you feel really good about your achievement."

"Isn't the achievement enough to make me feel good?" I ask.

"When you accomplish a huge goal, people may congratulate you and be happy for you, but it's short-lived. Boost that feeling with a plan outlining how you will celebrate your achievements. Set aside five percent of your net income to celebrate your victory. Money can't make you happy, but money can buy you profound experiences, and profound experiences *can* add to your happiness."

"Wow, that's a pretty mega celebration."

My mind races to all the unknowns I'll be facing. Right now, I'm just wondering where I'm going to live and how I'm going to continue rebuilding my business from the ground up, nevermind budgeting for celebrations, but I will take Arjun's advice and imagine myself already living the dream.

"I can see you are worried," he says, glancing at me. "It doesn't have to be a major savings. Just start with a tiny percent then gradually increase it."

I sigh and look out at the ocean. "I used to wonder how I'm going to implement all this advice you're giving me. But now, I think I'm just going to trust it. Trust the process. Have Faith that it will all work out. Visualize myself having this amazing celebration. Anything else I should do?"

"Yes." He nods. "The second thing is to give five percent of your net income to the less fortunate."

"Oh, man. The steps never end."

"You want to be successful, or not?"

"Yes!" I laugh, shaking my head. "You know I do. I'm just kidding you."

"Good, because giving back to the universe is important. Even better, start your own foundation! If you don't have much money, start small and give it anyway. There is no excuse. If you want more, give more. If you want to stay mediocre or even poor, stop giving."

"That sounds great, but what if I am in deep debt? What if I can't pay my bills on time?"

"Give it anyway," Arjun responds. "You would not believe what you will get in return. If there is one way to create luck, it is this. Give more than you receive. Giving selflessly is actually the most selfish thing one can do. The more you give, the happier, healthier, wealthier you become. Most of my friends are great philanthropists."

"Shouldn't I wait until I become one?" I ask. "I mean, I can't exactly help others until I help myself."

"Not true," he says. "You can always give. Even if you can't be charitable by giving money, give of your time, volunteer, give of yourself, give emotional support, give free advice...give, give, give."

He's right. Look at how kind Arjun has been to me. He raised me up when I needed help by giving me his time, advice, and attention. I could do the same for someone else in my position. It doesn't all have to be about money. Being successful is a mindset.

"I see."

Arjun picks up two rocks from the sand and pretends to weigh them manually. "Which is easier: giving fifty dollars from a thousand dollars, or giving fifty thousand from a million dollars?"

"Fifty dollars," I answer. "Because I can do it sooner."

"Right. Give it *now* and have Faith, and in no time, you will have fifty thousand to give."

I smile, because the man's confidence in me is contagious. If he can believe I will be in such a position, then why can't I?

"Yes, boss. What are the charities you support?"

He shares the charities he is involved in so I too can give and be fulfilled.

He throws the rocks into the ocean. They veer off into two different directions and plop into the waves. "Here is the third thing you should do: save or invest five percent of your income into assets."

"Assets like what?" I ask.

"Anything that produces cash flow," he says. "For example, your car is not an asset for you. It is an asset for your lender. So is the house you live in."

"Then, what is the purpose of investing?"

"The purpose of investment is to create cash flow. There are plenty of books that will strategically teach you how to create an investor's mindset. I strongly recommend a book by my friend Robert Kiyosaki, Rich Dad, Poor Dad, if you haven't read that already."

"I *have* read Rich Dad, Poor Dad," I respond. "It's a great book."

"Excellent. Then go ahead and read my friend Ray Dalio's Big Debt Crises. Ray is a multibillionaire, one of the best financial geniuses of all time, who manages the biggest hedge fund in the world with $151 billion and counting. Big Debt Crises is available on his website for free."

I open my iPad and jot those titles down. "Great. I'll definitely check it out. What's your best advice for someone like me, who knows little about investing?"

Arjun shrugs. "I can let you in on a two-step secret that I learned from Warren Buffet himself."

"Warren Buffet? I'll take that."

"Okay, well, here is the mindset: Try to be fearful when others are greedy and greedy only when others are fearful. And when you invest, here is his strategy regarding real estate or stocks. Rule One: Never lose money. Rule Two: Never forget Rule One." Arjun pauses dramatically, his eyebrows in the raised position.

"Ha, great advice." But where will I ever begin?

"And here is the final thing," Arjun says. "Invest five percent of your net income into yourself. Jim Rohn said, 'Work hard at your job, and you can make a living. Work hard on yourself, and you can make a fortune.' My suggestion to you, Lindsay, is to read, join trainings and courses in the most important areas of your life. Learn about investing, relationships, success, health, emotional well-being, everything before you even need it. Don't wait for your relationships to fall apart before you study about how to care for them. Become a master in the major things of life."

He looks over at me, body posture exuding confidence.

I wish I had the tiniest fraction of that.

He goes on. "Put ten dollars into celebrating your thirty-day goal. Give another ten dollars to someone who is less fortunate than you or to your favorite charity. Put another ten dollars into a savings account and then invest in your mind with ten dollars toward a phenomenal book."

"Got it. Got everything, actually." I exhale and close my eyes, absorbing it all. "Now, all I have to do is put everything you've told me together and practice what's been preached. No more losing money."

I stop walking at the point where I remember Arjun finding me that very first fateful day. I sit on the sand and sigh.

I must sigh pretty heavily, because he puts his hand on my shoulder.

"I can feel your frustration," Arjun says. "It's a lot of information. It's daunting. But…I promise you, it will work out. One step at a time. Keep the Faith, and it will all come, Lindsay. You are intelligent, you are kind, you are funny, you are hardworking."

"None of that has worked out for me in the past," I croak back.

"And it won't if you don't believe it. Really believe it. In here." He points to his chest, to where his generous heart lies. "It all might seem as large and overwhelming as this ocean, but you begin with a few drops. Then, a bucket. Then, a pool, and so on. Imagine the universe at your feet, and it will be."

"You make me feel like I can do it," I tell him, tears rising into my eyes. I blink them back before he can notice. Crying never solved anything for me.

"Because I've been where you are," he says, words which unlock the tears anyway. Just knowing that Arjun understands is enough to fill me with determination. If he could do it, I could do it.

I'm too choked to say anything else.

Arjun nods and looks away.

We sit on the sand, side by side, watching the waters that nearly took me that fateful day. No, they didn't almost take me, I almost gave myself to them.

I nearly threw away the most valuable thing in my life—myself.

For a long time, we're silent. Only the caw of seagulls and rushing sounds of flowing and ebbing waves fills the emptiness. Eyes closed, I meditate on the Pacific Ocean's lullaby, Arjun's ideas swirling around in my mind. I imagine my dreams all coming true, and they give me strength.

After a while, I feel the sun's energy waning as it drops behind the horizon. In my mind's eye, I'm as powerful as the sun, ready to begin a new life, ready to put the puzzle pieces together and build something great and wonderful. I imagine myself as confident as Arjun, as financially successful, not because I made it my goal, but because it came to me. For being generous, for being charitable, for being strong and hardworking, and all those things he mentioned about me.

I do feel it.

I am all those things.

I guess I had to come back to this spot and reclaim it as a victorious one for my journey to truly begin. I'm ready, and I imagine glancing at my friend, just as the golden light of our fading afternoon washes over his wise face.

But when I open my eyes to reach over and give his hand a grateful squeeze, Arjun is gone.

10 Years Later—

Morning brightness seeps under my eyelids.

When I open them, I'm treated to my daily view of waves crashing off the Pacific Ocean and the beach near San Francisco where I've lived for the last five years.

I chose this home specifically, to remind me of that day a little over ten years ago when I nearly took my life, when a friend and mentor called me away from the waters and dared me to discover my best self.

My call to action.

Seeing the ocean every morning keeps me grounded and grateful for who I have become. In Arjun's famous words—I am the next version of me.

I think about that day a lot, the day I met Arjun and everything that happened on that beach. I'm grateful for the amazing things I was able to accomplish after meeting him. He believed in me more than I did. Until I took back control of my life, that is. It makes me sad for people who don't have anyone to lift them up when they're on the verge of checking out, which is why I try to give back whenever I can.

I'm so glad I didn't check out. I wouldn't have all I have today.

And I have it all.

It has been an amazing journey since the afternoon he quietly stepped out of my life for a while. I've often wondered why he did that. At first, I was put off. But I quickly realized he had to do it. I would never learn to swim if I wore a life-jacket, I'd never learn to balance if I used a safety net, and I'd never walk on my own if he continued to be my crutch.

Once I had some time to process and apply all of his teachings, Arjun came back into my life. Both as a friend and one of my best clients. We didn't see one another as often as either of us would prefer, but the time we did spend together was precious to me.

My smartwatch chimes, reminding me about the Stanford graduation ceremony at noon today.

Guess who's giving the commencement address?

Nope, not me this time. Arjun! I'm happily looking forward to sitting in the audience as a guest and hearing him talk again. It will remind me of the old days, when I had the pleasure of sitting across from him once a week as his student. *The Arjun Days*, I think to myself with a smile.

As for Charlie, I never looked back. That man tried to suck all the life out of me. Now, I'm married to Liberato Domani, a venture capitalist in Silicon Valley. He's my partner in business, netting several million dollars a year. Money is not the most important thing in my life anymore, time is. We have three kids—Jake, Aiden, and Ava. Jake is eight, my twins Aiden and Ava are six, and they are *huge* handfuls, but I wouldn't change our life for anything in the world.

Many women think that, at forty, their life is over.

Well, mine had just begun that day ten years ago.

"Bye, guys. Mommy's off to see an old friend."

"Bye, Mommy!"

I kiss each of my kids before ending with a smooch for my husband, Lib. "See you in the office later?" Then, I pull the keys off the wall hook—the keys to my Ferrari F60.

"Sure. Tell Arjun we say hello." He smiles as he serves grilled cheese bites to the kids.

In the garage, the Ferrari's key smoothly slips into the ignition and easily turns, making the engine purr.

Ten years ago, I could only wish for this life. And now, here it is. The house, the family...the Ferrari. They're not just status symbols. For me, they're reminders of hope, persistence, and survival. I survived those dark times. I turned my life around using Arjun's techniques and reconditioning the way I approach life.

Anyone can do it. Brains are intelligent computers. Computers can be reprogrammed, brains can be reconditioned.

I wish I could find one hopeless person on a beach per day for the rest of my life and teach them what I now know.

It's about an hour's drive to Stanford on one of the busiest streets in the world, but I enjoy the drive because of the time to reflect it gives me. I've been in a reflective mood all morning. Thinking about seeing Arjun this afternoon, I remember the three things that stayed with me most: power ceremony, C^3 system for productivity, and my new identity that Arjun helped me build - 'Sara Blakely of Technology.'

It's funny, because the name actually stuck, and some of my close friends still call me that. After my learning period with Arjun, I went from a spiritual bankruptcy to employing three hundred of the smartest geeks on this planet. I see it as a turning point, a time that helped me stop and learn.

And to top it all off, today I have a big surprise for Arjun.

I can't wait to give it to him...

***

Sitting at the commencement ceremony surrounded by proud family members of the graduating class, I'm struck by the youth and innocence of the graduates. Even though they have suffered four to six years of higher education and are deemed ready for the world, they are only beginning their journeys, and I find myself proud of them as if they were my children.

And when Arjun is introduced by the dean, some rather unexpected emotion rises into my chest. The dean introduces him with grand words, words of which he is entirely deserving.

"And now...live from the Stanford University's graduation ceremonies, please welcome...Arjun Siddharth."

He begins with his usual mysterious smile, and I'm on the edge of my seat, the same as I was ten years ago.

"Thank you...thank you, Dean Levin, for inviting me here today. I want to tell you a story."

I laugh inwardly. Arjun and his stories are the best!

"There once was a famous guru who lived in a small ashram near Mount Kailash in the Himalayas. He was known for his insight, wisdom, peaceful teachings, and meditation. Although he lived alone in a remote area, many of his followers came to visit him. One day, a small, black cat made its way to the guru's ashram, and even though he made it clear to the cat that he didn't particularly like felines, the cat refused to leave."

In my mind's eye, I see Arjun as the guru; all bothered while being pestered by an annoying cat.

"Every day," Arjun continues to a rapt audience, "the cat would yowl at the top of its lungs until the guru left his chair and shooed the cat outside. Each time, the cat would return and continue to yowl just before the guru began his lessons. Finally, the guru got the idea to take a long string and tie the cat to a tree outside his ashram just before his lessons. That way, he wouldn't be interrupted again.

"But soon, the cat caught on to his method and began hiding right before the lessons were to begin, foiling the guru. But the guru was one step ahead—he began preparing fresh fish and milk for the cat, to tempt it out of its hiding place before taking it to its tree. Before long, the guru was preparing meals for the cat and running around his ashram every day to catch it, so that he could tie it to the tree. Only then could he have his peaceful time for teaching or meditating. His disciples were fascinated by his methodology, and he was proud of himself for his wits.

"But then, one day, the guru grew too old to go on and died, while his Faithful disciples took in the annoying, yowling cat. To them, they needed the feline beast around to preserve their master's legacy and built a beautiful temple for it. Because they felt sorry for the now confined cat, they bought two more to give the holy cat some company."

I chuckle along with those around me. *Holy cat!*

Arjun waits for the laughter to fade before going on, "They hired the finest chef in the country to prepare the cats' fish every day before taking them to the tree to be tied. They also bought a cow so the milk would be readily available for them. No preaching began until all the cats were located, taken to the cat temple, fed, and then tied to the tree. Once fastened to the tree, the disciples said a puja for them. At least three times a day, the entire group of disciples ran around the ashram saying this prayer to honor the cats before continuing their master's teachings.

"They believed these habits were a necessary part of their guru's routine and were convinced that anyone who participated in this puja and ran around the ashram seven times would all have their karmic debts cleansed. After the exhausting daily cat rituals, the disciples became very tired and took naps exactly the way their guru used to do when he was alive. Little did they know, their guru did all these things to **avoid** distractions for his powerful meditation."

A smile as wide as the Grand Canyon sits on my face as I sit listening to my favorite teacher and take delight in watching others in this sea of smiles around me enjoy him, too.

Arjun's tone turns a little somber, and I know he's about to drive the story home, with the same skill as he always did when I spent so much time learning from him.

"Over time, these disciples vigorously fought and sometimes killed infidels who did not respect their guru's strict rituals. The so-called infidels tried telling them the guru's teachings represented love, peace, and meditation, that people should reflect on their thoughts to become better human beings, but the 'cat disciples' wouldn't listen.

"'We saw our guru with our own eyes,' they said. 'We don't care what he wrote or said. We saw him chase the cat, run around the ashram doing everything we do to honor him today. We built our holy ritual around these actions—the cat-chasing, the sitting, the daydreaming, the lying down to sleep…'" Arjun folds his hands and waits for the audience to take in the message of his story. In a quieter voice, he says, "My friends, this is how most people perceive their culture and tribes today—through a limited viewpoint of fear. Fear of immigrants, the unfamiliar and the unknown. Once we are fearful, we lose the big picture and become superstitious and divisive."

After a round of enthusiastic applause, Arjun continues, "I am honored to be with you today at your commencement ceremony. You are graduating from one of the top universities in the world, so you might be wondering why I chose to tell you this story today. You see, we are about to enter the brightest era of human history. Self-driven cars are on the horizon and drone delivery is only awaiting FAA approval. Richard Branson, Jeff Bezos and Elon Musk are all planning commercial trips for you to visit space. It is truly an exciting time to live!"

That it is, Arjun. That it is.

"And yet, many people are still chasing the proverbial cat, tying it to a tree, then lying down to sleep…missing the entire point. As we embark on this journey into the future, our biggest challenges are extremism and divisiveness. Technology is ready—humans aren't, yet. Radical jihadists, like ISIS, are extreme examples. Their highest goal is to instill fear throughout the world through their dramatic cruelty. A lot of us have bought into this fear, which is exactly what they wanted. As a result, extremism has returned to being the driving force of the world, but I know it is only temporary. If you are sick and tired of terrorism," he goes on, "fundamentalism and extremism, believe me when I say this - the current period of darkness precedes the dawn of a new world order.

"Since I have been teaching business acceleration for the last thirty years, let me bring in a metaphor from my world. Imagine human race is like a well-oiled business. In order for any business to thrive, it needs world class innovation. For the human business, the greatest innovation is the acceleration of our collective consciousness. **If we become victims of fear, and focus on scarcity, we stop all the innovation.** Some people say we have nothing to fear but fear itself. I say psychological fear is not your enemy nor is she your friend. Use your fear as a tool or an assistant to create a bigger impact in your world, rather than letting it use you. What we need for that is a spiritual innovation. I am not asking you to change the current values and beliefs you have to fit my world. What I am asking you is to help accelerate consciousness forward by focusing on principles.

"Values are from the mind and for the mind, **principles are the food for your soul.** When our mind divides us as Christians and Muslims, blacks, and whites, Americans and Indians, young and old, and men and women, principles unite us. **Values are the creation of our mind. Principles are eternal.**"

"Hear, hear," I mutter under my breath. Some in the audience clap while Arjun pauses for a drink of water.

"Inside every one of you is a leader longing to find the next version of yourself. Your business or job needs to become the platform to finding that version. Once you do, you can lovingly open the eyes of those who are asleep in their self-created bubbles of limited beliefs.

"The message from my story is very simple—abandon fear and focus on principles, whether you want to be an entrepreneur or a professional. After studying the world's philosophies for more than twenty-five years, I have learned that these are the seven core principles which all tribes and cultures deeply embrace—principles of nature and the universe. If you look outside the rituals, you will see these principles forming the foundation by which your culture is shaped. Almost everything else is a distraction."

Truer words have never been spoken, I think to myself.

Arjun looks around the room, as if examining the soul of every individual in the auditorium.

Applause breaks out, and I know Arjun is about to bring this all together somehow. I've been there, done that.

"In summary, these are going to be the seven principles that will define the new dawn of civilization. Faith, *Ananda*, Forgiveness, Gratitude, Discipline, Love and Kindness. I did not invent these. Each of the world's holy books has a different emphasis for one principle over another, but all of them—the Bible, Quran, Torah, Bhagavad Gita, and Tripitaka—all talk about these principles. Let us have an even closer look at them.

"The first is Faith—Faith to believe what you don't see. Its reward is to see what you believed in the first place. Coincidently, applied Faith is the number one attribute needed for a successful entrepreneur, being able to see the unseen before anyone else and create it for others.

"The second principle is Ananda. Ananda is your inner joy. It is not pleasure; it is the dance within you, the true happiness that every human being brings to this world. When you see a cared-for infant, you see Ananda in her. Buddha said, 'When the mind is pure, joy follows like a shadow that never leaves.' We systematically undo this experience as we grow older, and it becomes our learned helplessness.

"The third principle is Forgiveness. Forgiveness liberates your mind and its limits. 'Forgive and you shall be forgiven'. In other words, in order for you to invite Forgiveness into you, you lead with it. If you have been struggling to forgive yourself, here is the medicine. **The extent to which you can forgive and appreciate others is the extent to which you can forgive and appreciate yourself.** Lack of Forgiveness is one of the single most negative forces that could stagnate our human consciousness.

"The next principle, Gratitude, is the bulk expander of human growth and consciousness. It is the humility to appreciate what you are given. At any level, Gratitude takes you to the next stratosphere of consciousness.

"The fifth principle, Discipline, is the thread that weaves them all together within you. It grounds you, helps you integrate your head and heart.

"The sixth principle is the ultimate expression of the human spirit—Love. Poet Kahlil Gibran said, 'Life without Love is a tree without blossoms or fruit.' Prophet Mohammed said, 'You will not complete your Faith until you Love one another.' Gautama Buddha said, 'Love is a gift of one's innermost soul to another, so both can be whole.' Krishna revealed in Bhagavatgeetha, 'Of all I could name, Love is truly the highest.' Twenty centuries ago, Christ proclaimed, 'Love your neighbor as you would thyself. There is no commandment greater than this'. He said that God is synonymous to Love and revolutionized our limiting metaphors in the process.

"And finally, the last principle is Kindness. That is what I want to emphasize here today. The Dalai Lama said, 'My religion is simple. My religion is Kindness.' Let us talk about the brutal reality we face today. In spite of all the advancement in technology, approximately 3.1 million children die from hunger each year. Poor nutrition is the cause of nearly half the deaths in children under five. According to UNICEF, eleven million child deaths every year are attributable to six causes, including diarrhea, malaria, neonatal infection, and pneumonia.

"According to World Food Programme, 795 million people in the world do not have enough food to lead a healthy, active life. This amounts to one in nine people on Earth. Eight hundred million people do not have access to clean water. That is why you and I are going to grow our businesses and make more money so that we can invest it back to our world community. I ask you all today to commit to giving back 5% of your income to the underprivileged, or if you start a business, 10% of your profit for these causes that inspire you. This way money can actually buy you happiness."

The audience breaks into supportive applause.

I have never been more proud of my mentor.

Arjun continues through the din of the auditorium. "When you are principle driven, the impossible will become your daily reality. As you walk across this stage today, graduates of one of the most prestigious universities in the world, I wish that for you.

"I believe that you being yourself is your greatest gift back to the Universe. I believe that your character is always more important than your charisma. I believe you can lead others by believing in them even more than they believe in themselves.

"Hunger is essential to success; stress is optional. And to that end, I say, 'Stay curious, stay hungry!' Today, you are receiving something that even Bill Gates, Steve Jobs, and Mark Zuckerberg did not receive—a Stanford degree. Congratulations, everyone!"

The whole room erupts into a roaring standing ovation, me included. At this moment, I've never felt so grateful than for the weeks I spent under Arjun's tutelage.

After the commencement, the happy crowds gather outside to congratulate each other, while I wander the campus, remembering when I first began my journey as a positive, hopeful graduate student. I remember my hard times, especially when I hit rock bottom. And then I remember Arjun, that effervescent observer standing on the beach—smiling. Oh, how that radiant smile bored straight through me, irritated me, challenged me, then changed my life.

At that moment, a familiar form emerges from the auditorium's double doors and strolls toward me with a smile. It never ceases to amaze me that, despite being a decade older and a little slower, Arjun still walks with amazing presence and confidence.

"It is great to see you again, Lindsay!" he calls out, crossing a stretch of green. It's a beautiful day, made even more beautiful now that I see my old friend.

"Hey, well, if it isn't my hero." I smile wide, and we give each other a firm hug. "And now the hero of every young person in that stadium."

"Thank you, Lindsay," he says, bowing slightly. "Tell me, how is business going lately?"

"Terrible. I'm bankrupt again, my kids have replaced the employees, and I've been arrested twice for child labor."

Arjun cocks his head with narrowed eyes. "Lindsay, your sense of humor has not changed. I am glad to see that."

I laugh, happiness and triumph bubbling up from inside me. "It's great, Arjun. Never better. You already know, we're the largest software provider for small businesses in California today." Just saying it out loud fills me with pride, and for some reason, having Arjun in front of me when I vocalize it brings a wave of emotion into my chest. "Everything I have, I owe to you."

"Thank you, I appreciate you," he says. "I am even more proud of you, Lindsay, for letting me lead you. You could have given up, but you chose the path of learning instead, and that took courage."

I'm humbled, but at the same time, I know the truth—*my* truth: I couldn't have done it without Arjun's help. I *do* owe him. And something my mother taught me when I was little was always to pay my debts. Reaching into my purse, I pull out an envelope and hand it to him.

"What's this?"

"Just something."

With a curious eye, he opens the envelope and pulls out a check for one million dollars. Signed by me. I couldn't always do that and can't help but smile.

"What is this, Lindsay?" He stares at me like a father who doesn't want or need any cash from his child.

"It's a small gift for your foundation. Think of it as Gratitude."

"More like Kindness," he replies, bowing his head. "Thank you so much. This could help well over one thousand five hundred blind children with cataracts to see and five million friends who are starving for food."

For several years now, I've thought of this moment and how it would go, and now that it's here, it couldn't have played out more perfectly. "It's my pleasure. Really. But there's more there…" I point to the envelope, realizing he only took out one of the two checks.

With a chastising expression, he slides the other one out. "Three hundred in my name? What is this for?" he asks.

"The day we met, you took me to the store to buy me new clothes. I'm paying you back." I smile. "Now, we're even. Make sure you deposit the million into your foundation and the three hundred into your account, Arjun, not the other way around." I wink, holding down a laugh.

He grins. "Funny girl."

***

I am driving on the Pacific Coast Highway that symbolizes the dream-like life of mine. The turquoise color of the water reminds me of the same Pacific Ocean where I signed a contract for my soul. The one with Arjun around ten years ago to extend my life by ninety days. Today, I am far beyond anything I could dream of at the time. My parents are proud of me. My husband, Lib, adores me. My children are the pride of my life. I am friends with the movers and shakers of the world. This life is totally worth **reliving** and celebrating. I am grateful for each moment of it.

After all, it was a good contract to live and celebrate.

THE END

If you haven't already, here is your last chance to get instant access to 90 Days to Life Complementary Training.

Or Visit
https://rublechandy.com/accelerator

Acknowledgements:

First of all, I thank you, for investing in yourself and entrusting me to serve you on this journey. I hope I get to meet you someday so you can share your story of how 90 Days to Life helped your business, career or life.

I thank my mentors, Vattayilachan, Tony Robbins, and Eben Pagan for their advice and guidance. Thank you my dear friends, Antochan, Vivish, Titto, Fr. Jaison, Tas, Mony, Abhilash, George, Mariamma, Siby, Chad, Kelly, Dana, and Sal for supporting me through this journey called life. I am grateful to my sisters, Sonia and Joan, for all their love and support.

My content researchers and creative writers, Nisha Chandy, Maria Cardenas, Mariah Patterson, Gaby Triana, Christine Bell, Rachel Dew, and Toni LaGree who all contributed to this project. Thank you to my publicist, Devra Ann Jacobs.

I am thankful for a million other people in my life, including my team members and everyone from my culturally rich hometown, Rampuram in India.

Made in the USA
Columbia, SC
03 May 2019